IMAGES
of America

RACINE

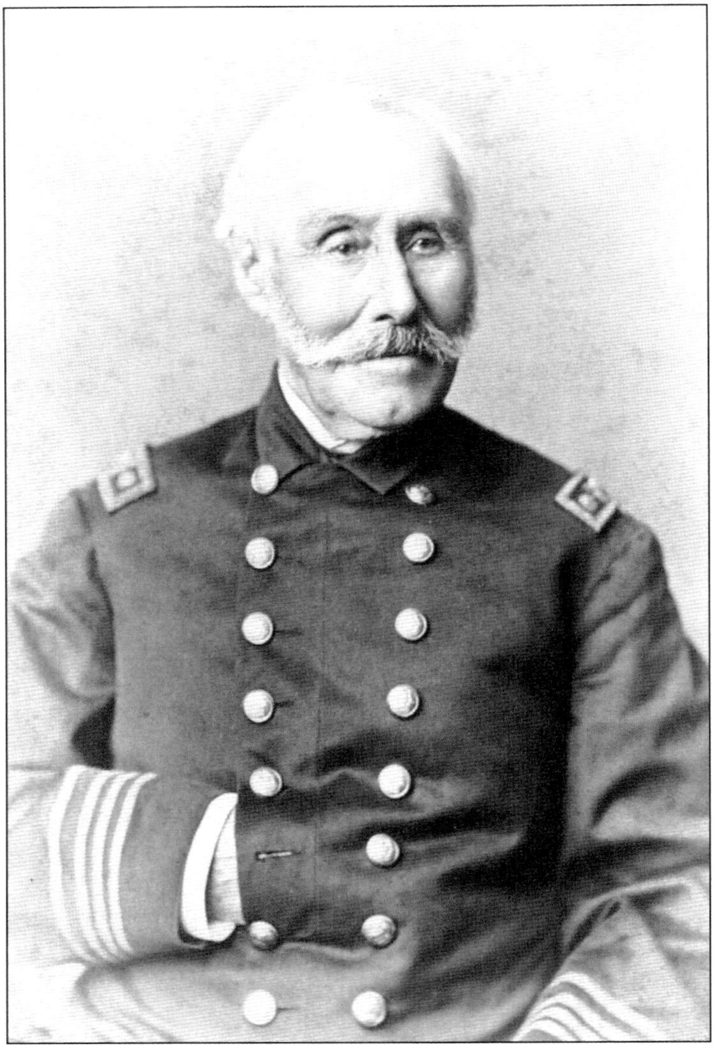

Gilbert Knapp, above, is the founder of the city of Racine. He was born on December 3, 1798, in Chatham on Cape Cod, Massachusetts. Knapp went to sea in a ship commanded by his uncle when he was 15 years old, and he served in the War of 1812 aboard the *Leo*; a ship chartered by the government to carry dispatches to France. After the war, Knapp, who had been commissioned a captain in the US Revenue Service, patrolled the Great Lakes while searching for illicit fur traffickers. It was during this service in 1819 that he anchored in Lake Michigan off the mouth of the Root River and realized the area's potential as a harbor. Once the Potawatomi relinquished title to this land, Knapp, along with two partners, filed a claim for about 140 acres at the mouth of Root River. Upon this claim, the owners established Port Gilbert in November 1834. On February 13, 1841, Port Gilbert incorporated as the Village of Racine. (Courtesy of the Racine Heritage Museum.)

On the Cover: The Schulte Band, organized in 1877 by Adolph Schulte, is seen here on Monument Square around 1915 getting ready to lead a parade. The Schulte Band first gave public concerts in East Park in 1879. In 1923, the Schulte Band became the Racine Park Board Band. Since 1967, it has been called the Racine Municipal Band. (Courtesy of the Racine Heritage Museum.)

IMAGES
of America

RACINE

George D. Fennell with the Racine Heritage Museum

ARCADIA
PUBLISHING

ISBN 978-1-4671-1219-2

Published by Arcadia Publishing
Charleston, South Carolina

Printed in the United States of America

Library of Congress Control Number: 2014945555

For all general information, please contact Arcadia Publishing:
Telephone 843-853-2070
Fax 843-853-0044
E-mail sales@arcadiapublishing.com
For customer service and orders:
Toll-Free 1-888-313-2665

Visit us on the Internet at www.arcadiapublishing.com

To my wonderful wife, Liz, thank you for your love and encouragement—not just on this project, but in everything. I would also like to thank you for your patience and understanding, as there were times during this project that I was so focused that I was unable to talk, think, or do little else. You are the best!
To my faithful Australian shepherd companion, Ellie, thank you for all of the countless hours you patiently laid on my feet in the den, waiting for a walk or a ball playing session in the backyard that didn't happen because I was diligently working on this book. It's time, Ellie. Go get the ball!

Contents

Acknowledgments

First of all, I want to thank the Racine Heritage Museum's executive director, Christopher Poulson, for allowing me access to the museum's archives and giving me permission to use the images in this book. His faith in me to successfully produce this wonderful book is something that I will cherish forever.

I also want to thank the following staff at the Racine Heritage Museum for taking their precious time to help me in all aspects of making this book:

Karen Braun, curator/assistant director, for her total support. Anything that I needed for this project she would either get for me or make it happen—including coffee. Karen always took the time to listen, which was as invaluable as the ideas and advice that I continually sought.

Mary Kay Mandli Nelson, archivist, for always having a supply of chocolate candy on hand to share and, more importantly, for her help in finding and interpreting images, scanning and copying. Mary Kay was always very accommodating in allowing me access to the archives when it was convenient for me.

Norah McCue, volunteer museum assistant, for her complete authorship of Chapter 7: Education and Schools. Norah picked out the photographs and did all of the research for the captions she wrote. Unfortunately, due to space limitations, much of her work on this chapter had to be left out.

Andrew Kogutkiewicz and Raven Larson, museum assistants, for scanning many of the photographs used in this book.

Evelyn Lajiness and Harold Ralston, volunteer museum assistants, and Laura Carlson, office manager, for their help with research, photocopying, and advice.

I also wish to thank my editors at Arcadia Publishing, Jesse Darland and Jacel Egan. The expert guidance and encouragement I received from them was most appreciated.

Additionally, I would like to note that almost all of the research for this book came from the searchable newspapers available online at newspaperarchives.com. This service is well worth the money when doing historical research and they are to be applauded for making history so accessible and convenient. I would not have taken on this book project without having been familiar with this invaluable service.

All images in this book were graciously provided by the Racine Heritage Museum.

INTRODUCTION

Racine is located in southeastern Wisconsin, where the Root River empties into Lake Michigan. It is the county seat and leading community of Racine County. Root is the English translation of Kipikaoui, the name that the Miami tribe gave the river when they settled at its mouth.

The Potawatomi began moving into southeastern Wisconsin in the early 1700s, replacing the Miami who left the area and moved to southern Michigan and northern Indiana. The Potawatomi remained in the area until after the Treaty of Chicago in 1833, when they agreed to cede their lands in northeastern Illinois and southeastern Wisconsin in exchange for a similar amount of land in western Iowa. By 1838, when the US government had removed most of the Potawatomi, white settlers had already established themselves in various parts of Racine County.

Gilbert Knapp was born in Chatham, Massachusetts, in 1798. He grew up and attended school there, but when he was 15 he went to sea on a merchant ship. In 1818, Knapp became a captain, commanding a boat on the Great Lakes and policing the fur trade for the US Revenue Service. In 1819, Captain Knapp anchored off the mouth of the Root River and went ashore to explore the area. It was at this time that he realized the potential for the development of a harbor and became intrigued with the idea of establishing a settlement here. Knapp left government employment in 1828 and settled on Lake Erie in Chautauqua County, New York, going into business as a merchant and shipper. Long interested in the possibility of settling at the mouth of the Root River, Knapp sold his interests in western New York State in 1834 and headed for the Root River via Chicago.

In the summer of 1834, Gilbert Knapp, together with Gurdon S. Hubbard of Chicago, came to the Root River area on horseback from Chicago. They spent two days exploring the country and studying the river for possible harbor development. Gilbert Knapp returned again that November, bringing with him two brothers, William and A.J. Luce. They erected a small cabin on the lake shore south of the river. Knapp did not remain there during the winter, but he left his cabin in charge of the Luce brothers. Knapp went back to Chicago, filed a formal claim, and entered into a partnership with Gurdon S. Hubbard, one of Chicago's leading land speculators, to develop a village site called Port Gilbert. Knapp then returned briefly to the East where he sold a third share in the business of developing Port Gilbert to a friend, Jacob A. Barker, a merchant and shipper based in Buffalo, New York. The three claimed 140 acres on both sides of the river mouth; 74 of which were north of the river. In 1836, surveyors laid out their claim in lots, blocks, and streets. Knapp and his partners then began to promote the development of Port Gilbert.

Among the original three claimants, Gilbert Knapp was the only one to become a resident of Racine. Knapp remained a business and civic leader in Racine until his death in 1887. He never acquired great wealth, but Knapp lived comfortably here and enjoyed the respect of the community.

Other settlers began arriving in the Port Gilbert area as early as January 1835; however, they respected the Port Gilbert town site claim and made their own claims beyond its boundaries.

One settler who made a large claim beyond the area controlled by Gilbert Knapp and his partners was Joel Sage. Sage, who had recently arrived in Chicago from New England, met Knapp in 1835. At their meeting in Chicago, Knapp encouraged Sage to settle in Port Gilbert. Sage took Knapp's advice and established his claim of 107 acres on the north side of the river, west of the land already taken by Knapp and his partners. This area became known as "Sage Town."

By the fall of 1835, about a dozen families had settled near the mouth of the Root River. By 1840, over 300 people were living in Port Gilbert.

On February 13, 1841, Port Gilbert incorporated into the Village of Racine. In doing research for this book, there appears to be some confusion about why the village was incorporated as Racine and not as Port Gilbert. Suppositions have previously been made that early pioneers objected to the name of Port Gilbert for some reason. However, the article "Racine's First Name was Port Gilbert," which appeared in the May 26, 1925, issue of the *Racine Times-Call*, clears up this matter. This article states that "the title of Racine was substituted for that of Port Gilbert at the request of Captain Knapp, who was worried as to whether his title to the land on which he hoped to build a city would be questioned."

Knapp and his associates apparently did experience some title problems with their claim because of claiming and settling the land before it was actually for sale. These difficulties were not resolved until 1845. It is also important to note that when the village was being incorporated in 1841, the title problems on his claim were not cleared up yet. Therefore, it is very plausible that Knapp had the village's name changed from Port Gilbert to Racine in an effort to somehow protect his claim.

Racine's growth during its early years was largely the result of it being a service center. As the area's population grew, so did the need for all sorts of business and governmental services.

By the early 1840s, there was a tremendous need for a harbor. At first, arrivals to Racine by water were put ashore with their luggage in the boat's landing craft, landing on a beach between Third and Sixth Streets. Rafts were used to bring ashore to the beach household furniture and other heavy merchandise and freight. Later, as traffic increased and the settlement grew, piers 600 or 700 feet long were built out into the lake from Third and Fourth Streets.

Construction of Racine's first harbor began in 1843. The first piers were finished and the channel of the Root River was dredged by July 1844. On the 14th of that month, the steamer *Chesapeake* entered Racine's new harbor and tied up at the warehouse of Taylor & Cather. This was the first ship seen in the Root River, and it was reportedly the first to enter an artificial harbor in Wisconsin.

On August 8, 1848, Racine was incorporated as a city. Five years later, in 1853, Dr. J.W. Hunt of Madison, a writer for the *Wisconsin Gazetteer*, visited Racine and described the city in glowing terms. He commented on Racine's beautiful location, excellent harbor, thriving commerce, the number and beauty of its public buildings, the many churches, and the new Racine College. Dr. Hunt gave Racine the title "La Belle City of the Lakes," stating that it was justly entitled to the name.

In the 1850s, two railroads came to Racine. The first, the Racine, Janesville & Mississippi Railroad, was chartered on April 17, 1852. Its purpose was to connect Racine and Janesville to the Mississippi River. By 1856, it had track laid from Racine west to Janesville and, from there, south to Beloit. It was not until 1859 that it completed the last quarter mile of track from Beloit to the Illinois state line, where it connected to tracks it had acquired through two mergers with other railroads operating in northwestern Illinois. This finally gave it a route from Racine and Janesville to the Mississippi River.

A second railroad came to Racine in 1855, when the Green Bay, Milwaukee & Chicago Railroad completed 40.40 miles of track from Milwaukee to the Illinois state line where it connected to tracks in northeastern Illinois. This line gave Racine railroad access to all of the western Lake Michigan communities from Green Bay to Chicago.

A developed harbor and two railroads set the stage for the rapid growth of industry in Racine during the late 1800s. People flocked to Racine because there were jobs. Manufacturing became the main economic activity, and Racine became known as a "factory town."

One man who was prominent in early manufacturing in Racine was Henry Mitchell; a Scot schooled in wagon building. He came to Fort Dearborn, soon to be known as Chicago, in 1835. In 1838, he relocated to Southport, which later became Kenosha, to be closer to the large stands of oak and other hardwoods necessary for wagon building. There, he established a thriving wagon making business. After 15 years, he sold the business and moved a few miles north to Racine where, in 1854, he established another wagon building business.

Initially, the Mitchell Wagon Works in Racine built cultivators and plows, in addition to farm wagons, carriages and bobsleds. However, during the 1860s, Mitchell switched to the exclusive production of wagons.

By 1871, Mitchell & Lewis Wagon Company was Racine's third-largest manufacturer, with 165 employees. Its annual sales of $450,000 in 1871 ranked it second in Racine, behind only the J.I. Case Threshing Machine Company.

Timing is everything, and the westward migration in the United States created a huge demand for sturdy, well-made wagons. Known as *The Monarch of the Road*, Mitchell wagons sold very well.

In 1900, Mitchell & Lewis Wagon Company remained as Racine's third largest manufacturing company, with 430 employees.

Prior to going bankrupt in 1923, the Mitchell family business expanded to include bicycles, motorcycles, and automobiles. The company's story is further presented in Chapter 9.

Racine has experienced its share of ups and downs, and has seen tremendous changes. However, today finds Racine a unique and vibrant lakefront community. It is currently home to about 78,000 people, making it the fifth-largest city in Wisconsin. The historic charm of its downtown, with its boutiques, art galleries, festivals, fine dining, and museums, attracts visitors from all over.

Racine also has many architectural interests; including five Frank Lloyd Wright–designed buildings. Racine's beautiful lakefront is home to a large marina and two of the finest parks in the area: North Beach and the Racine Zoo.

This book is not meant to be a thorough and complete history of Racine. Rather, it is a collection of images, with each one providing a glimpse into Racine's past.

About the Racine Heritage Museum

A great starting point for exploring Racine County's history is the Racine Heritage Museum at 701 Main Street, Racine, WI 53403. The museum contains exhibits that tell stories of the fascinating, innovative people who have called Racine County home. Other exhibits detail the Racine area's many inventions and share stories of sailing and shipbuilding on Lake Michigan. The museum also includes a look at Racine's abolitionists and their underground railroad. A newer feature is the Racine County Sports Hall of Fame, which celebrates the accomplishments of the county's athletes.

The Racine Heritage Museum is open Tuesday through Friday from 9:00 a.m. to 5:00 p.m., Saturdays from 10:00 a.m. to 3:00 p.m., and Sundays from 12:00 p.m. to 4:00 p.m. Admission is free, though donations are always welcome.

This book was written as a fundraising project for the Racine Heritage Museum. All of the author's royalties will be used to continue its operation. Thank you very much for your purchase. It is most appreciated!

All of the photographs that appear in this book come from the Research Center at the Racine Heritage Museum. They represent only a very small fraction of the photographs that are contained there. Copies of photographs can be purchased there, and archive staff members are available during hours of operation to answer your questions and guide you in your research. Hours of operation are Tuesdays, from 1:00 p.m. to 4:30 p.m., and Saturdays, from 10:00 a.m. to 1:00 p.m.

Appointments for individual research can be scheduled outside of regular hours by advance appointment with the archivist at (262) 636-3926, or inquire@racineheritagemuseum.org.

If you have materials that you would like to see preserved and shared with generations to come, please consider donating them to the Racine Heritage Museum.

One

THE HARBOR

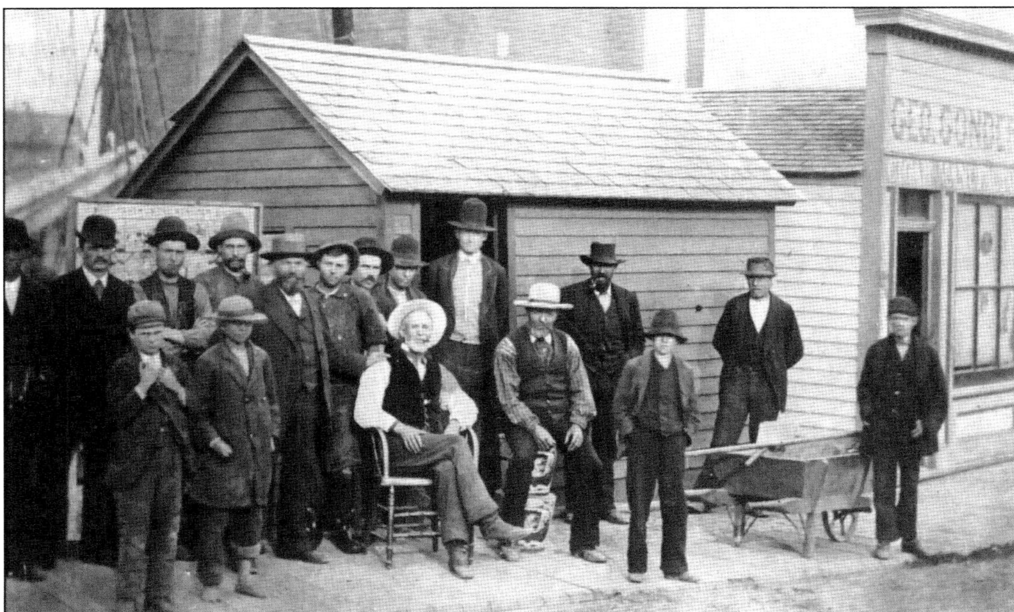

Racine's harbormaster, Capt. John Powers (seated in the chair) is pictured in front of his shanty dwelling at the Main Street Bridge around 1880. The shanty was located just south of the bridge, on the east side of the street. George Gondert's cigar factory is at the right of it. The old grain elevator, which burned in the great fire on May 5, 1882, looms up in the background. Others pictured are crewmembers of the various boats docked in the harbor at the time and dock workers.

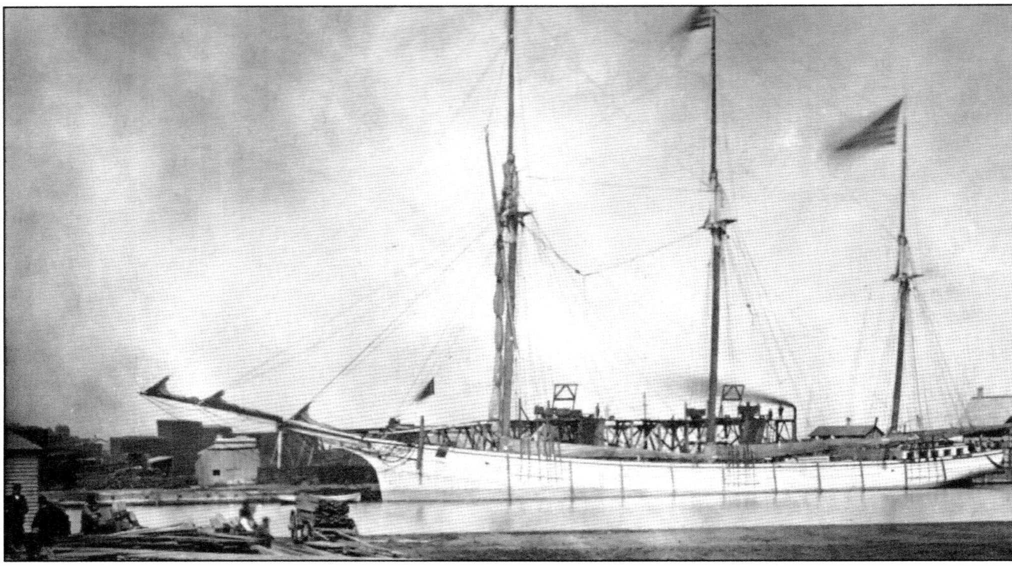

The schooner *J.I. Case* was built in Manitowoc in 1874 and, at first, was used mainly to carry grain out east. On the return, it was usually loaded with coal. For its time, it was the fastest vessel on the Great Lakes. On its three masts, the boat carried the letters "J.I. C." on the fore, main, and mizzen masts. The letters were made of highly polished bronze and, on clear days, were visible for miles.

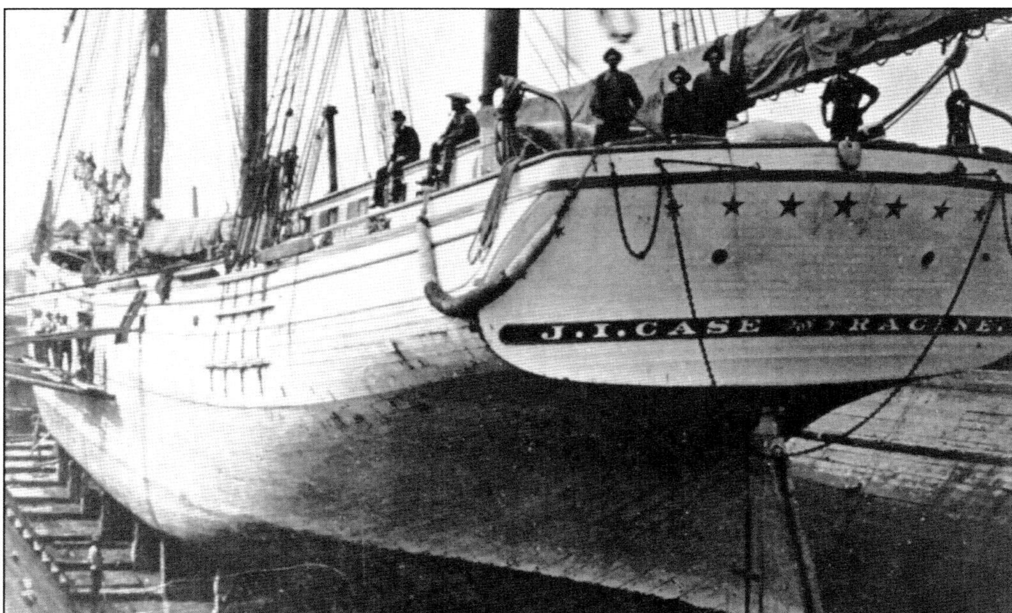

In the early 1890s, the *J.I. Case* was made a tow barge and belonged to John Corrigan of Cleveland. Later, she was put in the lumber trade and, in 1917, belonged to the Hamilton Transport Co. of Chicago. In the spring of 1920, she was sold to the Sincennes-McNaughton Line of Montreal. In 1932, the company towed the boat out into the St. Lawrence River, near Quebec, and she was sunk out of the path of traffic.

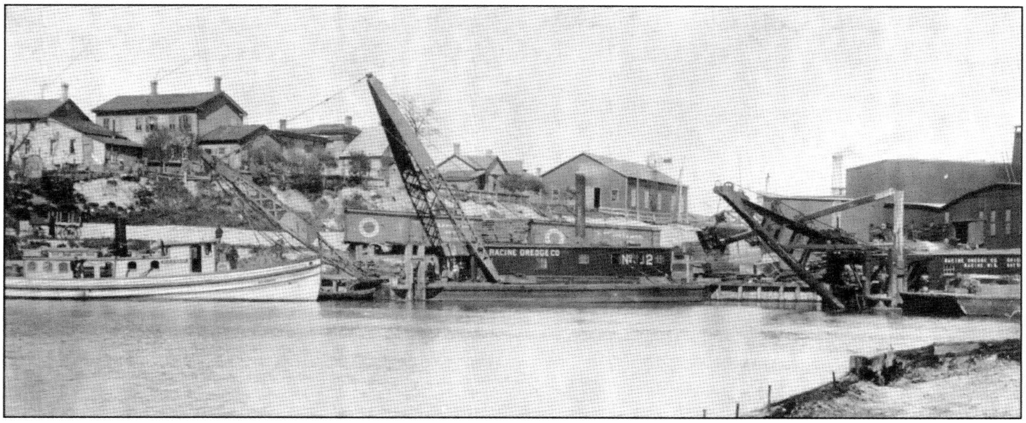

Samuel O. Dixon organized the Racine Dredge Company in 1872. In 1900, it merged with the Starke Dredge & Dock Company of Milwaukee, and Dixon became associated with that company. Frederick M. Knapp, treasurer of the Racine Dredge Company for a number of years, was the owner of the tug *F.M. Knapp*, seen on the left in this photograph.

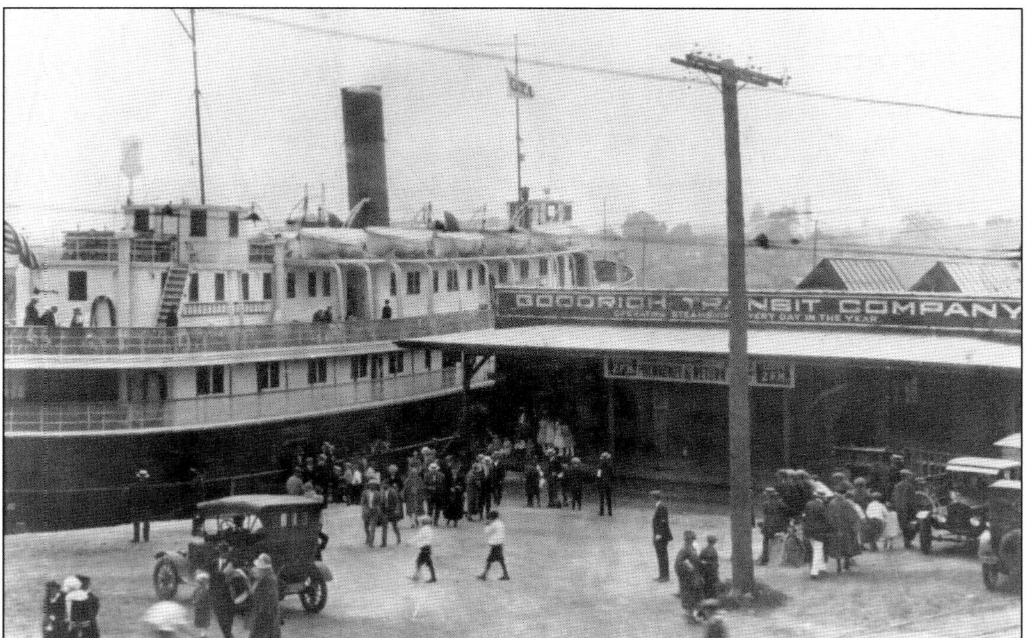

The Goodrich Transit Company's dock was located west of the Main Street Bridge, on the north side of Root River. They provided daily round-trip passenger service to Milwaukee. One of the steamers in Goodrich's fleet in the early 1900s was the *City of Racine*. In early December of each year, it would make runs to Sturgeon Bay, Wisconsin, where it would pick up loads of Christmas trees for the Milwaukee, Racine, and Chicago markets.

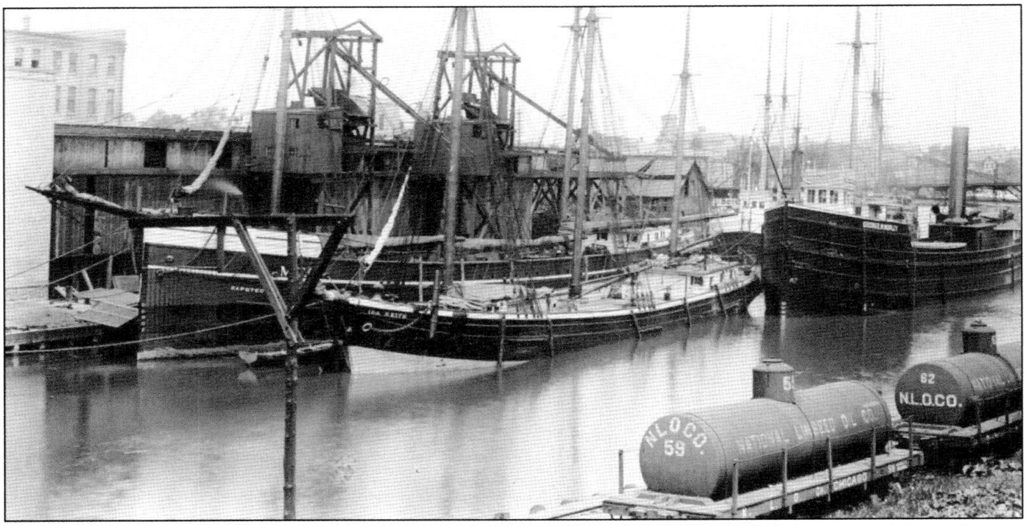

This view of the harbor, taken from behind the D.P. Wigley Company, located at Third Street and Wisconsin Avenue, looks northwest. The two railroad cars in the foreground are owned by the National Linseed Oil Co. They owned and operated a plant for about five years, beginning around 1891, in what is today known as the D.P. Wigley building. Much of the flax seed used was grown within 20 miles of Racine.

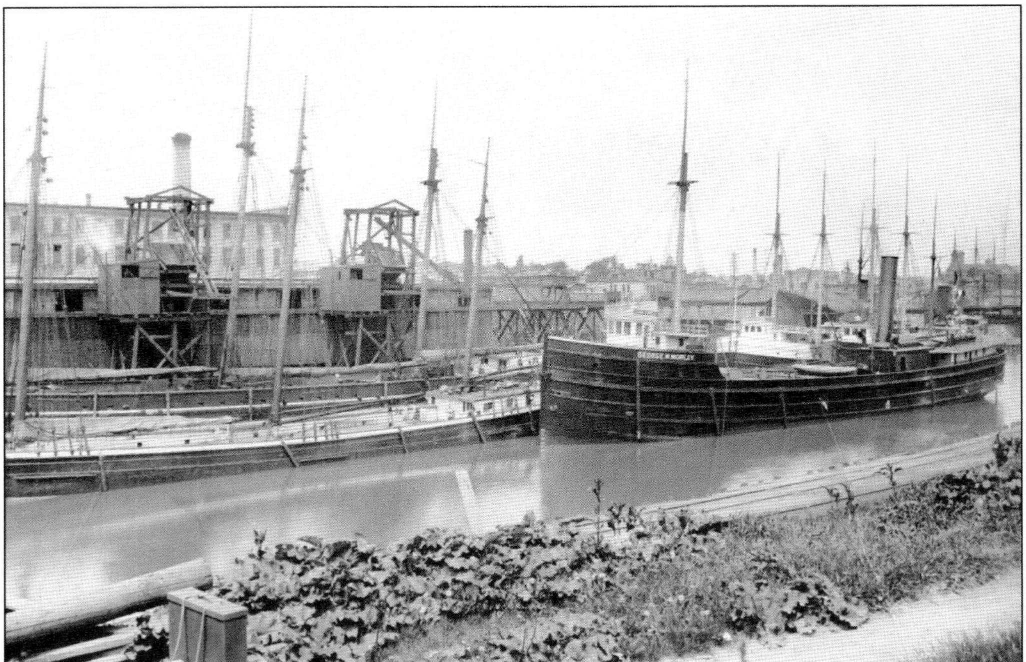

Looking northwest from Fourth Street around 1900, schooners and steamers are seen docked side by side along the west bank of Root River. From 1850 to 1875, warehouses, docks, and lumberyards sprang up all along the river and the harbor was packed with ships. Shipping started to decline here in the 1880s, when area farmers began switching from wheat to dairying, and when railroads started to offer competitive rates.

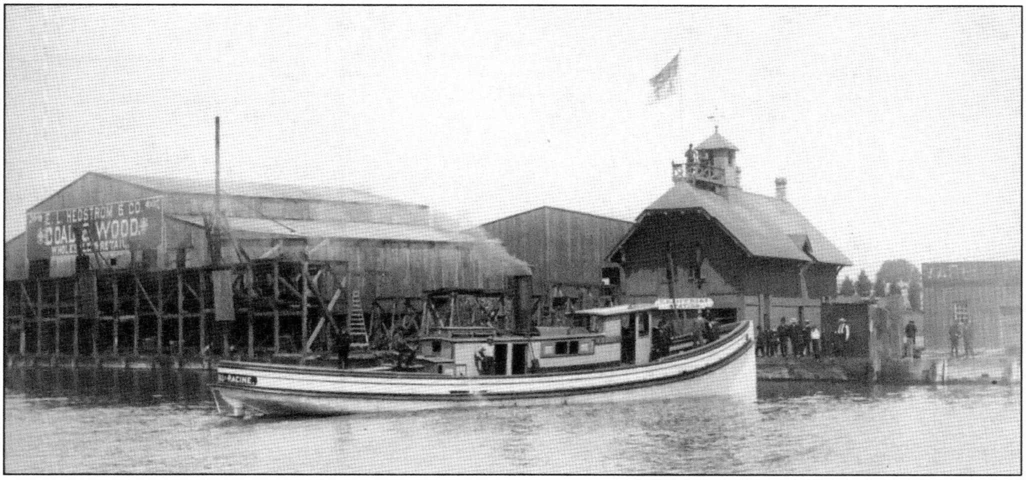

E.L. Hedstrom and Company was a Chicago firm that had a branch in Racine in the late 1800s, as well as in the ports of other cities throughout the Great Lakes, selling coal and wood for heating. In the fall of 1880, E.L. Hedstrom and Company had 12 teams delivering coal to customers in Racine, but by around 1900 they were no longer in business here.

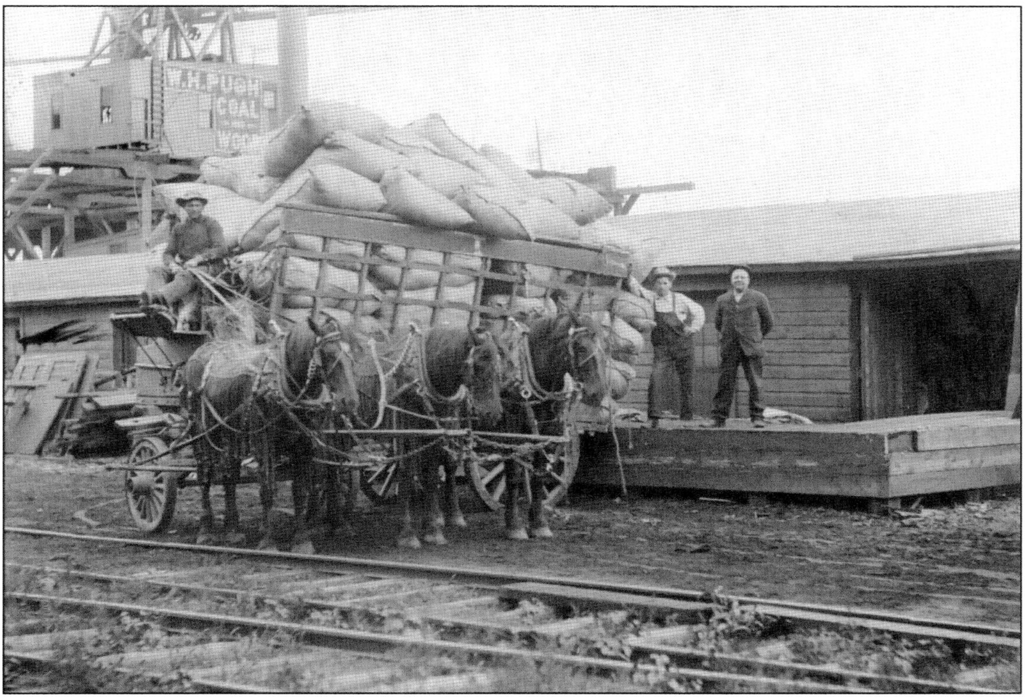

After the harbor was adequately developed in 1844, it became a very active and important element to Racine's growth. The city quickly developed into a bustling place, with grain elevators, coal yards, lumber warehouses, and shipbuilders. By the late 1840s, Racine had become the fifth-busiest port on the Great Lakes in terms of tonnage, behind only Buffalo, Cleveland, Detroit, and Chicago.

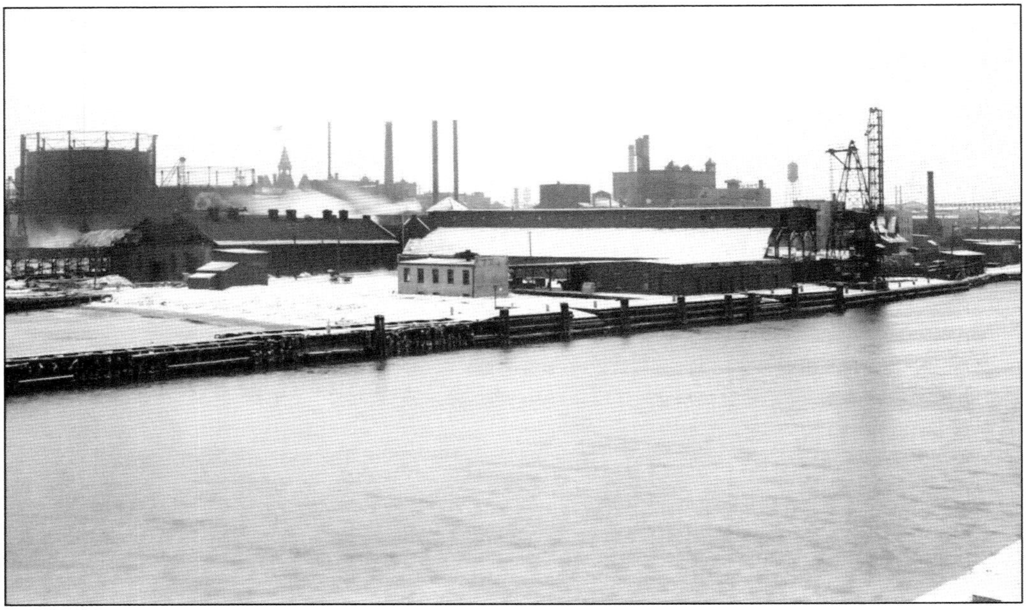

Racine is pictured as it looked from the mouth of the Root River, on a cold, winter day in the 1920s. Looking southwest across the harbor, the Goodrich Transit Company's warehouse can be seen in the foreground, with the Wisconsin Natural Gas and Electric Company's coal yard and coke plant beyond. The flag flying atop the spire in the background marks the location of Racine's city hall.

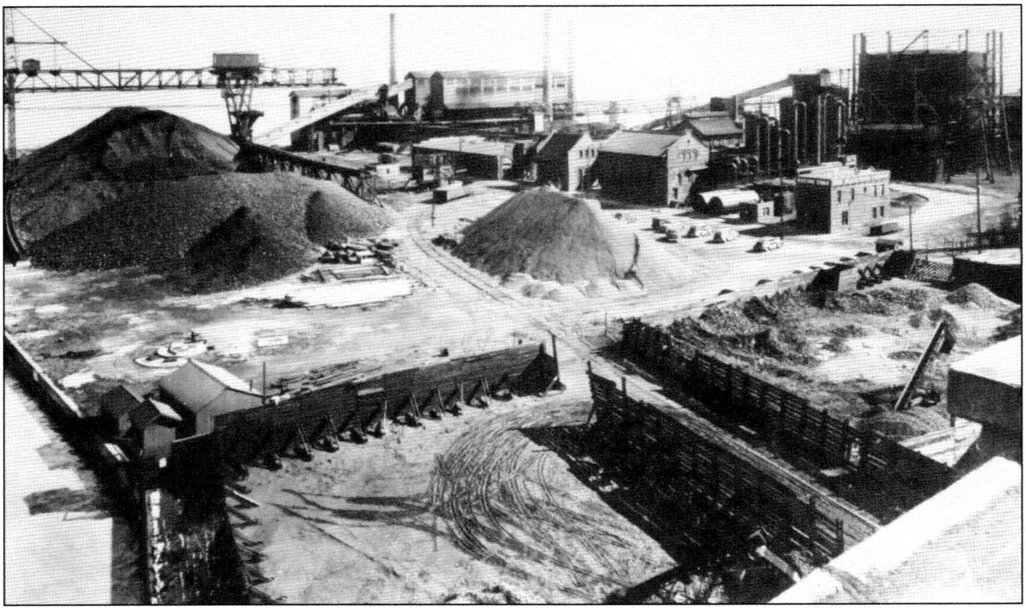

The Wisconsin Natural Gas and Electric Company, once located on the south side of the Root River where it empties into Lake Michigan, looked like this in 1939. Here, coke had been made since 1905 from the large piles of coal, which, under the name of Racine Coke, was sold to homeowners to heat their homes. It burned cleaner than coal. This plant was eliminated in 1950, when natural gas became available in Racine.

This westward view of the Fourth Street Bridge was taken in the late 1860s. The original woolen mill, which burned in 1870, can be seen in the background. In the left foreground is a rickety wood stairway leading down to the river. This bridge, built in 1857, was kept painted white, making it boldly stand out. It was replaced in 1878 by a new steel bridge.

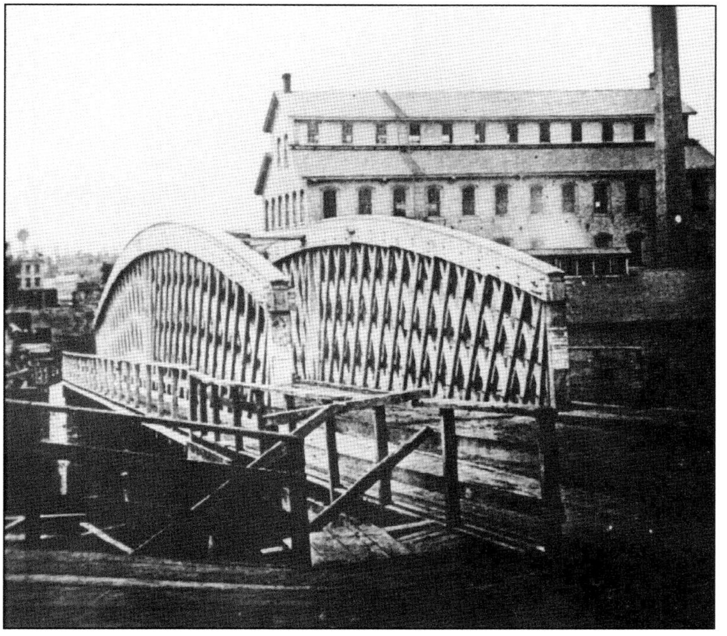

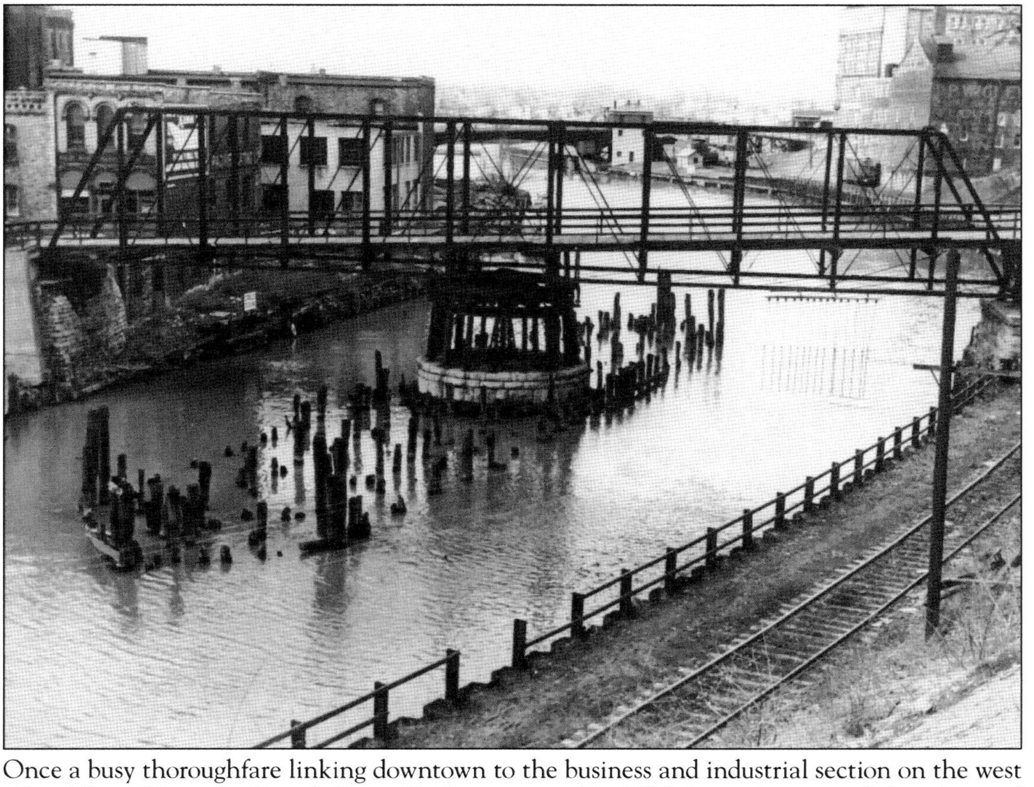

Once a busy thoroughfare linking downtown to the business and industrial section on the west side of Root River, the Fourth Street Bridge was razed in 1954 due to its age and the advent of heavy motor vehicles. Constructed in 1878, it had steel supports with a wooden deck. The bridge was condemned in 1936 and, after that, was designated for pedestrian use only.

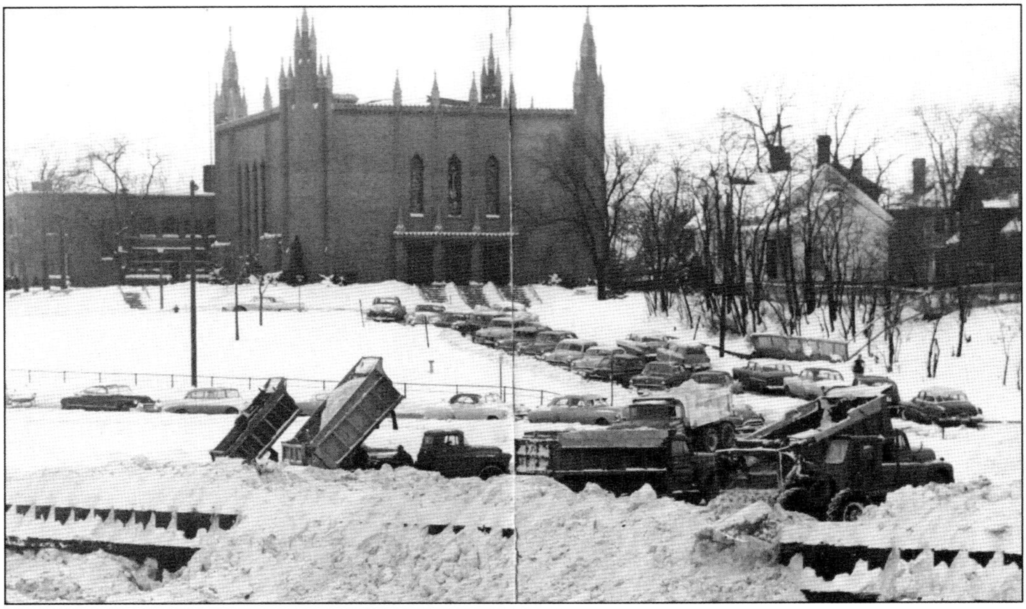

Truckloads of snow are seen here, being dumped at the Goodrich Dock bank along the Root River in January 1959. After 19 inches of snowfall, hundreds of truckloads of snow were removed from city streets and dumped in various areas of town including the lakefront, behind the Howell School, and at Graceland Cemetery. At the lakefront, a bulldozer was used to push the snow into the lake.

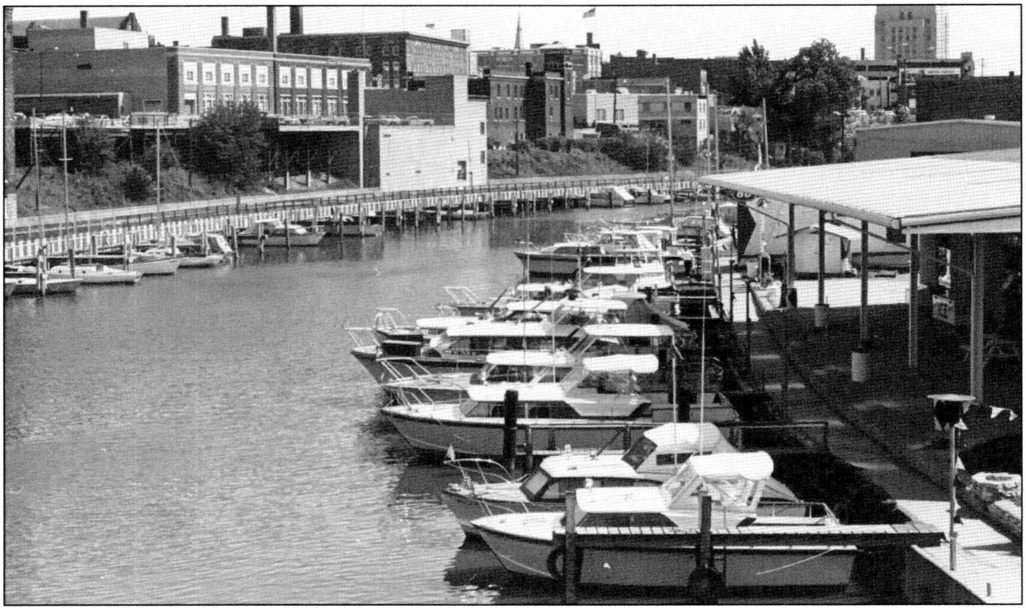

Looking south from the State Street Bridge around 1970, this part of the Root River is now lined with pleasure boats. Palmer Johnson's marina can be seen on the west side of the river. Lake Michigan's water level, which cycles unpredictably up and down, rose to the highest level recorded during the 1900s in 1973. The rise was more than five feet over nine years, with the high water lasting through 1976.

Two

Monument Square

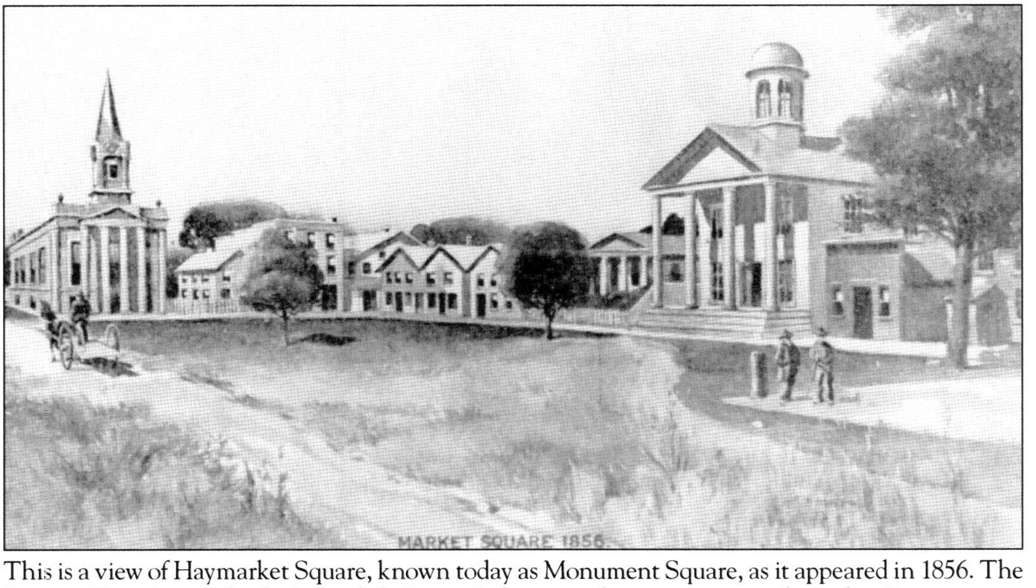

This is a view of Haymarket Square, known today as Monument Square, as it appeared in 1856. The Baptist Church is at the far left, while Racine's first courthouse is seen on the right. Construction on the Baptist Church building was completed in 1846. The bell in the belfry was used as the fire alarm for the city of Racine until the church burned down in 1862.

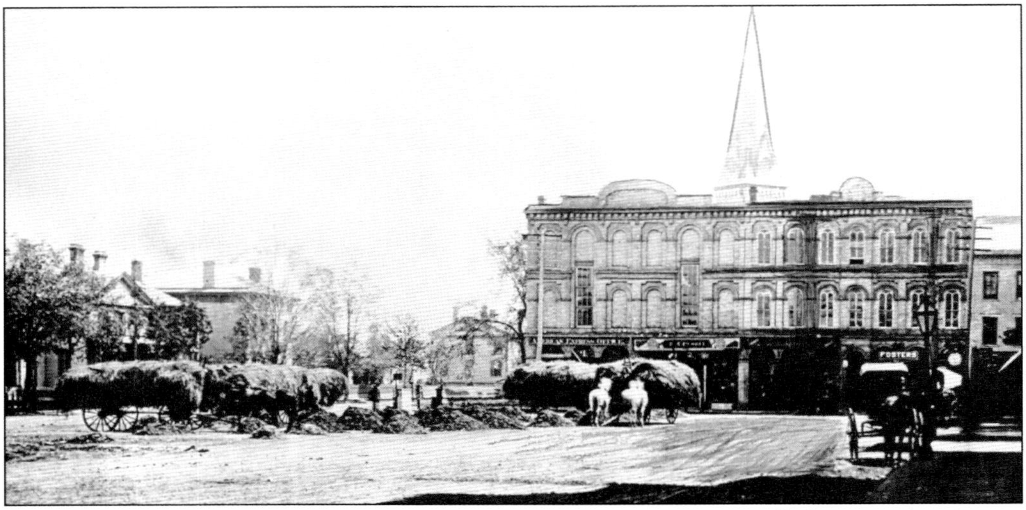

This c. 1870 photograph of Haymarket Square illustrates why it was called Haymarket Square in the early days and shows the southeast intersection of Main and Sixth Streets—present site of the post office. Many people at that time believed that Haymarket Square should be cleared of its loads of hay, produce, and its wagons and that the area should be transformed into a spot of beauty.

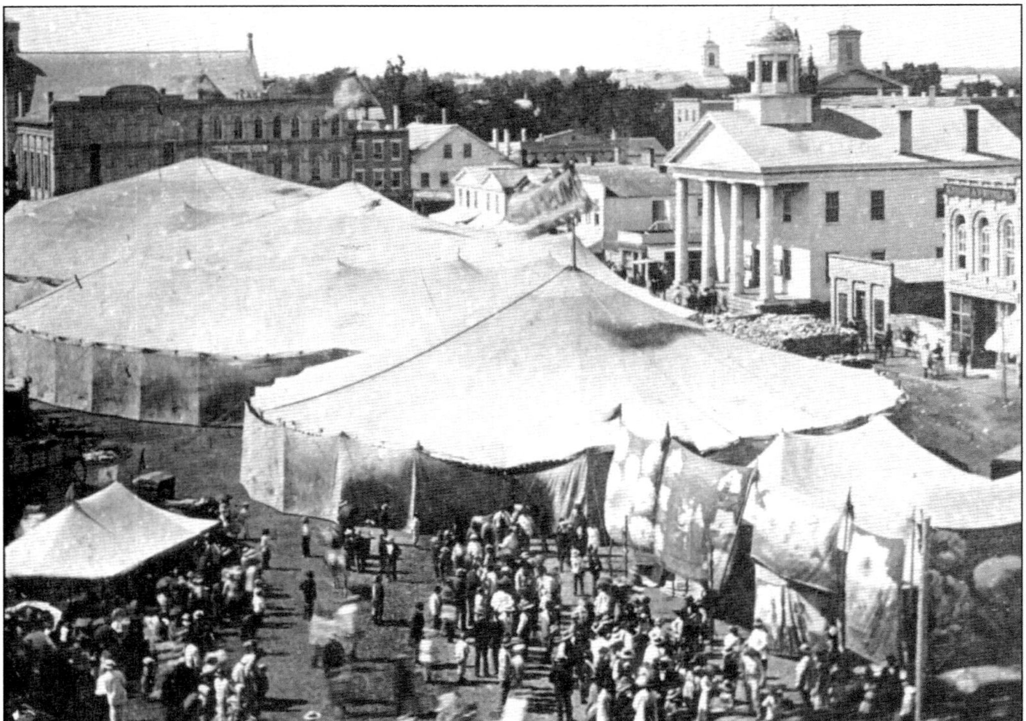

Haymarket Square was the site of a circus sometime around 1870. Looking south from what, today, would be near the corner of Fifth and Main Streets, the canvas tents of the Forepaugh Circus are seen here. During the 1870s, Adam Forepaugh and P.T. Barnum had the two largest circuses in the nation.

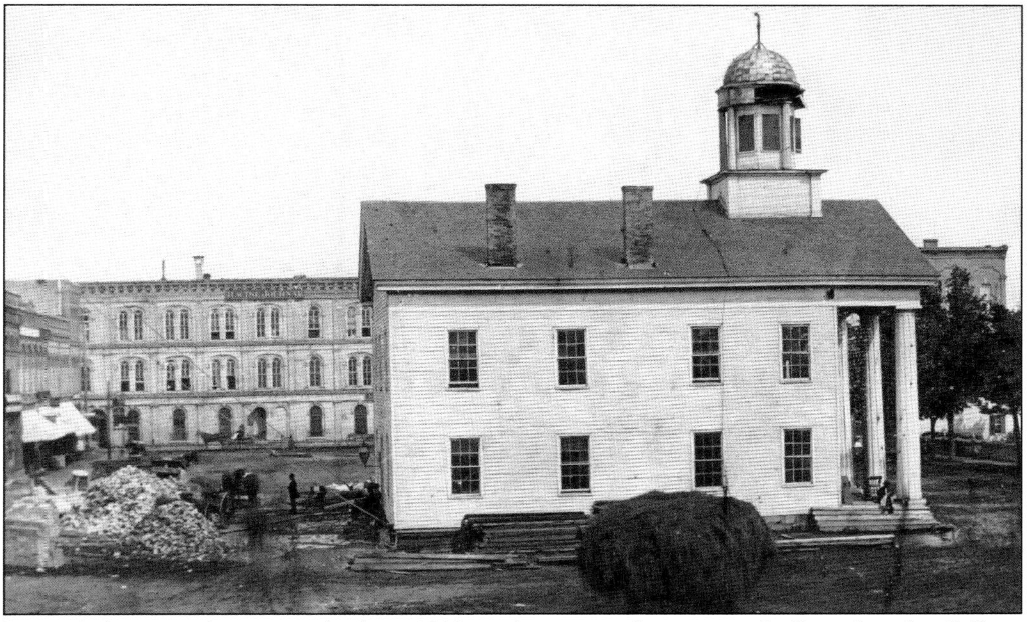

Racine's first courthouse was built in 1839, at the personal expense of village founder Gilbert Knapp. It was used until 1876, when it was moved to the center of Haymarket Square, as shown here, so that the second courthouse could be built on the original site. After being moved, the original courthouse remained in use until construction of the second one was completed.

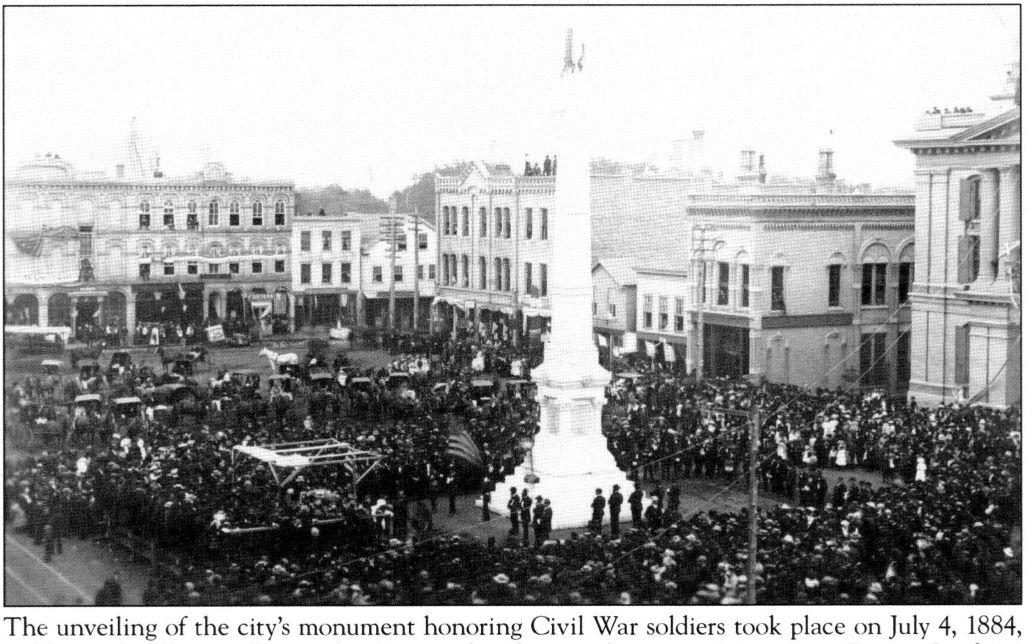

The unveiling of the city's monument honoring Civil War soldiers took place on July 4, 1884, in Haymarket Square. Haymarket Square then became known as Monument Square. Looking southwest across Monument Square, part of the front of Racine's second courthouse can be seen at the far right.

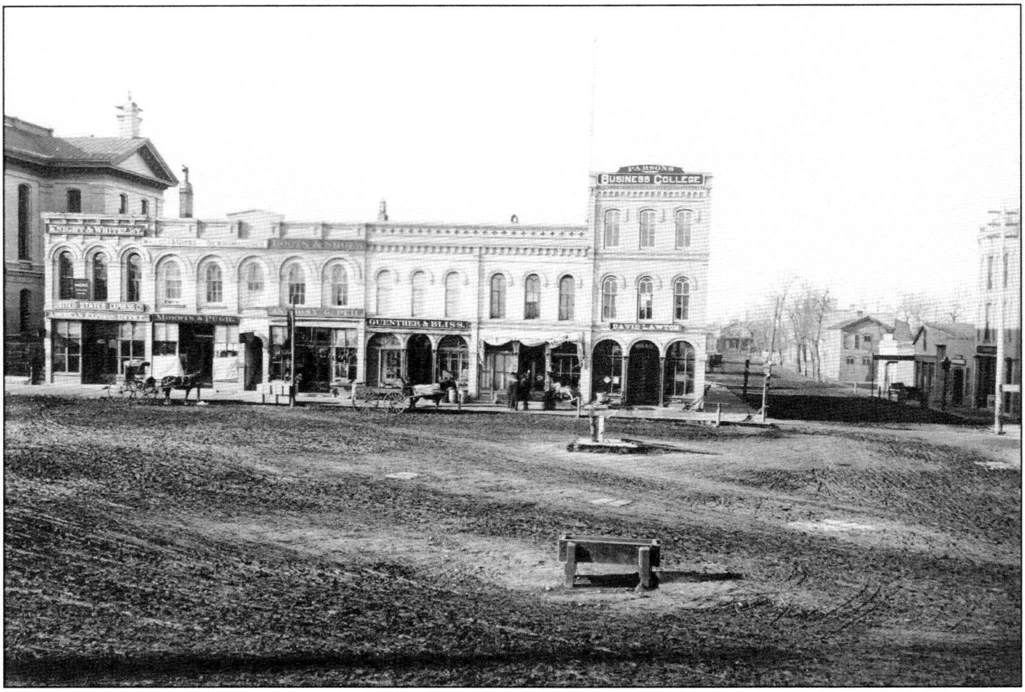

This incredible view features the buildings north of the courthouse and west on Fifth Street from the late 1800s. For a time, Racine was the site of a number of private business colleges. Professor Parsons' Business College, on the far right, was opened in 1877 at Fifth Street and Monument Square. By 1900, four business colleges were in operation. Today, none remain.

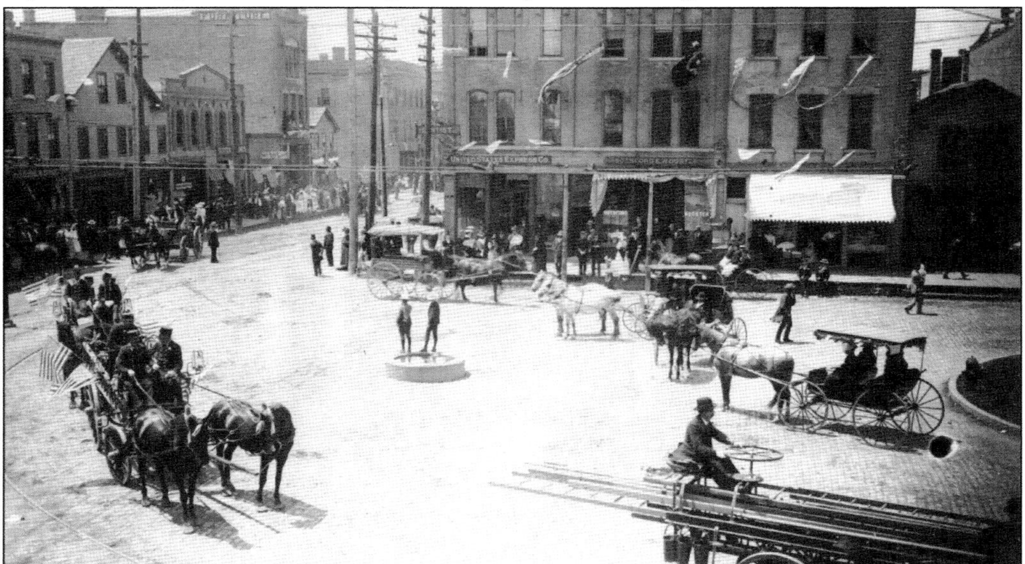

The city of Racine's fire equipment is seen here, leading a parade east on Sixth Street where it turns north onto Main Street at Monument Square. Pictured from left to right, the United States Express Co. and Botsford & Wooster booksellers were located at the south end of Monument Square in the late 1890s.

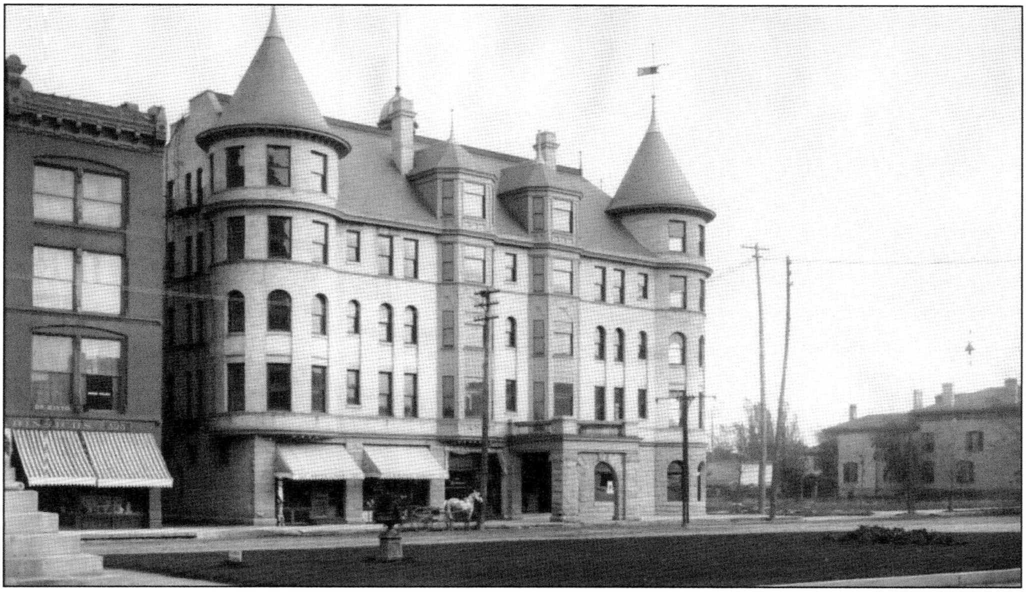

When it was completed in 1892, the first Hotel Racine pictured above was considered the ultimate in comfort and gracious living. Spanning the block of Sixth Street between Main Street and Lake Avenue, it provided its guests with wonderful views of Monument Square and Lake Michigan. It was razed in 1925, and the second Hotel Racine was built in its place.

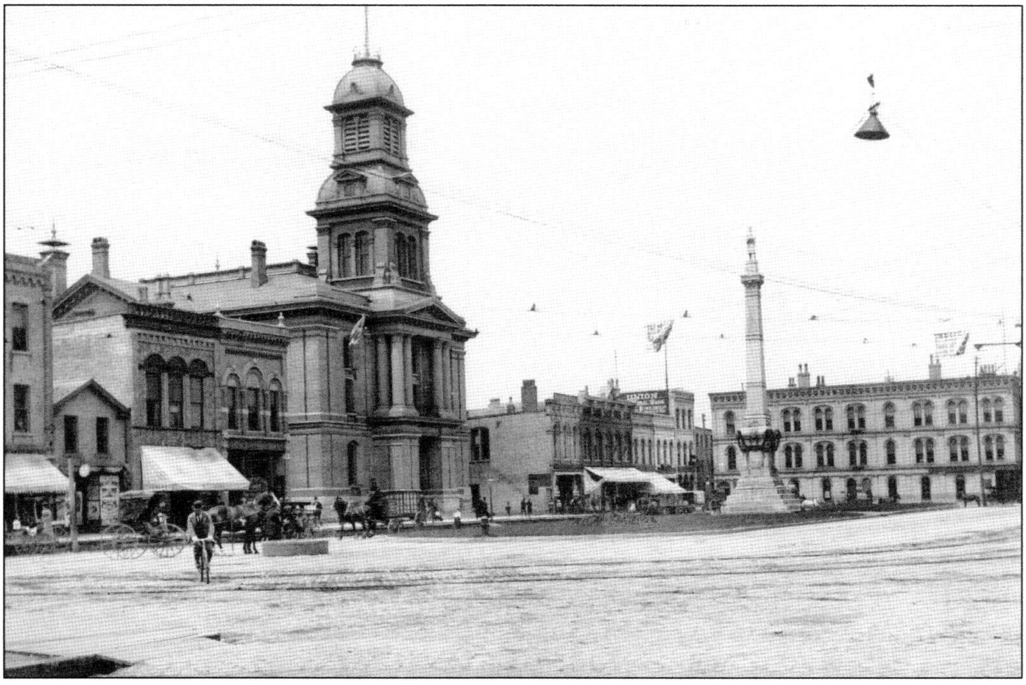

Looking northwest from the corner of Sixth and Main Streets, this image offers a sweeping view of Monument Square as it appeared in 1898. By this time, a grassy parklike area with flower gardens had been developed around the Civil War Soldier's Monument. Racine's second courthouse can be seen standing proudly as the tallest building on the west side of Monument Square.

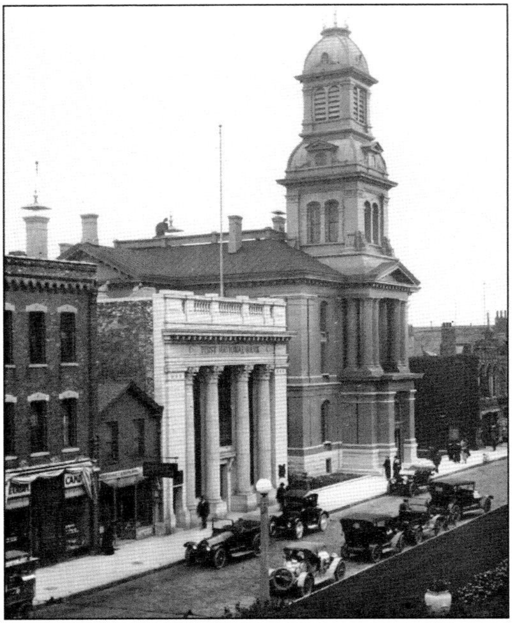

The First National Bank building, constructed in 1913 on the south side of the courthouse, was three stories high and shut off all natural light to offices on the south side of the courthouse. As a result, the county board decided that any new courthouse would be built quite a distance from other buildings, so as to allow it to receive natural light and for safety in case of fire.

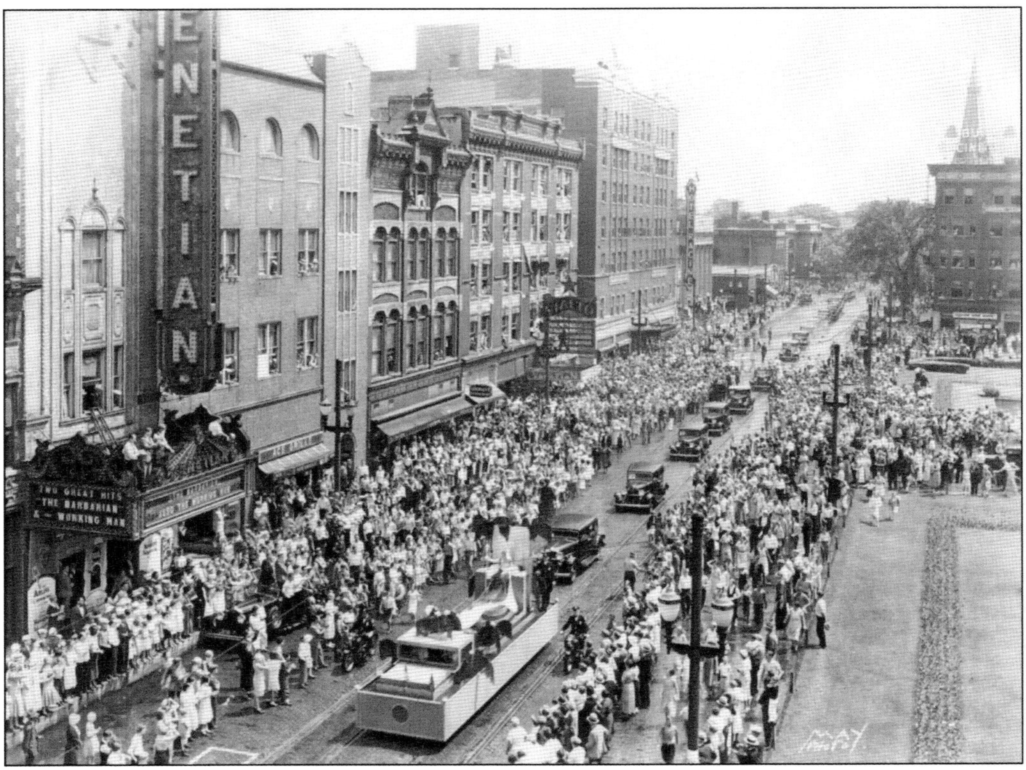

In 1933, Lillian Anderson was chosen to serve as queen of the Century of Progress celebration in Chicago. Friends entered her picture in the competition, and she was chosen as the first-place winner from more than 100,000 entries. Her homecoming to Racine with her court of honor, pictured here, drew thousands along the reception route.

This 1938 photograph looks northeast across Monument Square from Sixth Street. Buses and electric streetcars are seen in operation on Main Street. Bus service was operated at this time by the Milwaukee Electric Railway and Transport Company. The Venetian theater (pictured at center) is playing *The Affairs of Annabelle* and *Tenth Avenue Kid*, while the nearby Rialto (three buildings to the right) screens *Too Hot to Handle* and *Freshman Year.* All four of these films were released in September 1938.

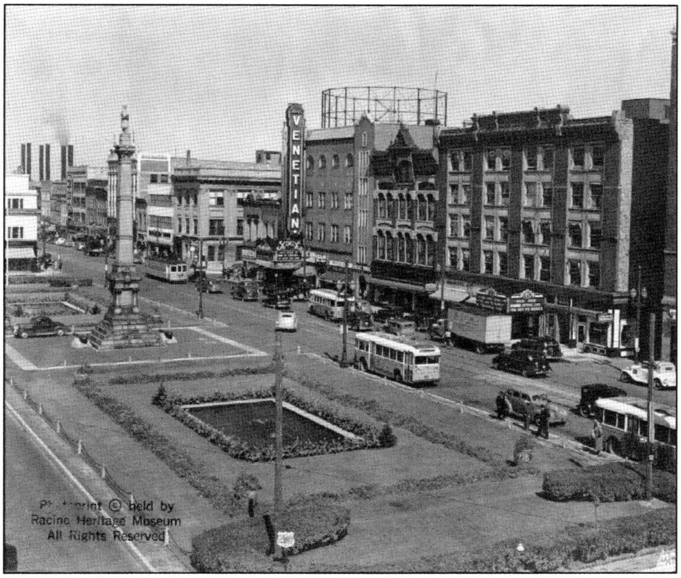

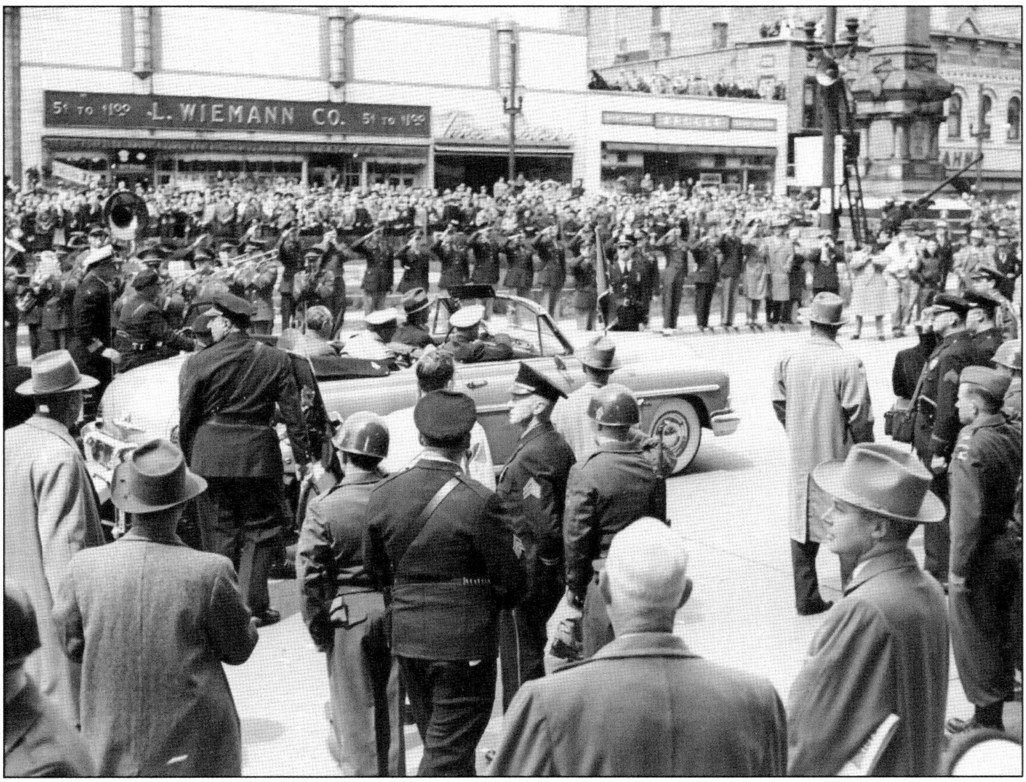

Gen. Douglas MacArthur stopped at Monument Square Friday morning, April 27, 1951, on his way from Chicago to Milwaukee. The general rode with Wisconsin governor Walter Kohler, who met him at the state line and is seated in the back seat, to the general's left. Police had to surround the car to hold back the crowds that broke through the lines at Monument Square and milled around the car.

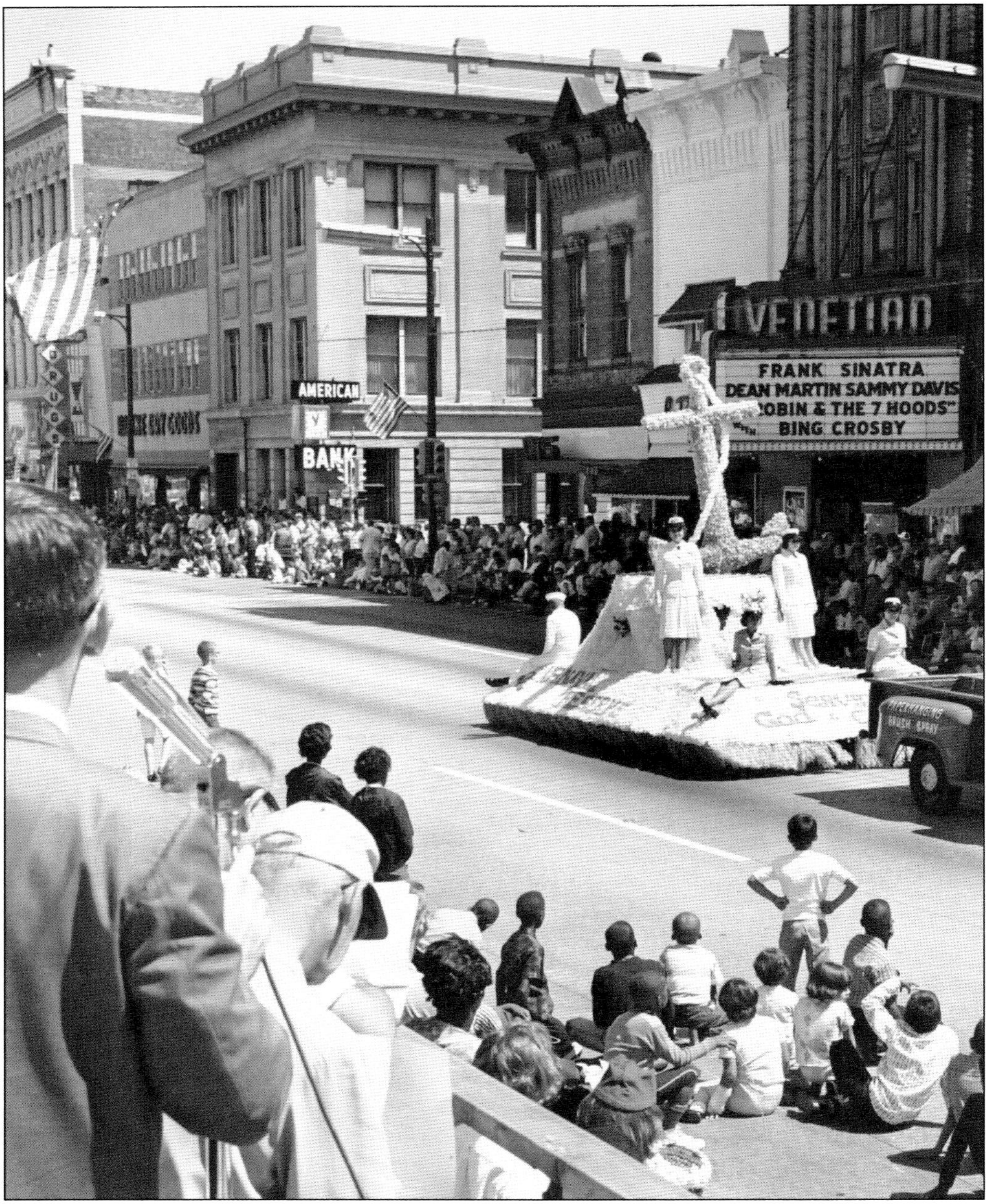

A crowd estimated at 100,000 persons lined Racine's Main Street to watch the 28th-annual Goodwill Fourth of July Parade in 1964. This is the view from the reviewing stand on Monument Square, where the judges for the floats were located. An announcer on the stand would broadcast details about the floats and other units to the surrounding crowd as the parade passed by.

This fabulous view of Monument Square in 1955 is looking north from Sixth Street. The billboard on Monument Square is advertising the Racine Kiwanis Club's annual Pancake and Sausage Day at Memorial Hall on Saturday, May 28. *Strategic Air Command*, seen playing at the Venetian Theater, opened there on Wednesday, May 25, 1955.

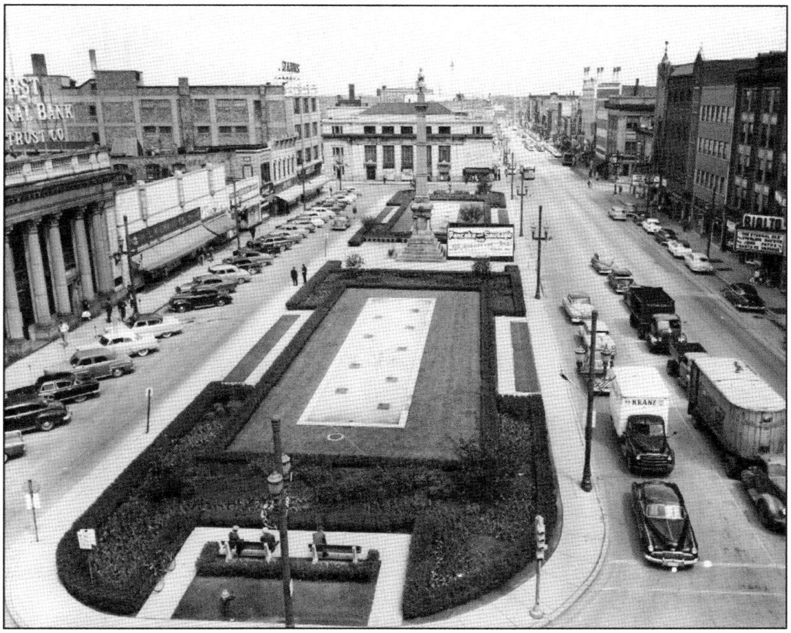

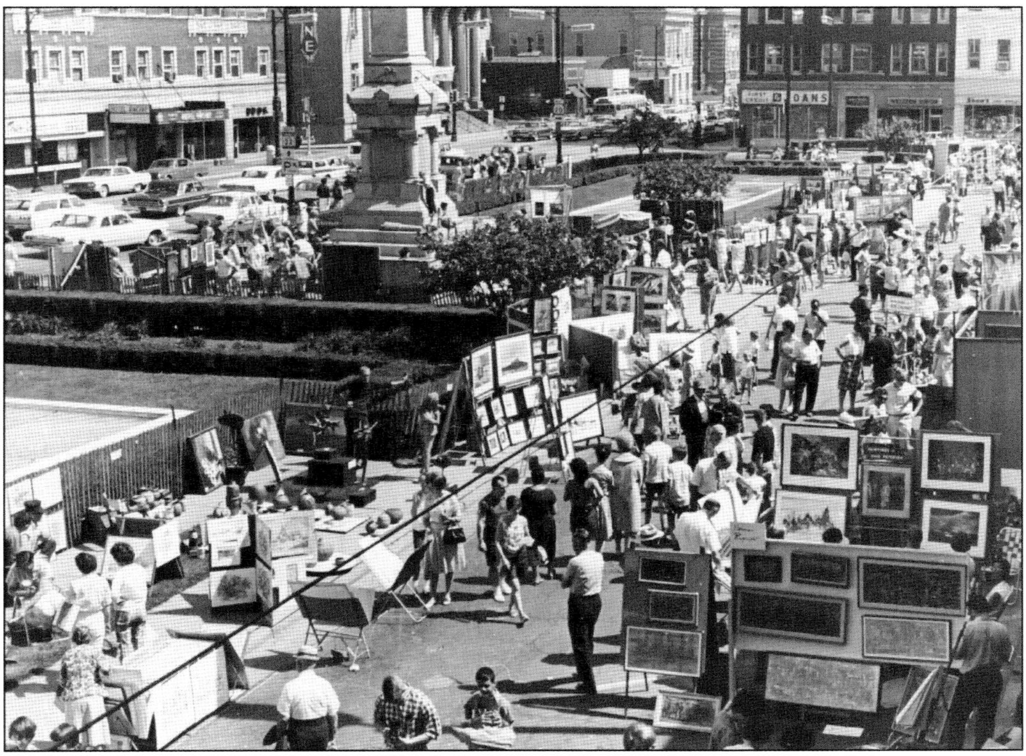

The first-annual Monument Square Art Fair was held on Saturday, June 22, 1963, and is now one of the oldest and most respected art events in Wisconsin. It has been held at various locations over the years, but in 2013 it returned to its original location on Monument Square. This photograph of the Monument Square Art Fair was taken in 1965.

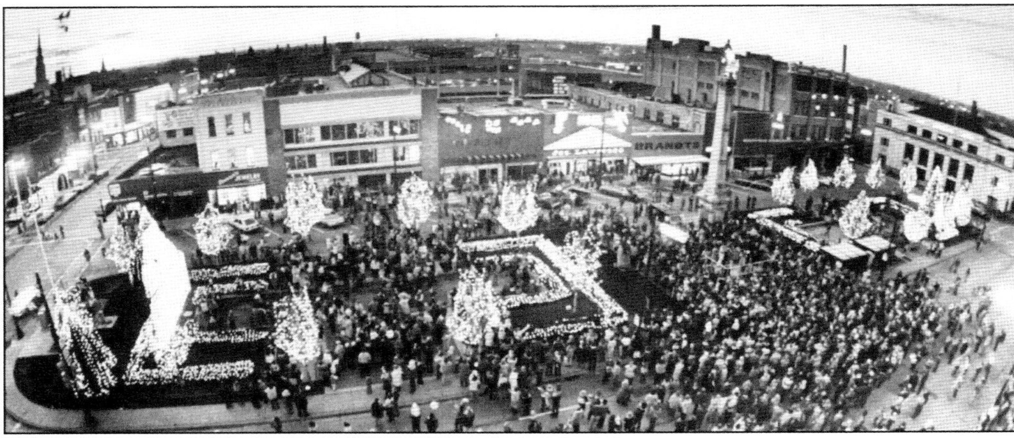

The viewing of the Wheary Lights, a Racine holiday tradition, began in the 1960s as a large light display at the home of local industrialist George Wheary. Around 1980, Wheary donated the lights to the City of Racine, who installed them annually on Monument Square, as seen here in 1982. In 1985, the Kiwanis Club took over the event and moved the display to the Racine Zoological Gardens.

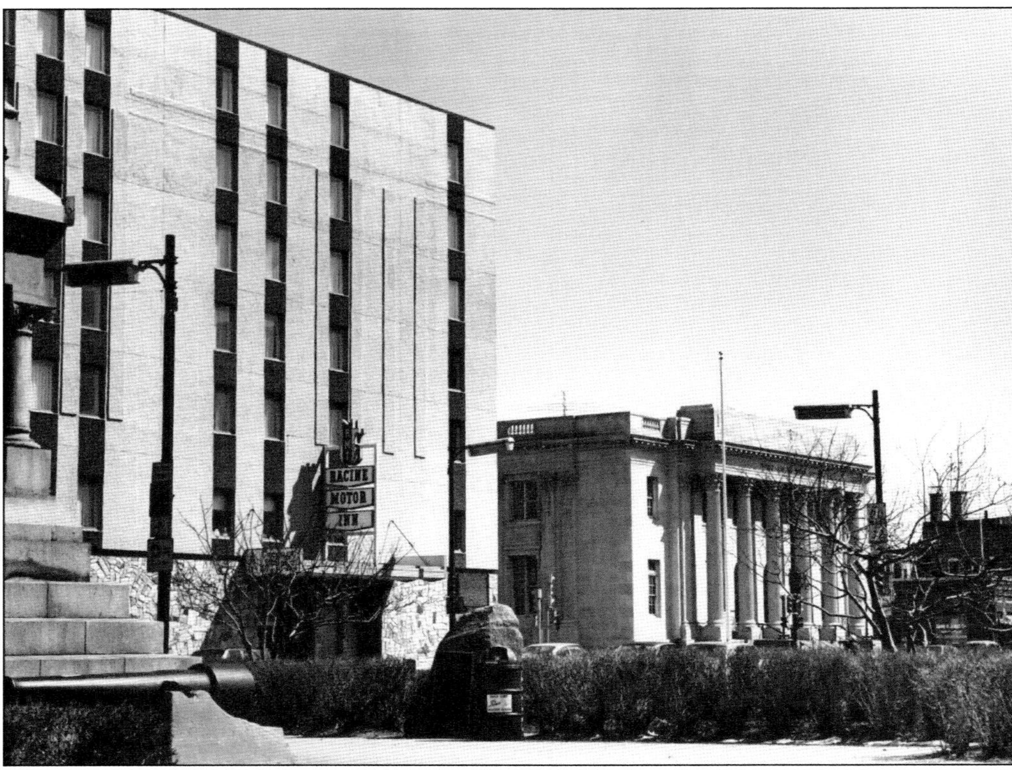

Looking southeast across Monument Square, the Racine Motor Inn occupied a prime location. Guests with rooms on the west side of the hotel had a wonderful view of Monument Square. Originally known as the Hotel Racine, the structure was acquired by a group of Milwaukee investors who closed it for rebuilding in mid-1965. After numerous delays, the hotel finally reopened as the Racine Motor Inn in 1968.

Three

Street Scenes

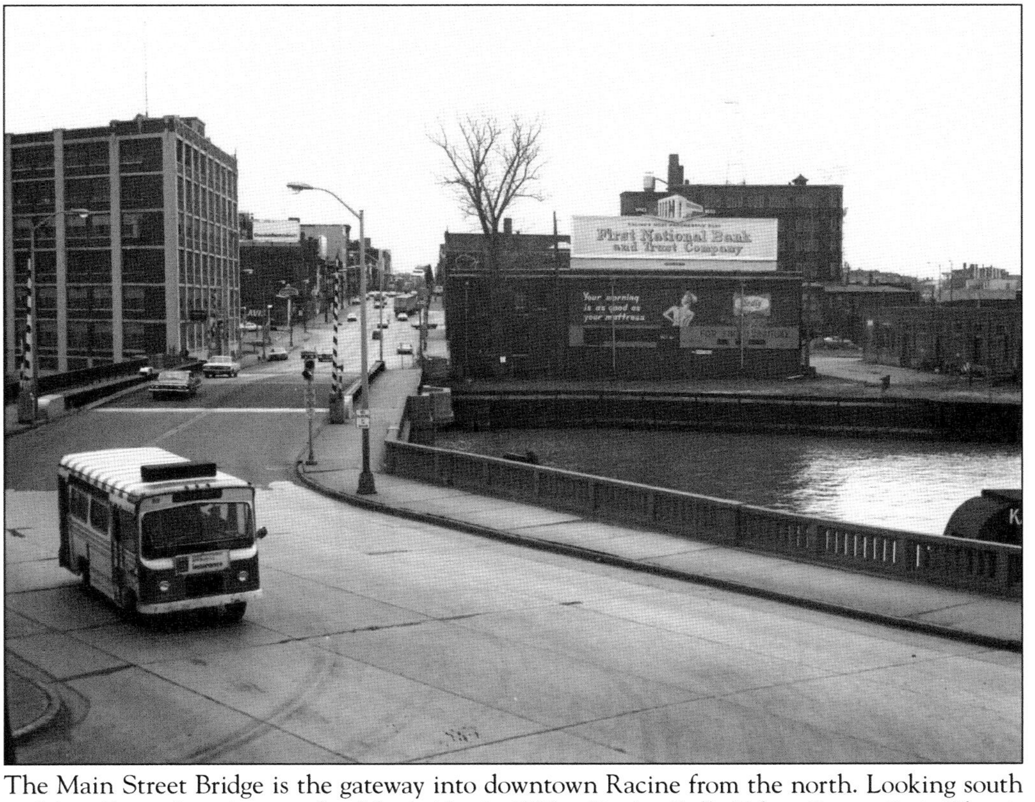

The Main Street Bridge is the gateway into downtown Racine from the north. Looking south on Main Street from just north of the bridge in 1972, a Racine Belle Urban System "mini" bus is seen in the foreground heading north. The six-story Terminal Building, across the bridge on the left, was built in 1919 and purchased by the Oster Manufacturing Company in 1944.

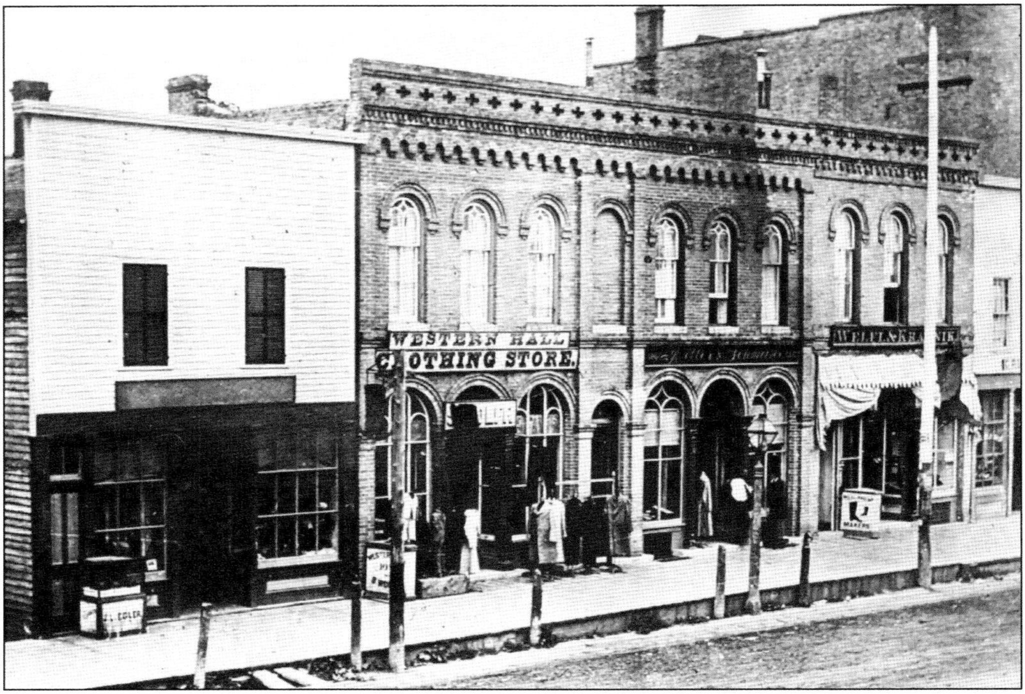

Hitching posts lined the wood sidewalks on the west side of Main Street between Third and Fourth Streets in the 1870s. Welfl & Kraynik operated a boot and shoe store in 1877, which is seen on the far right. These four buildings, on the southeast corner of Main and Third Streets, were replaced by Racine's first city hall in 1885.

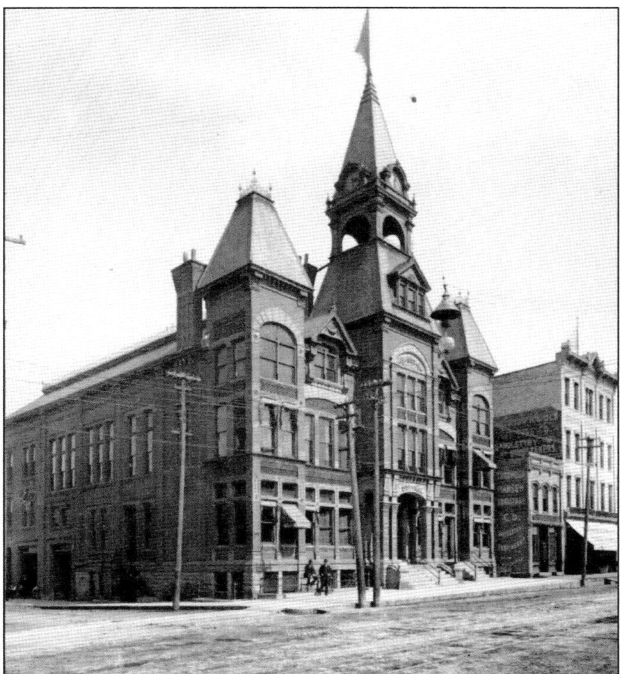

Racine's first city hall at Third and Main Streets is pictured in 1898. Racine's city council first met in the courthouse, and then it rented rooms in the Masonic Block on Main Street, south of Fourth Street. For the 11 years prior to the city hall building's completion in 1885, aldermen met on the third floor of the Merchants National Bank at the northwest corner of Fifth and Main Streets.

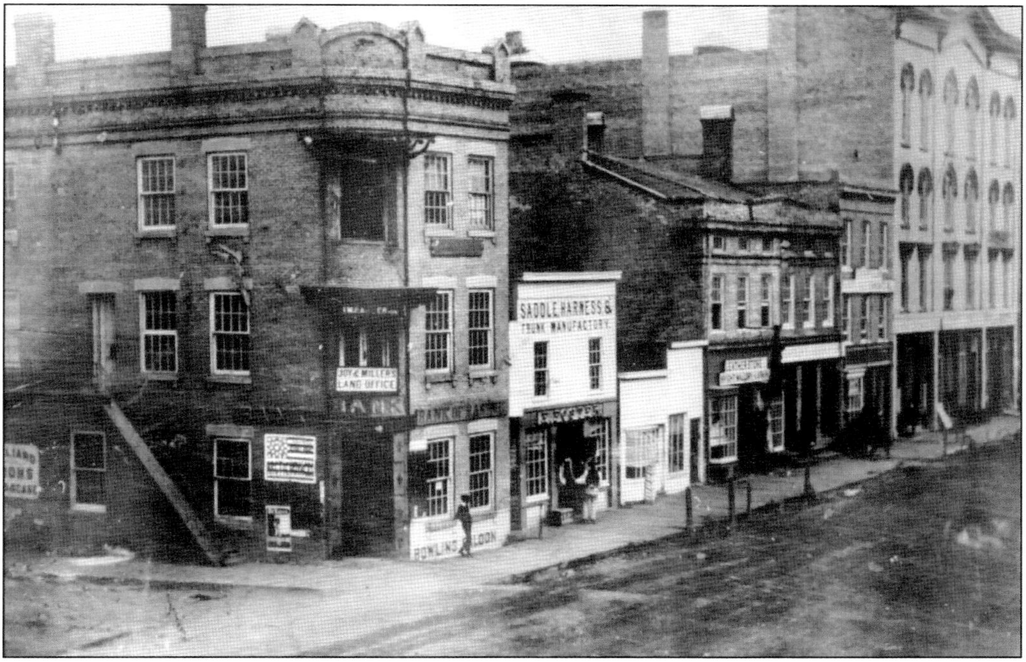

This is the southeast corner of Main and Fourth Streets. The building on the corner is the City Bank of Racine. Established in 1853, it failed in 1857. Edwin Foster opened his shop next to the bank in March 1853, making trunks, harnesses, saddles, and whips. By the end of 1866, he was out of business completely.

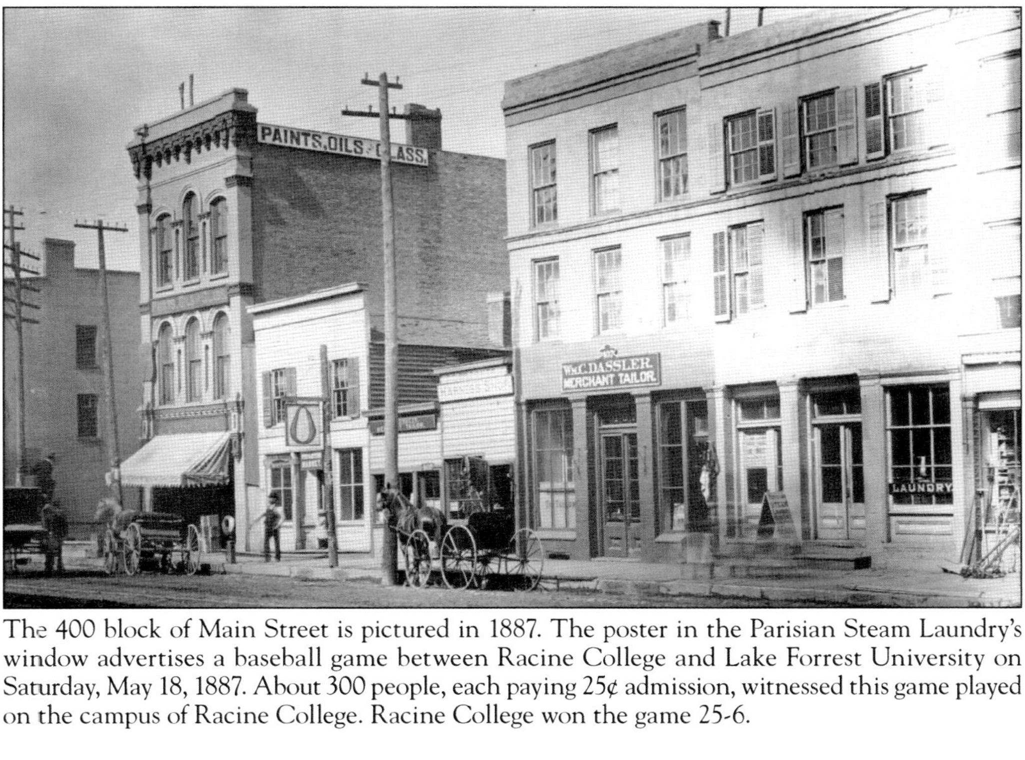

The 400 block of Main Street is pictured in 1887. The poster in the Parisian Steam Laundry's window advertises a baseball game between Racine College and Lake Forrest University on Saturday, May 18, 1887. About 300 people, each paying 25¢ admission, witnessed this game played on the campus of Racine College. Racine College won the game 25-6.

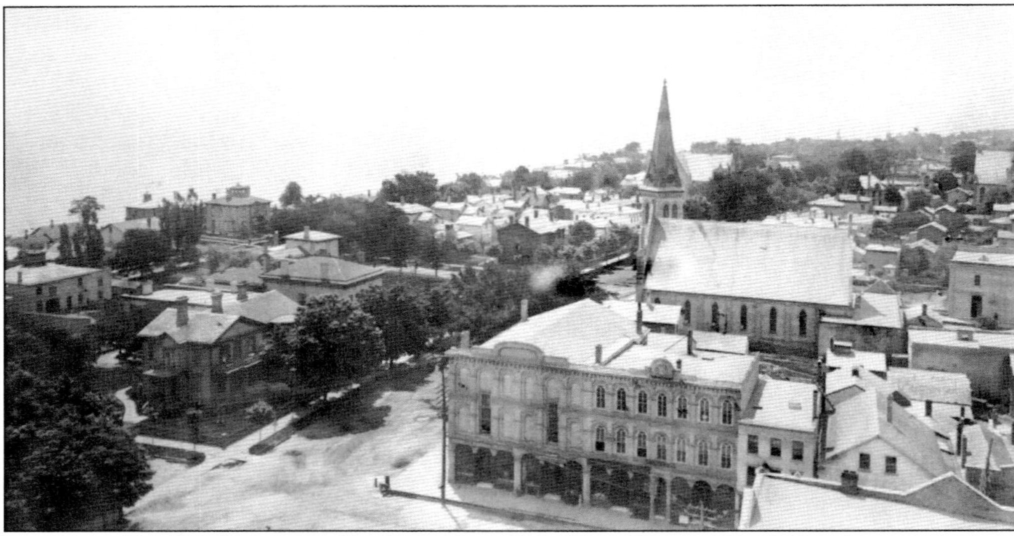

This c. 1882 aerial view is of the south side of Sixth and Main Streets as well as the area just to the southeast of it. At the time, this area was primarily residential. Today, the intersection of Sixth and Main Streets is in the heart of the business district of downtown.

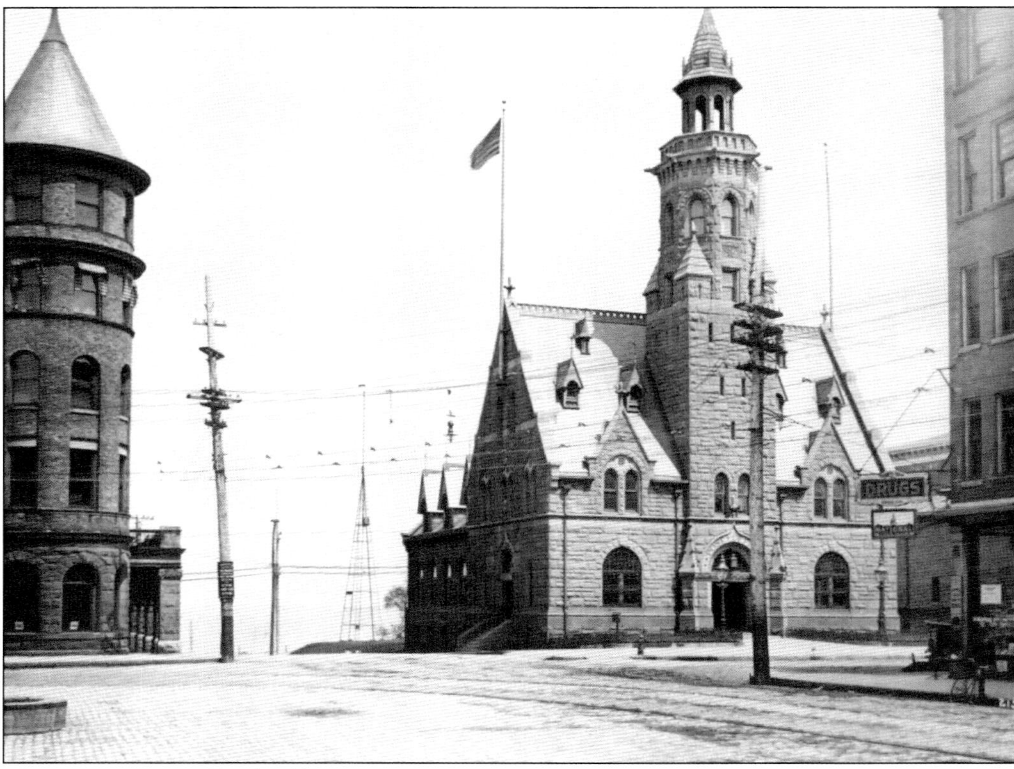

This Racine Post Office building at Sixth and Main Streets was the first federal building in Racine. Constructed in 1897 and built completely of stone, the building drew considerable criticism. Many felt it resembled a church more than a post office building, which finally caused the government to chisel the words "Post Office" over the front entrance.

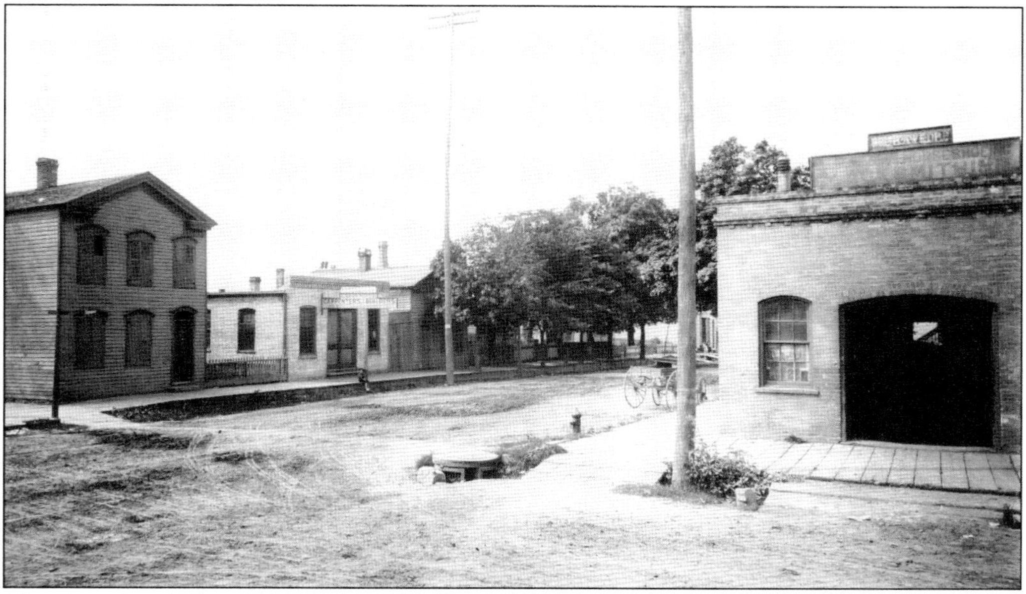

This photograph shows the corner of Fifth and Wisconsin Streets, looking northwest, in 1885. The blacksmith shop on the northeast corner (at the far right) is now where the *Racine Journal Times* building is located. Racine Fire Station No. 5 would later be built on the northwest corner of Fourth Street and Wisconsin Avenue.

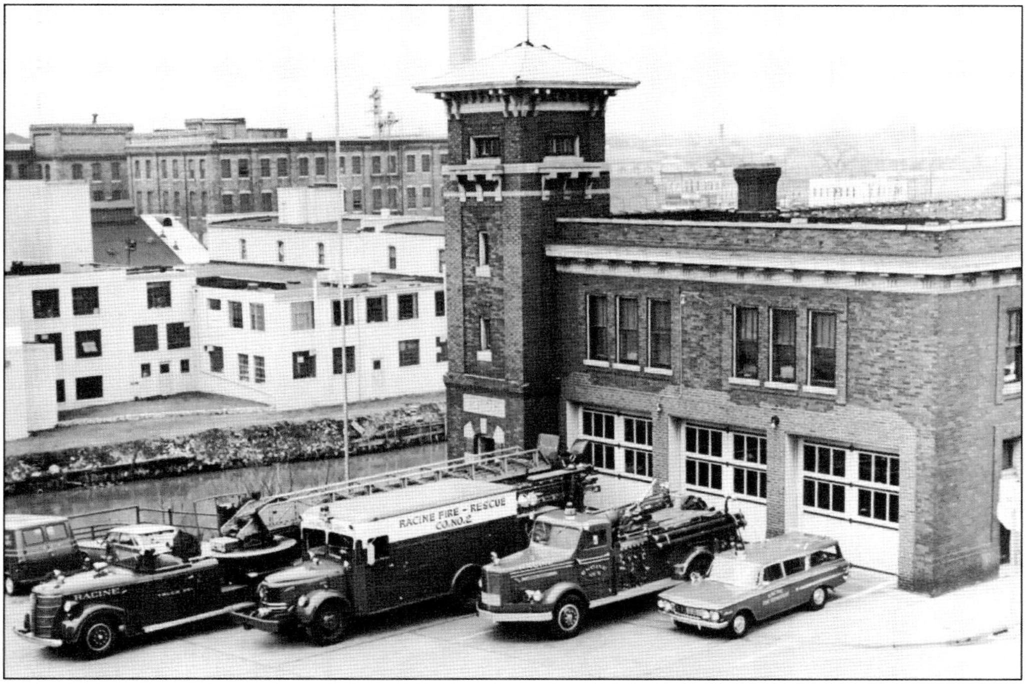

Before completion of the new Safety Building in 1968, the headquarters and main station of the Racine Fire Department was located on Fourth Street between Wisconsin Avenue and the Root River. Pictured is the motorized fire equipment utilized by this station in 1966. It has since been torn down and is now a parking lot owned by the *Racine Journal Times*.

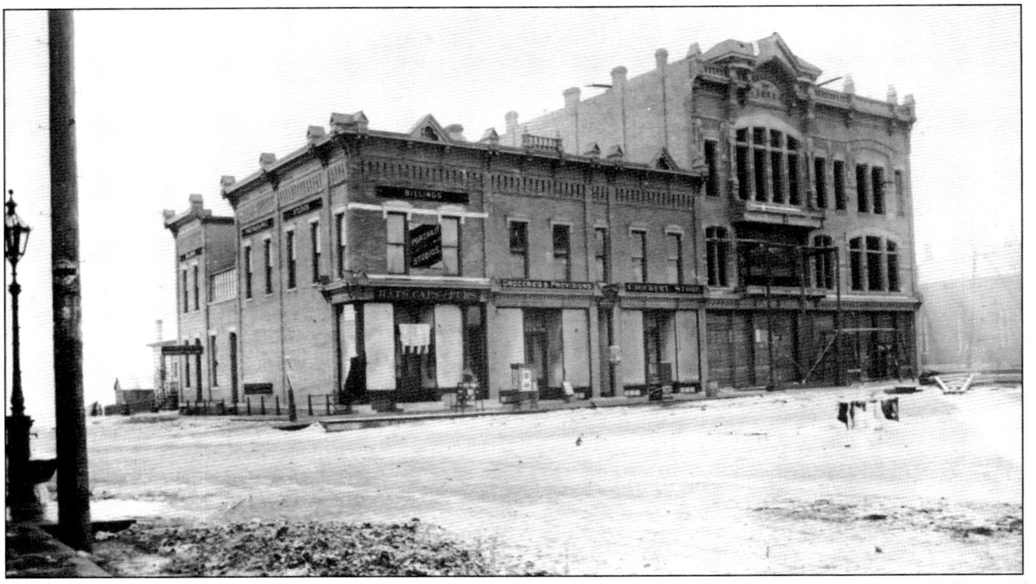

This is how the southeast corner of Fifth and Main Streets looked in 1882. The ground floor of the corner building was occupied by Frank Hubachek's hat, cap, and fur store, while the floor above furnished quarters for the E.T. Billings Studio. The three-story building under construction was the Lathrop Block. It became the local Masonic Temple in 1902.

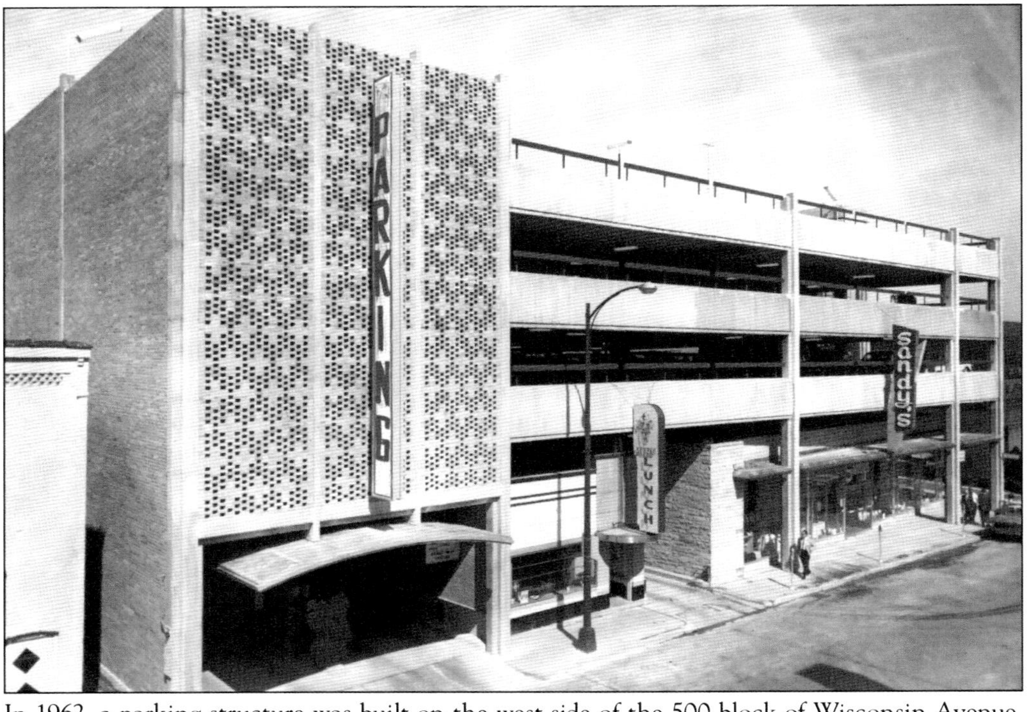

In 1962, a parking structure was built on the west side of the 500 block of Wisconsin Avenue, directly over two existing businesses: Kewpee's Restaurant, and Sandy's Gift and Appliance Store. In 1997, the entire complex was razed for safety reasons. A new Kewpee's was immediately built on its same site, while a surface parking lot replaced the old Sandy's building.

In this photograph, taken on October 17, 1953, two workmen can be seen dismantling the Racine Water Tower brick by brick. Located at Tenth and Pearl Streets, the old structure had been deemed hazardous and was promptly removed. The tower was built in 1887 and was used until 1931. This historic landmark stood 153 feet high and was dismantled in layers at the rate of two feet per day.

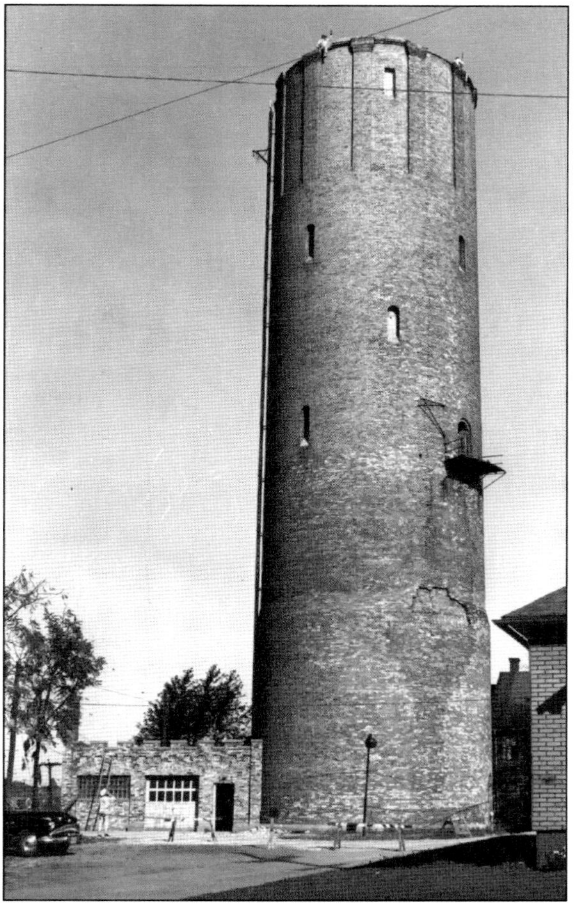

This 137-foot water tank, located just north of the Regency Mall, was completed in the spring of 1981. It has a capacity of 2 million gallons of water and serves parts of the city of Racine and the village of Mount Pleasant. Looking down, the High Ridge Health Care Center is seen. Today this area is a commercial development which includes Kmart, Home Depot, and Toys "R" Us.

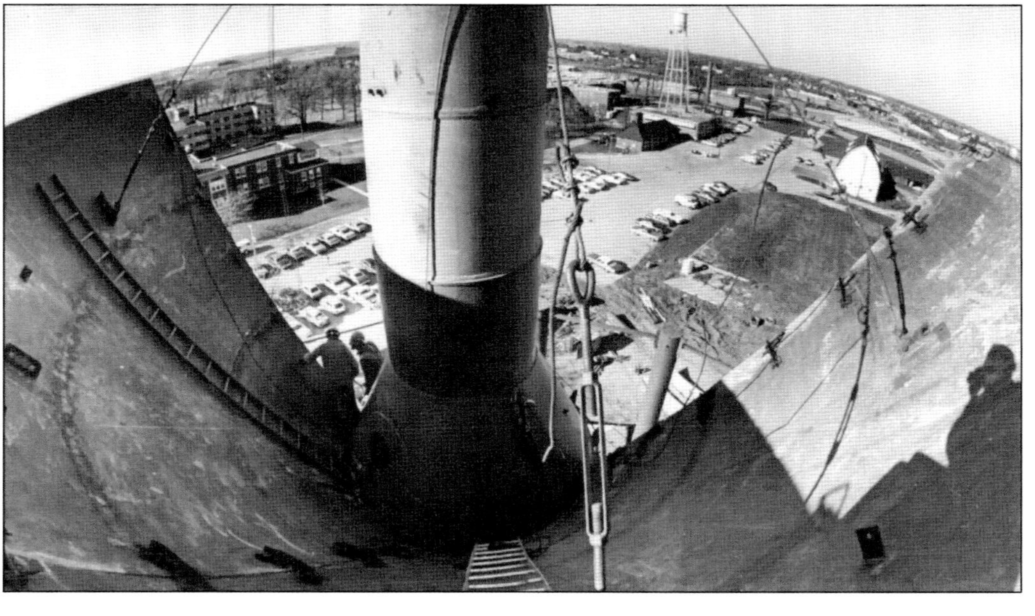

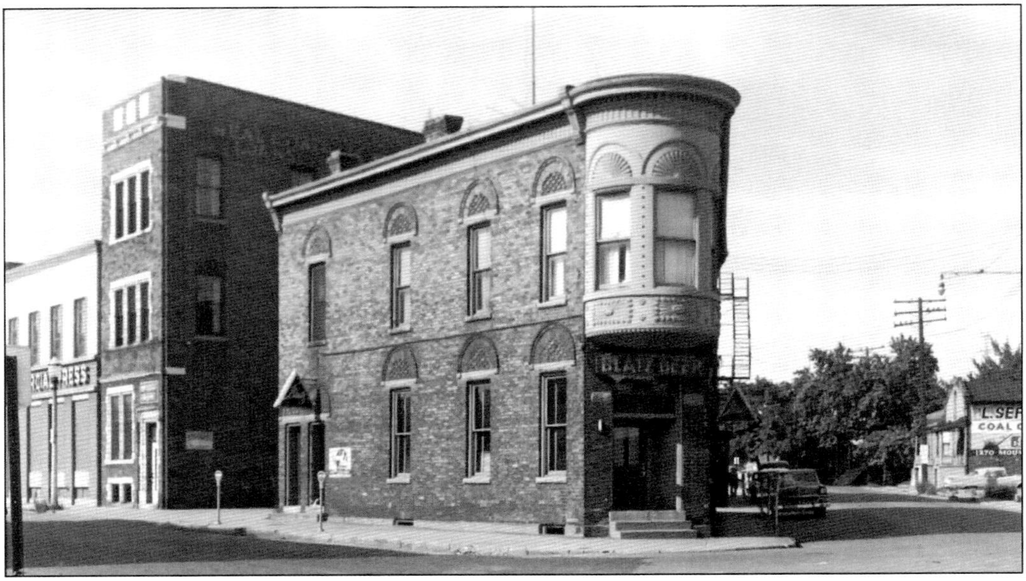

The Klinkert building, located on the corner of Fifth Street and College Avenue, spent its entire life as a tavern. Both the Klinkert building and the Boy Scout headquarters building next to it at 468 College Avenue were razed in June 1958, to allow for construction to begin on a new Union Savings and Loan building.

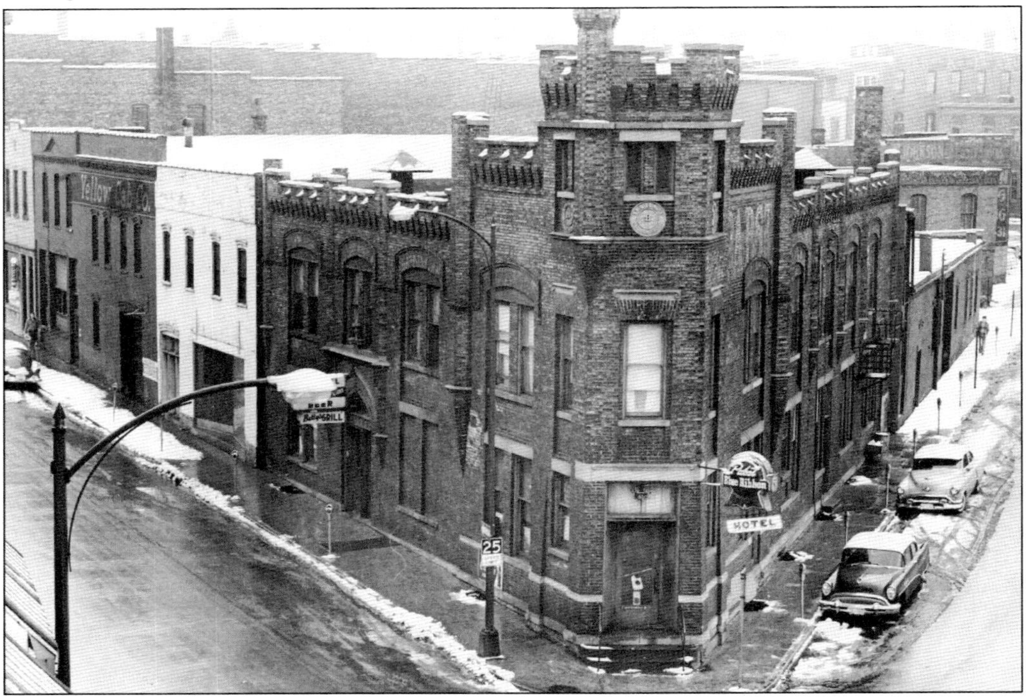

This was the southwest corner of Wisconsin Avenue and Water Street before wreckers razed the "Pabst Castle" hotel building in 1957. This corner building was 108 years old and had been built to house one of Racine's first volunteer fire companies. It was last a hotel and tavern. It made way for a new Racine Savings and Loan Association building.

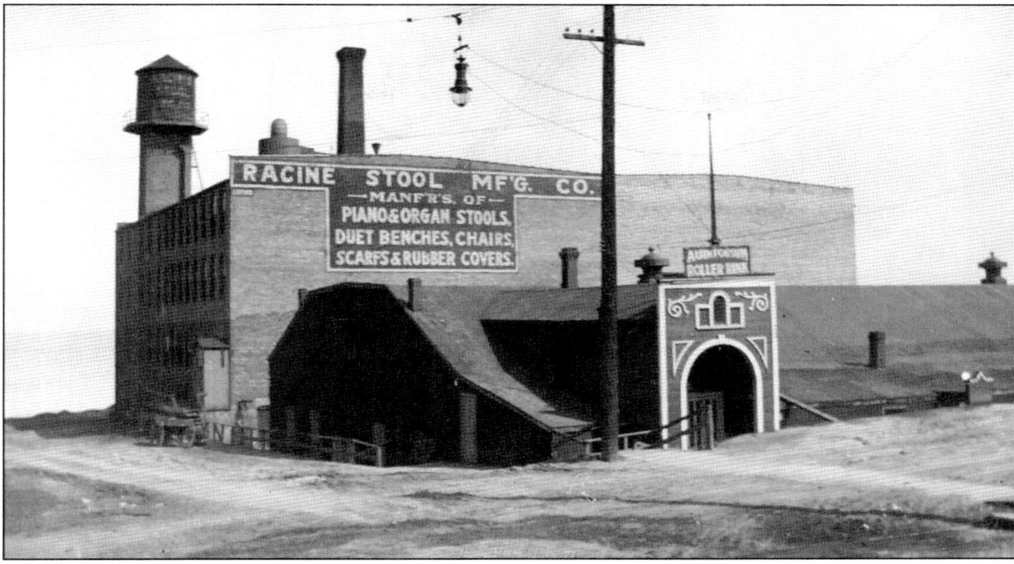

Racine Stool Manufacturing Company was incorporated in January 1910. It immediately purchased the pictured brick building on Third Street, which once housed the Belle City Sash and Door Company. New equipment was installed, and the company began making piano stools and benches in March. The company went bankrupt in December 1915.

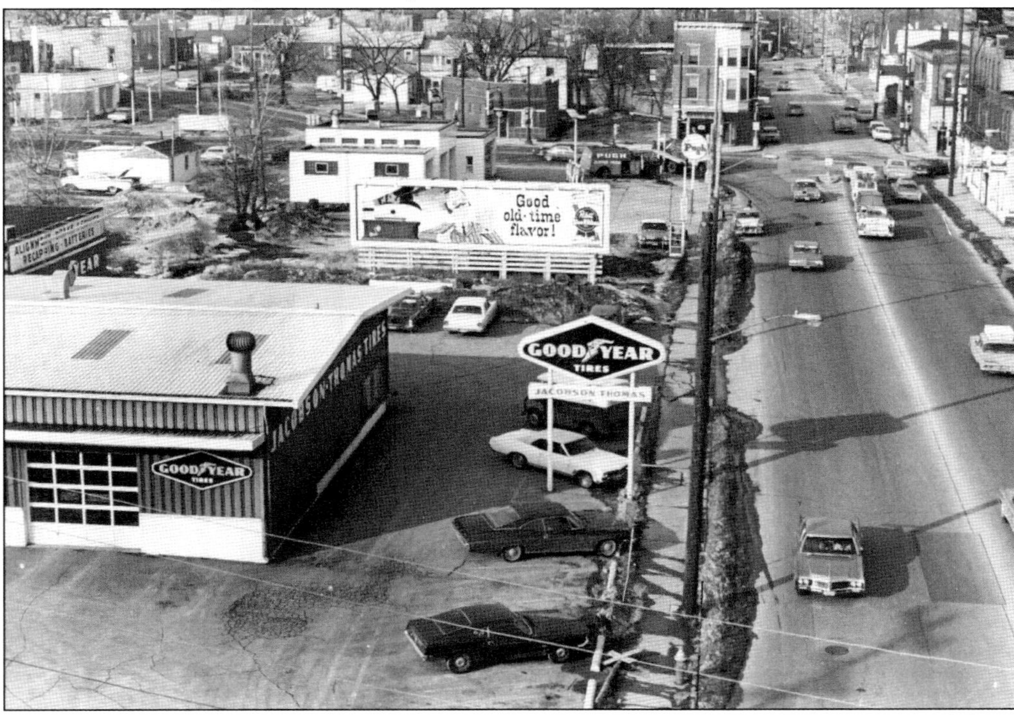

This wonderful aerial photograph, taken about 1970, looks north from Liberty Street and shows the intersection of Dr. Martin Luther King Drive, Marquette Street, and State Street. A statue of Dr. Martin Luther King Jr. (not pictured) is located in a plaza on the north side of State Street, between Dr. Martin Luther King Drive and Marquette Street.

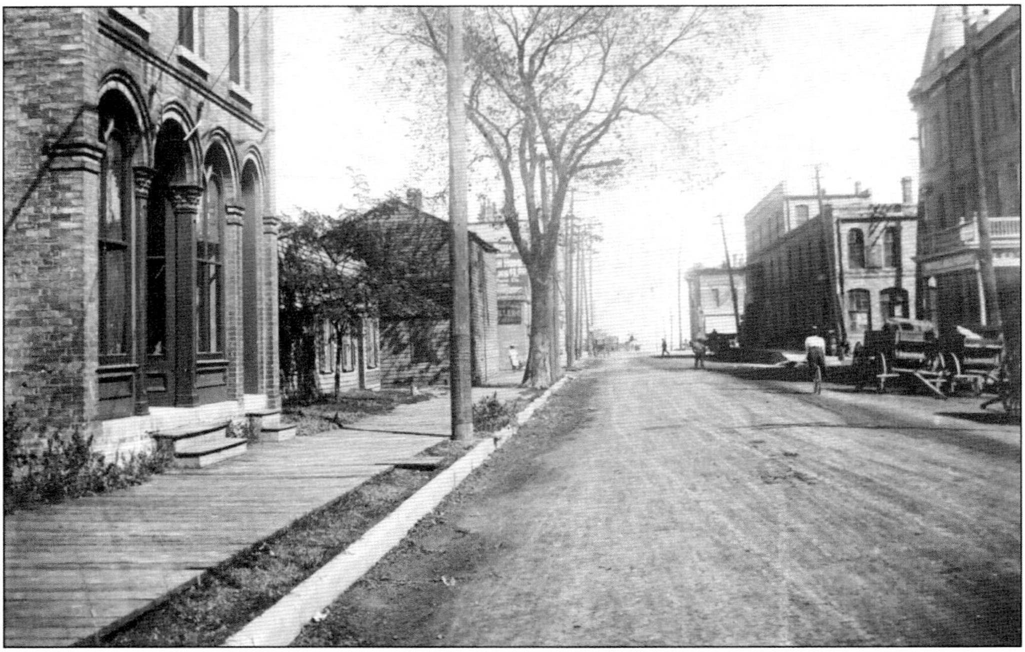

This view looks east on Fifth Street from College Avenue in 1900. The building with the wagons in front of it, on the right, is the Hotel Belvidere. It was located on the southwest corner of Wisconsin Avenue, at Fifth Street.

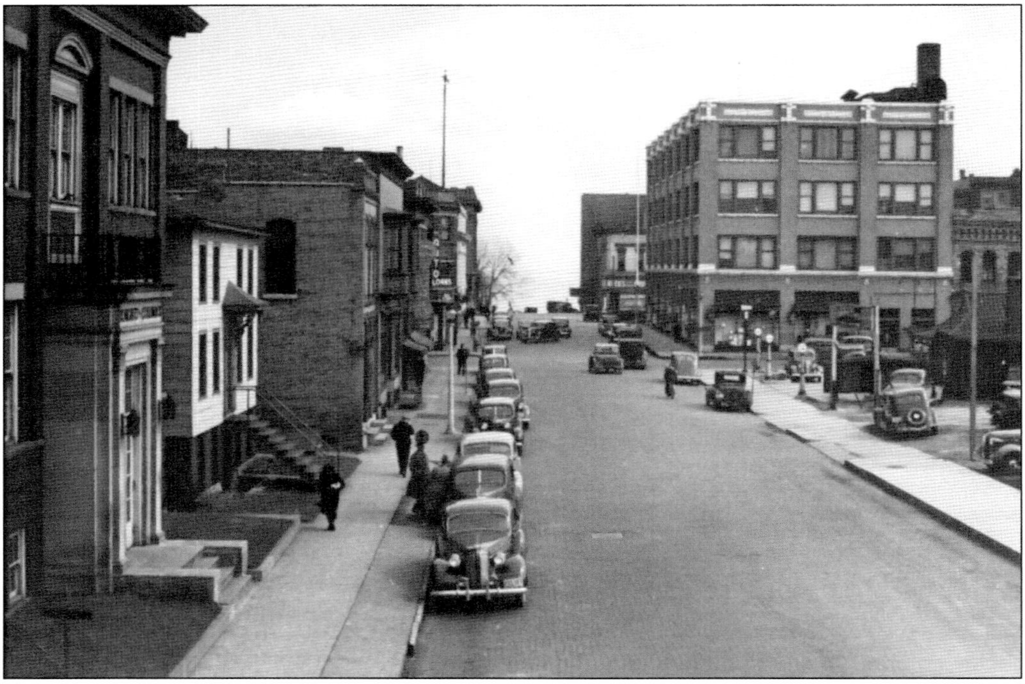

Fifth Street is viewed from College Avenue in May 1938. The two-story brick building immediately on the left was owned by the Knights of Columbus, while the four-story building dominating the vista on the right is the now vacant Zahns Department Store building.

Four

Early Commerce

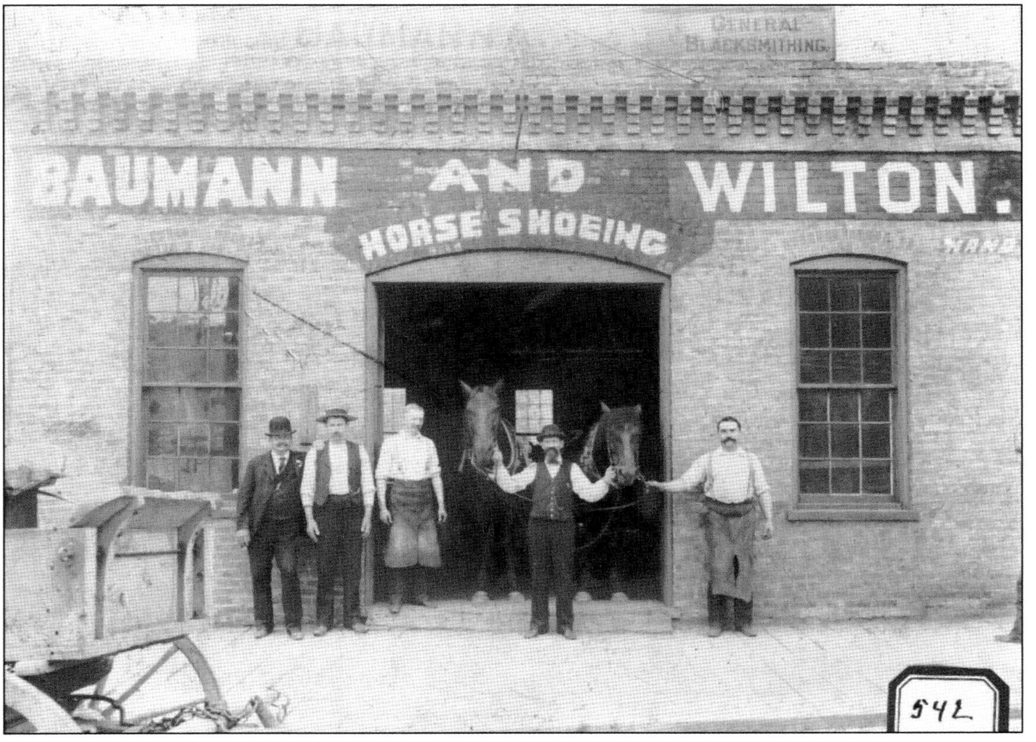

Bauman and Wilton, a blacksmith and horse shoeing shop, is pictured in 1898 when it was located on the south side of State Street, east of the State Street Bridge. It moved to the corner of Lake Avenue and Fourth Street in September 1902, after the property was purchased by Dr. Shoop. From left to right are Edward Schumacher, police officer; Peter Matson, police officer; William Baumann; Patrick Shaughnessy, driver for No. 2 Hose Company; and William Wilton.

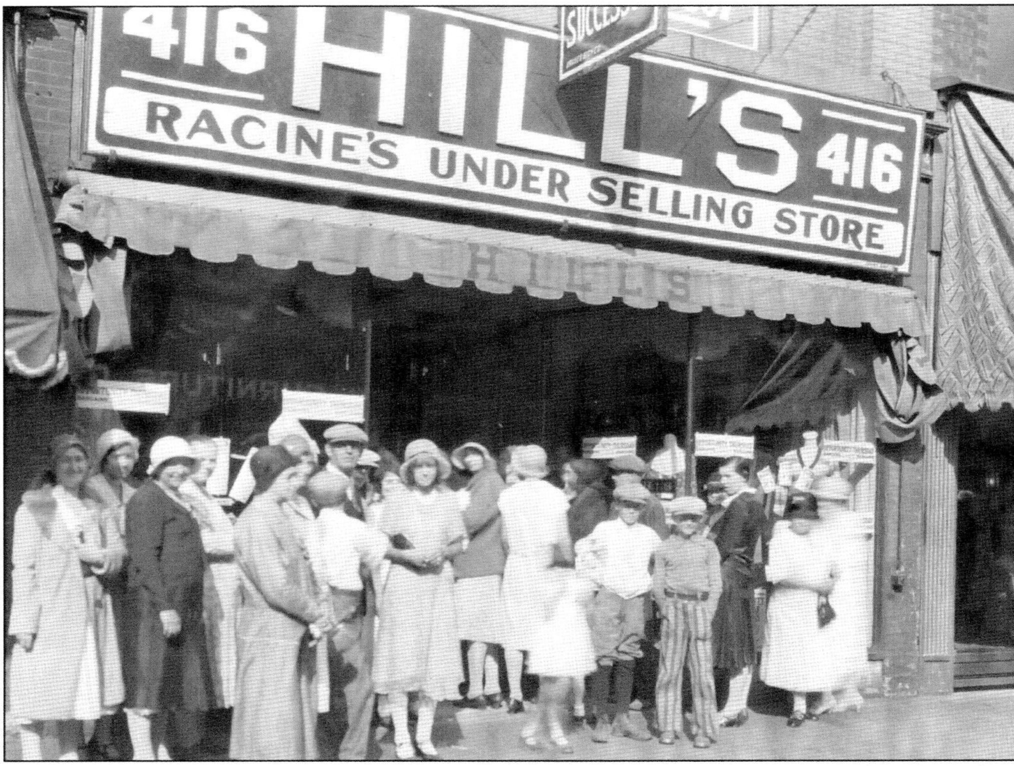

A crowd outside of Hill's waits patiently for the store to open on Opportunity Thursday, where bargains on ladies, misses, and children's clothing would all be available. Hill's was located at 416 South Main Street from 1925, through about 1931.

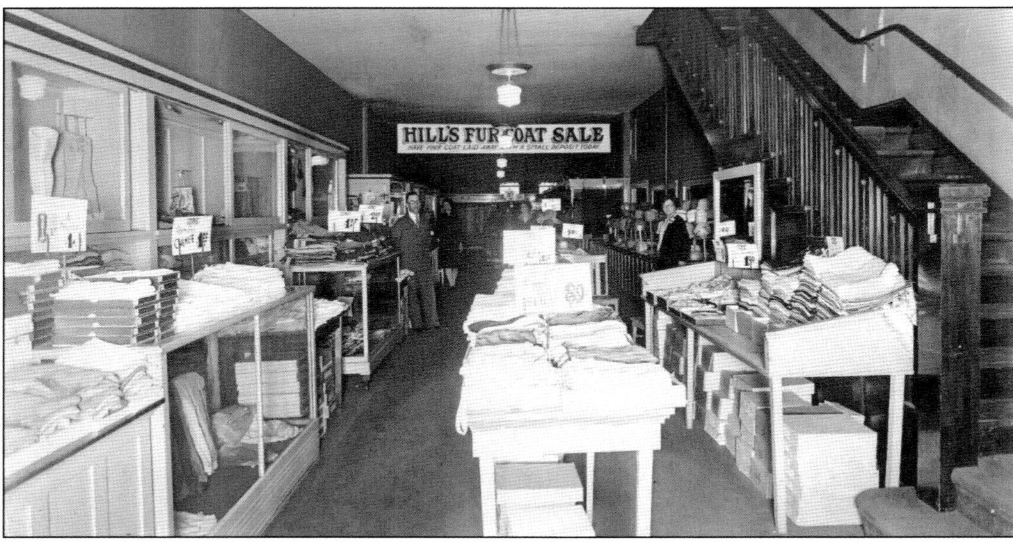

Inside, Hill's is found to be a neat and tidy clothing store, typical of its time. This style of long and narrow store was commonly found in downtown Racine and featured an indoor stairway to the second floor. In the case of Hill's, the upstairs featured more retail space, and the stairway did not lead directly to a living quarters.

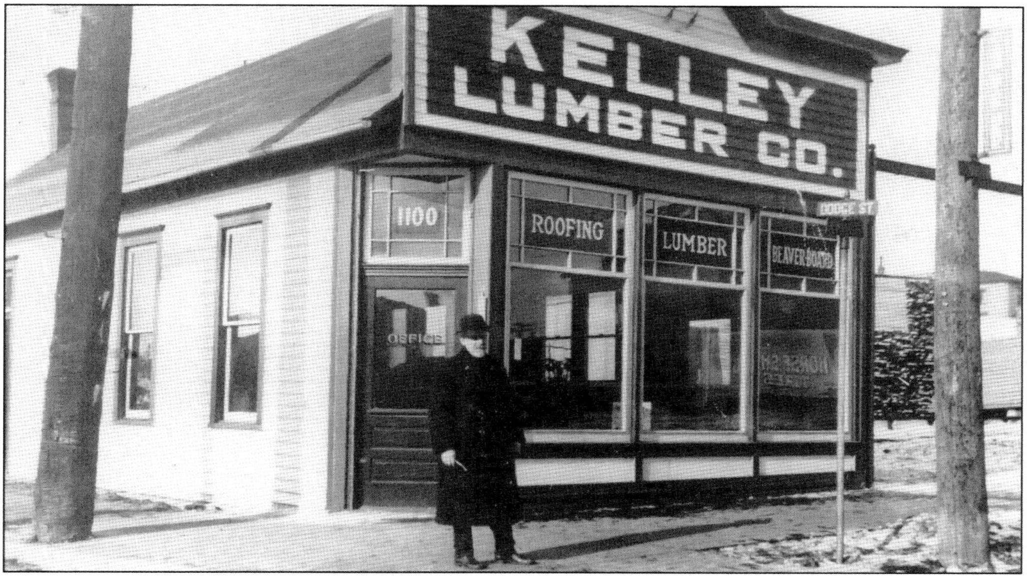

The Kelley Lumber Company's office had been located at 1100 North Main Street since around 1920; however, the business dates back to the 1800s. In January 1966, the Kelley Lumber Company was purchased by the Brannum Lumber Company, and it was closed. The above office building was razed, and a Dunkin' Donuts opened in a new building at this location on October 31, 1969.

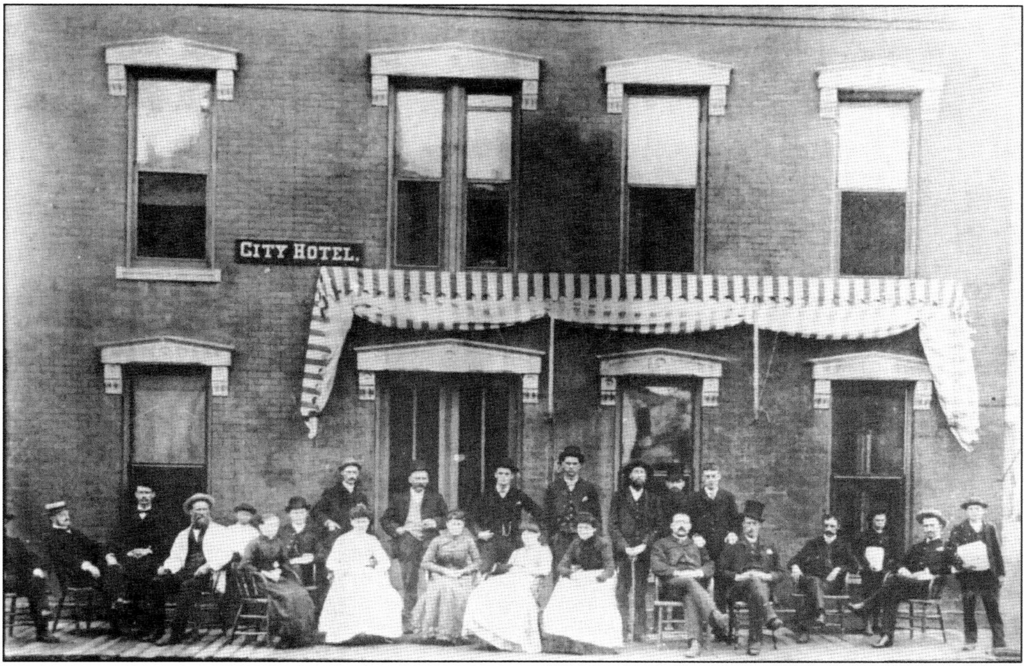

This 1886 photograph, taken in 1886, shows the City Hotel at 523 College Avenue. Built in 1855, it operated under that name until 1888. It then, as it changed hands, was known as the Asby House, the Phipps House, the Jones Hotel, and the Palisade. It finally housed the Racine County Welfare Department until it was razed to allow construction of the First National Bank and Trust Co. building.

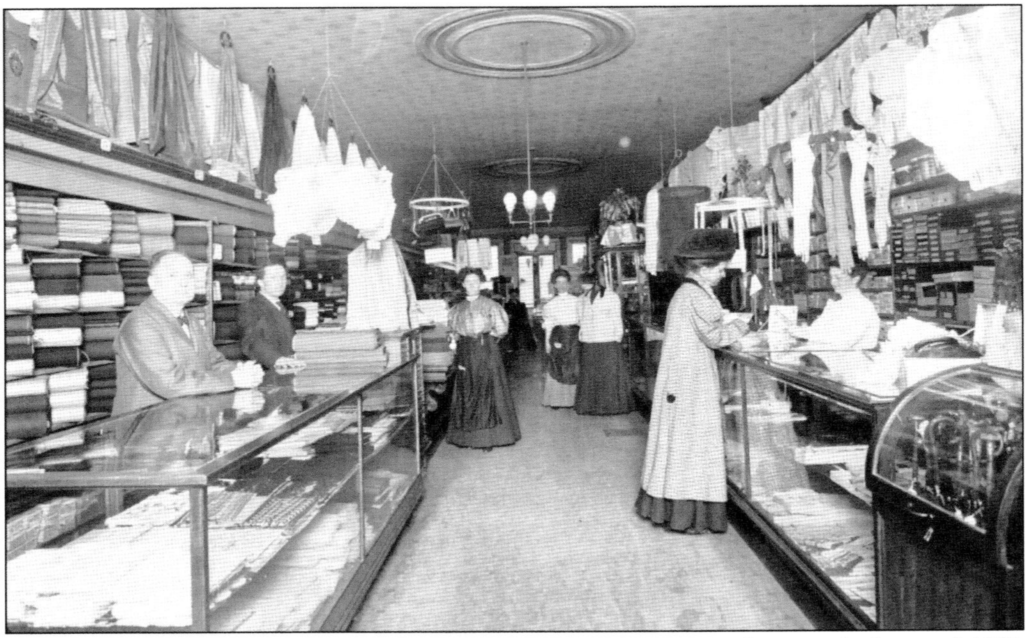

This Vandergrind-Dolister Dry Goods Store at 410 Main Street was photographed around 1910. A branch store was opened at 1300 Villa Street in October 1912, and in 1921 the downtown store moved to 338 Main Street after the Schulte Clothing Company vacated that space. In 1926, Harry Vandergrind sold his interest in the business to his partner, Joseph Dolister.

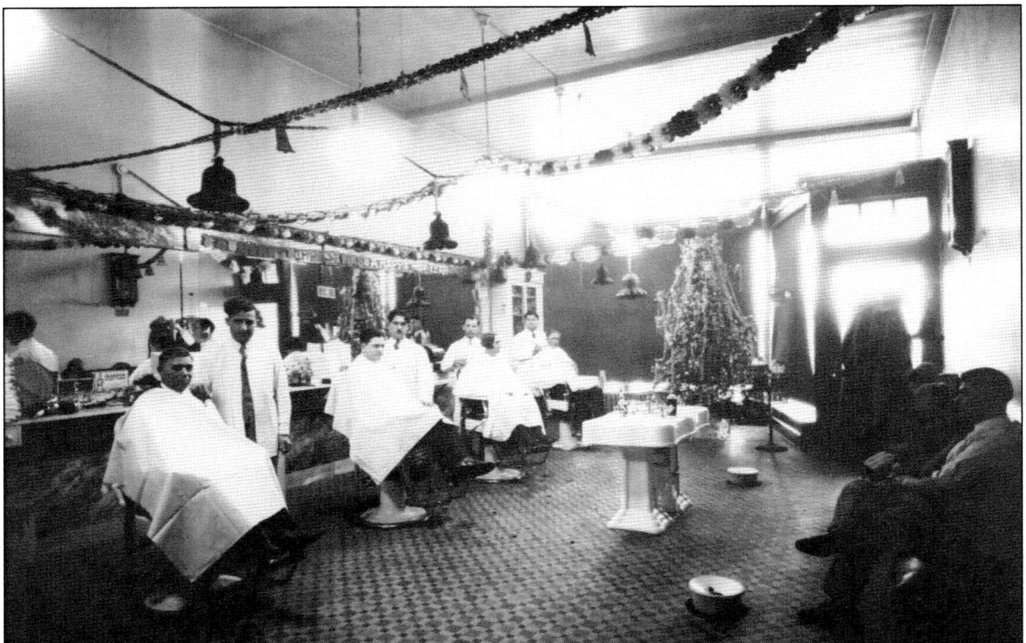

The interior of the White Star Barber Shop, located at 617 Sixth Street, is seen here decorated for Christmas. Dennis Parashis, first barber from the left, owned the business from 1918 until he retired in 1954. His cousin, Nick Maroplous, is the second barber from the left.

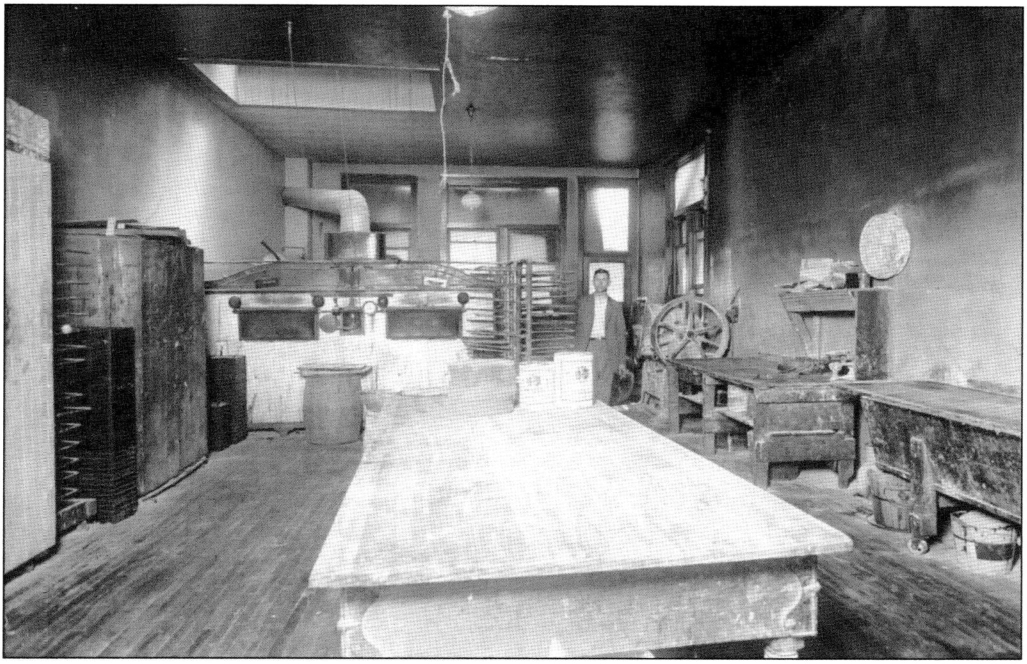

Magnus C. Winther opened a bakery at 1528 Washington Avenue in 1919, after he completed his service during World War I. In 1926, Winther's Bakery moved across the street to 1505 Washington Avenue, where it remained until it was forced to close by the Great Depression in 1930. Not giving up, Magnus stored his equipment and ovens, and went to work for the Washington Bakery. He reopened Winther's Bakery in 1934, this time at 2703 Washington Avenue, where he remained until retiring in 1959.

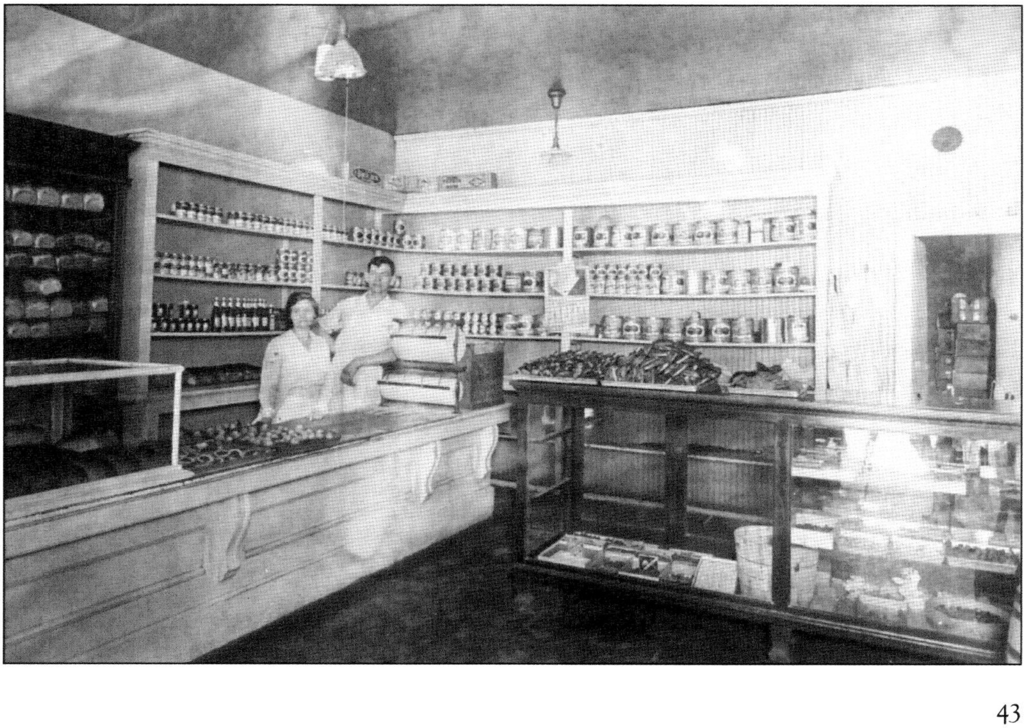

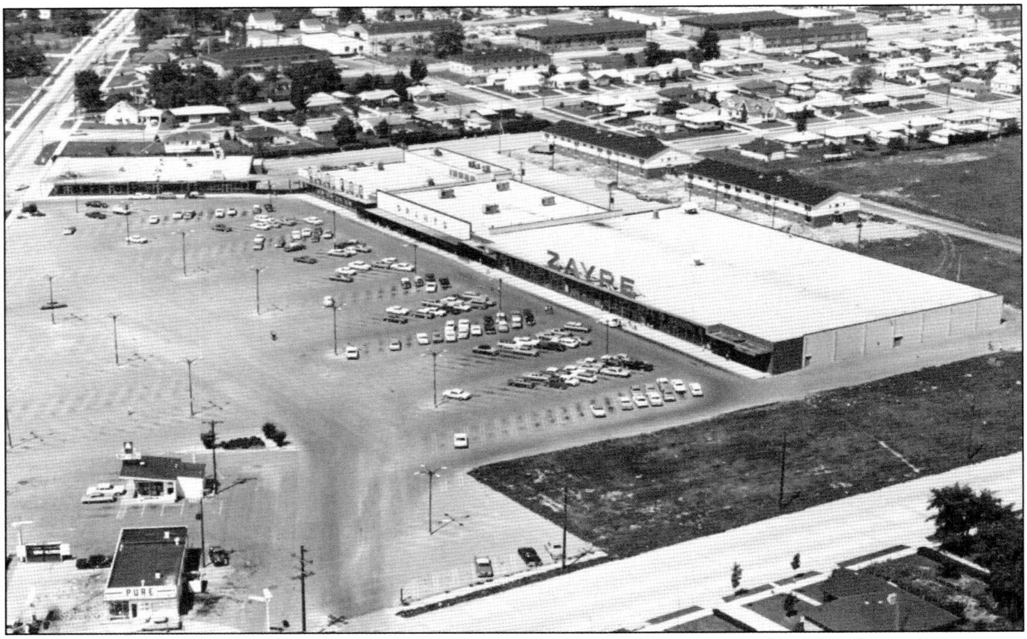

Rapids Drive Plaza is located on a 12-acre site at 2400 Rapids Drive. Its four-day Grand Opening began on Thursday, March 28, 1963 with Zayre, W.T. Grant, Sentry Foods, Red Cross Drugs, Poly Clean Laundry Center, and Rapids Drive Barber Shop as tenants. This aerial photograph was taken in October 1966.

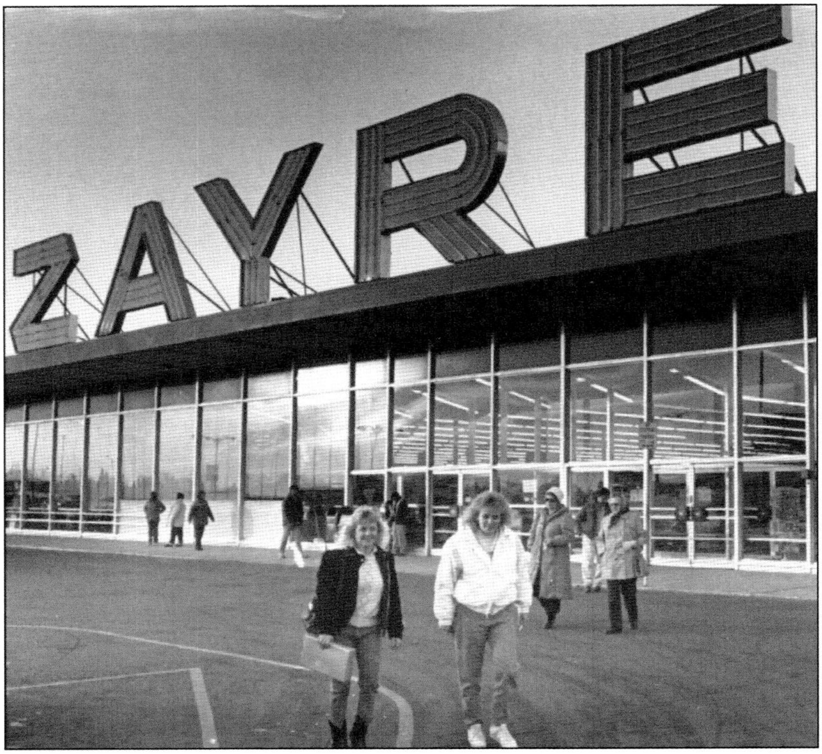

This Zayre store, located in Rapids Drive Plaza, was the first one in Wisconsin. The Zayre Corporation was a small department store chain based in Boston, MA. Seen here on December 31, 1988, the store closed just five weeks later on February 7, 1989.

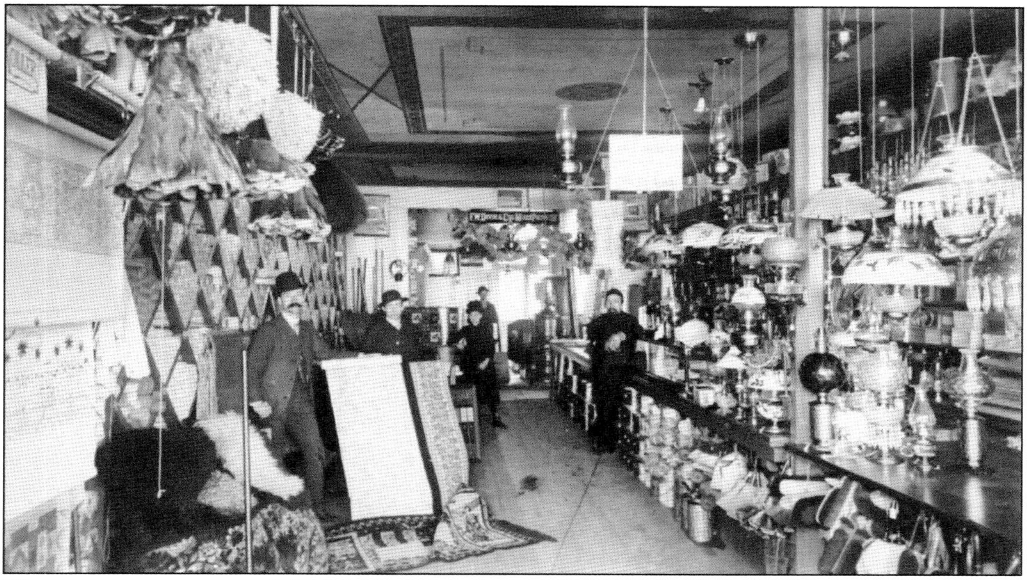

This is an interior view of the John R. Jones store at 213 Sixth Street, October 5, 1886. From left to right are E.V. Pushee, John R. Jones, Annie Jones, and John Harrington. The man in the far background is unidentified. Items for sale included paint, oils, wallpaper, and fixtures.

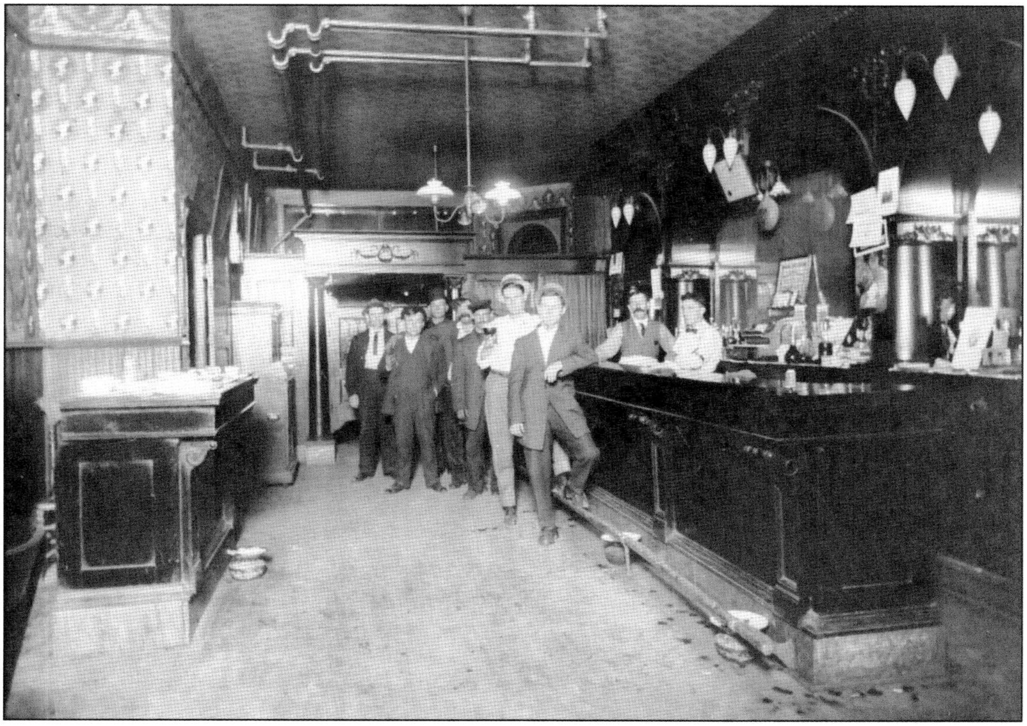

Pictured in the 1890s is the saloon in the Belle City Hotel, at 224 Main Street. The building, located on the west side of Main Street between Second and State Streets, was entirely rebuilt in 1901 and leased to the Schulte Clothing Company. On September 3, 1902, the Belle City Hotel opened for business at 1224–1226 Sixteenth Street.

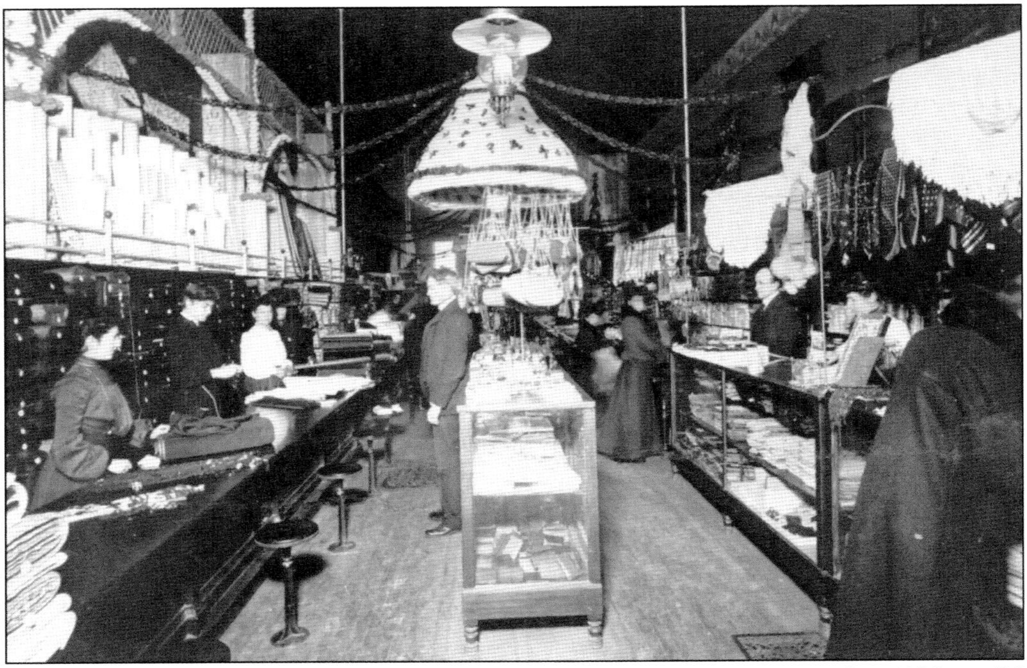

Edward Zahn Sr. opened his first store, pictured above, in Racine in September 1898, at 428 Main Street. Two years later, in 1900, the second floor of this building was rented for additional store space.

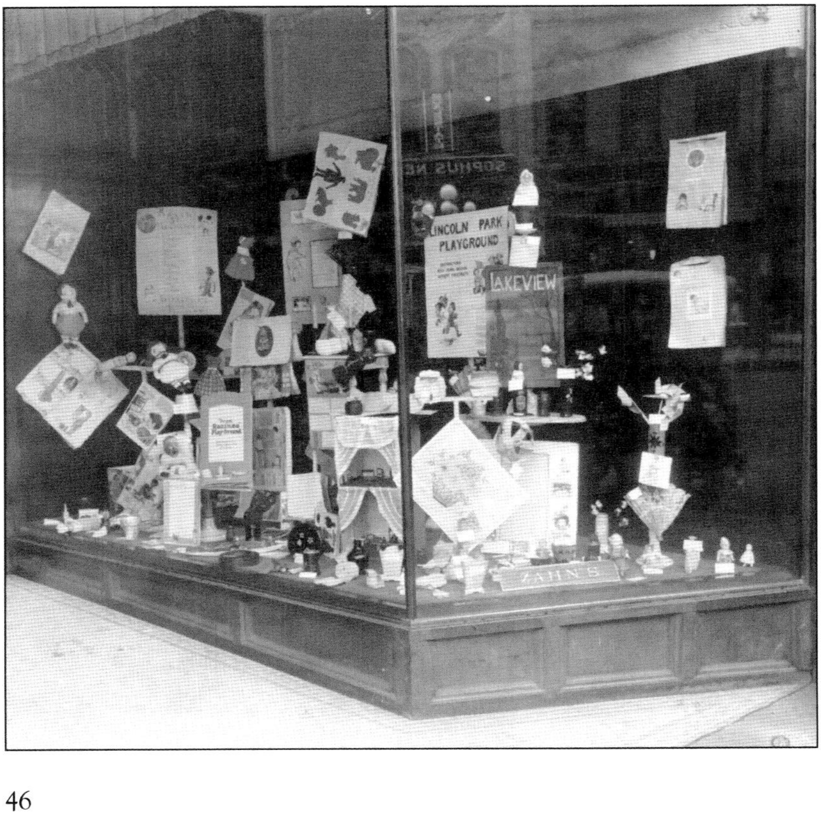

To keep pace with the constantly growing sales volume, Zahns leased the double store at 434–436 Main Street in May 1916. After five months of remodeling the three-story building, the store was opened to the public with brand new furniture and fixtures. Left is a display widow at the entrance to Zahns at 434 Main Street.

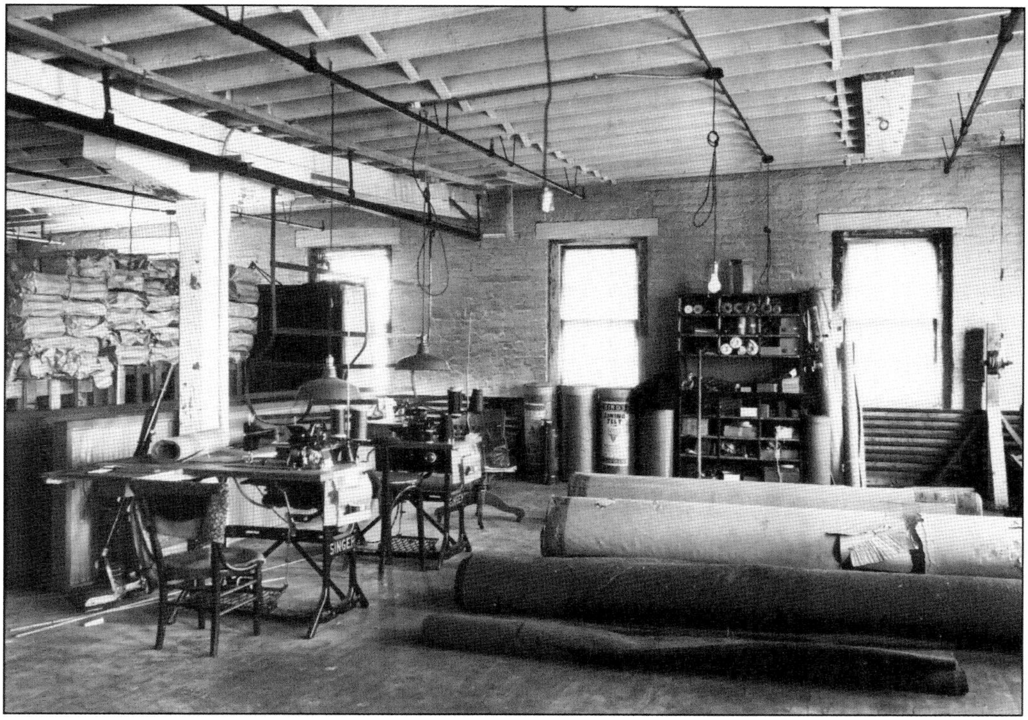

During the 1920s, Zahns also rented space in the Lake View building at Fourth Street and Lake Avenue for workrooms and storage. Above is the carpet workroom as it appeared in 1926; below is the drapery workroom at about the same time.

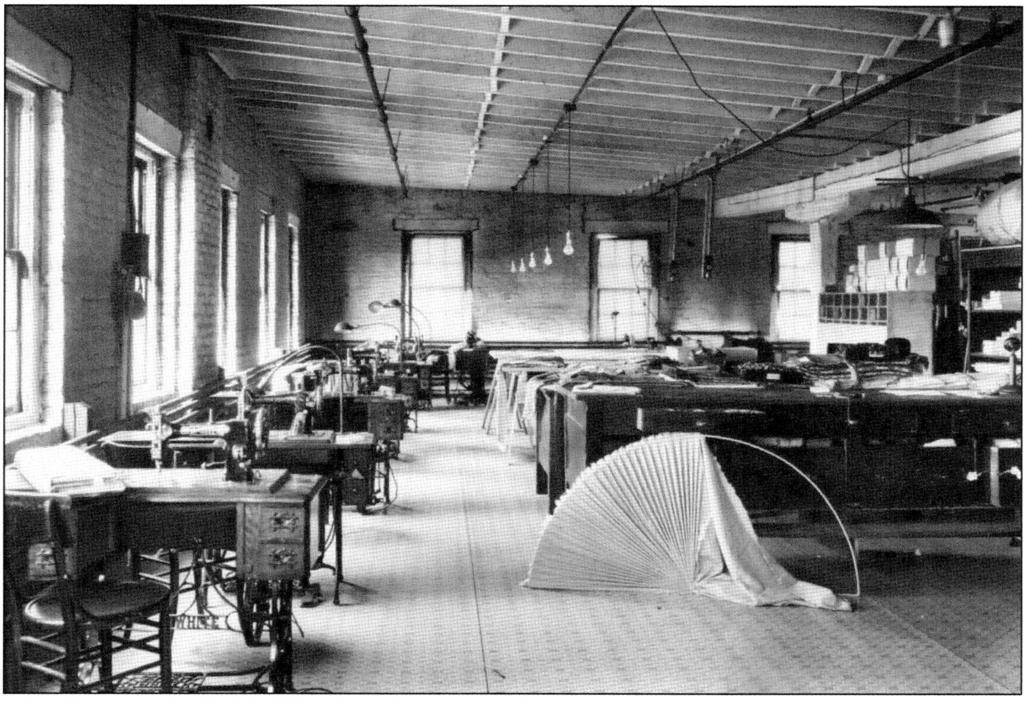

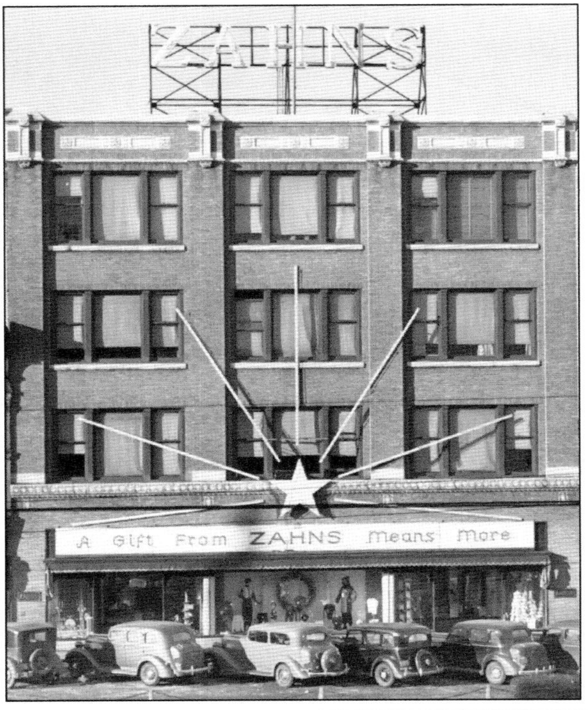

In 1925, Zahns constructed this four-story building at the corner of Fifth Street and Monument Square. Seen here decorated for Christmas in the late 1930s, this new building gave Zahns 42,000 feet of merchandising space.

In 1930, the two buildings adjacent to Zahns on Monument Square were purchased, giving Zahns much needed additional space. In September 1931, the building immediately to the south of Zahns was opened as Zahns Food Shop. Lloyd's Jewelry Store remained in the second newly purchased building at this time.

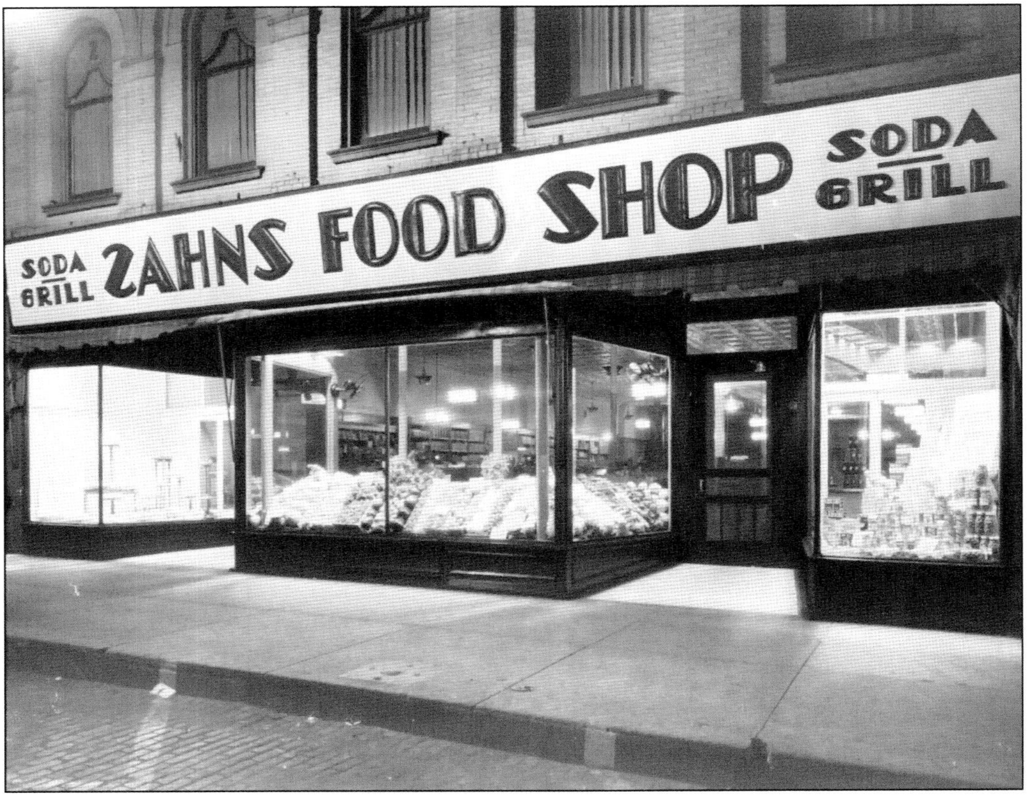

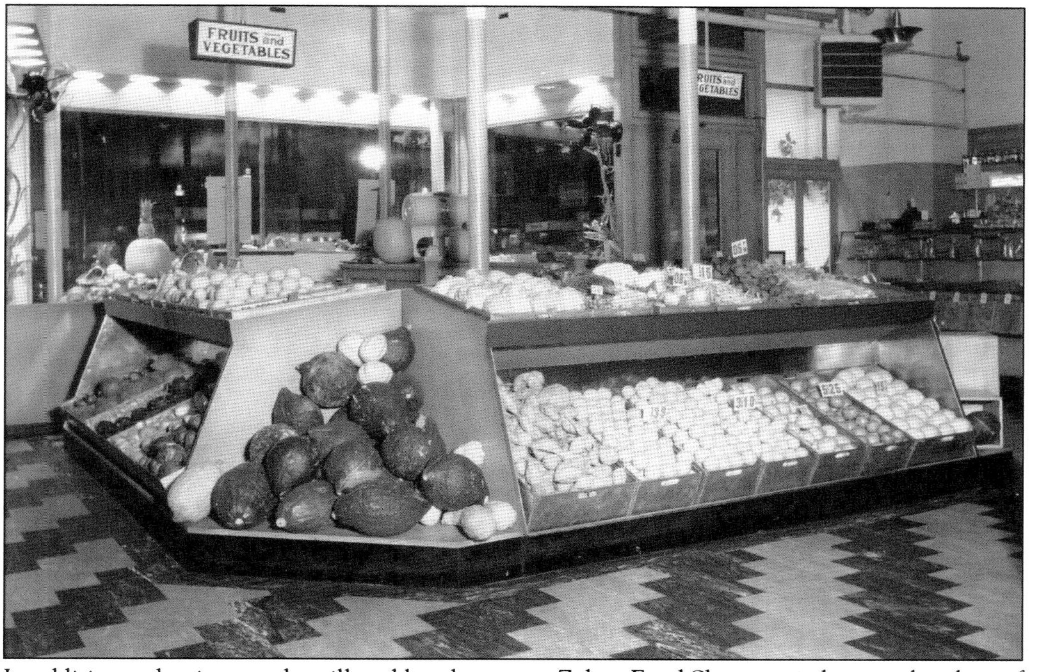

In addition to having a soda grill and luncheonette, Zahns Food Shop carried a complete line of groceries. The gift department was located in that building. At Christmas, the toy department was located in the basement.

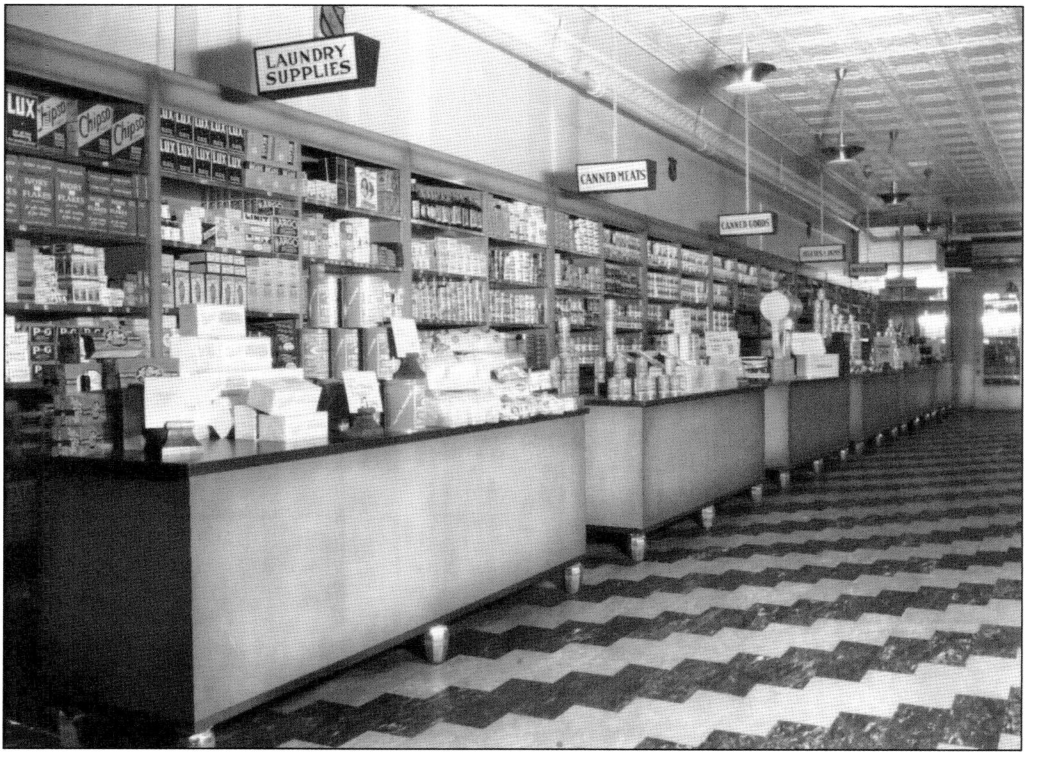

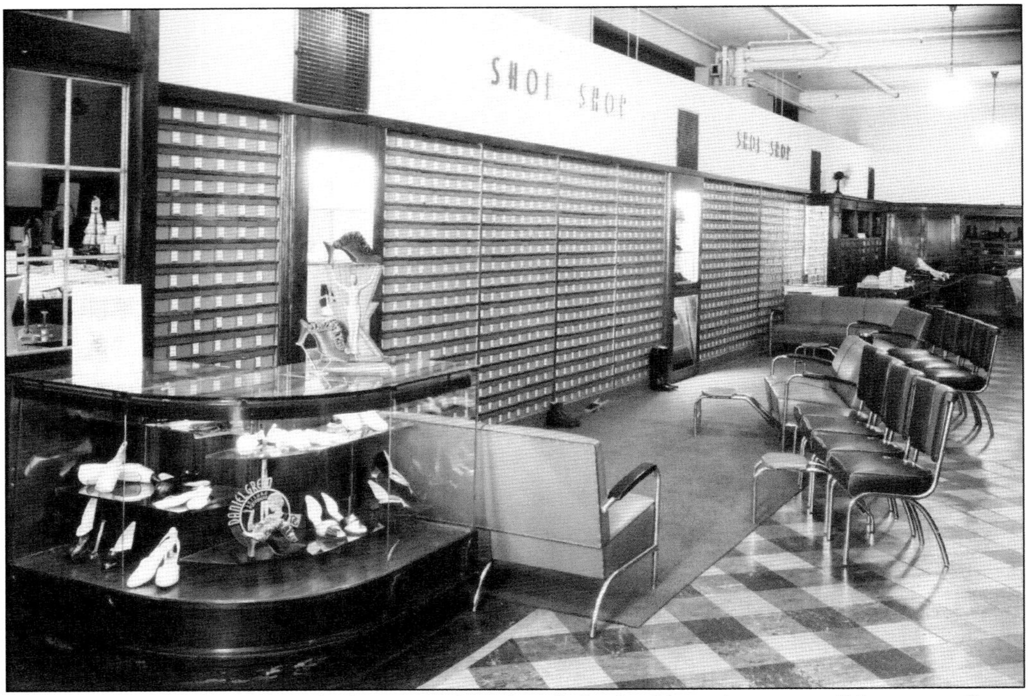

In August 1947, Zahns Food Shop was closed and the building, known as "the annex," was remodeled. The shoe shop was moved there, making it one of the largest and finest in southern Wisconsin. This is how the new shoe department in the annex building looked until 1960.

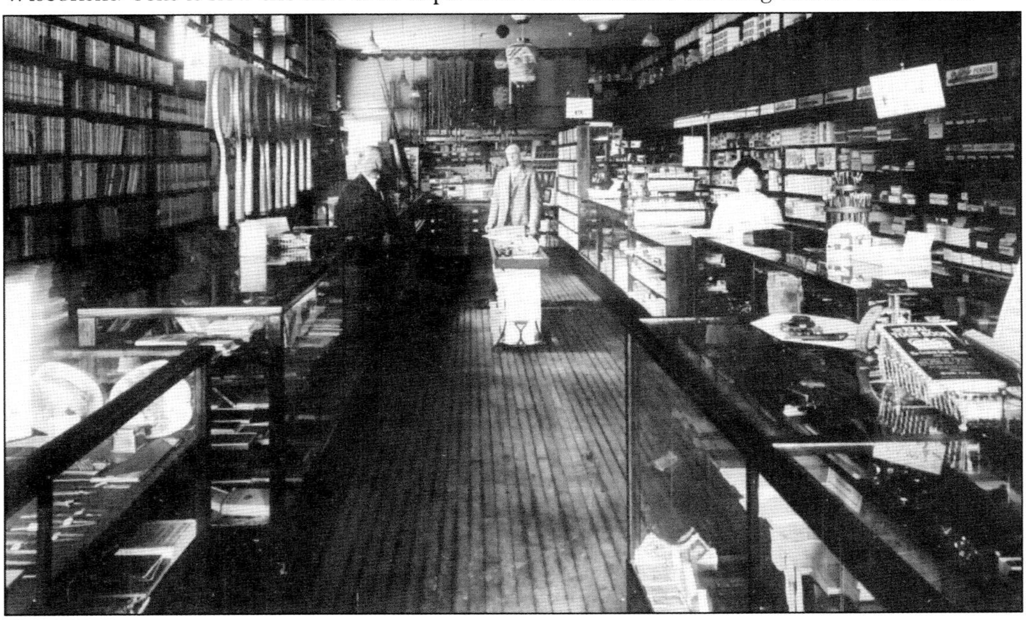

The interior of the Botsford and Wooster store, located at 532 Monument Square since 1884, is pictured in 1892. Although its main business was selling books and stationery, during the 1890s it also sold fishing tackle, guns and, sporting goods. Park Wooster became the sole owner in 1912, and Matt Woelky bought the store in 1935.

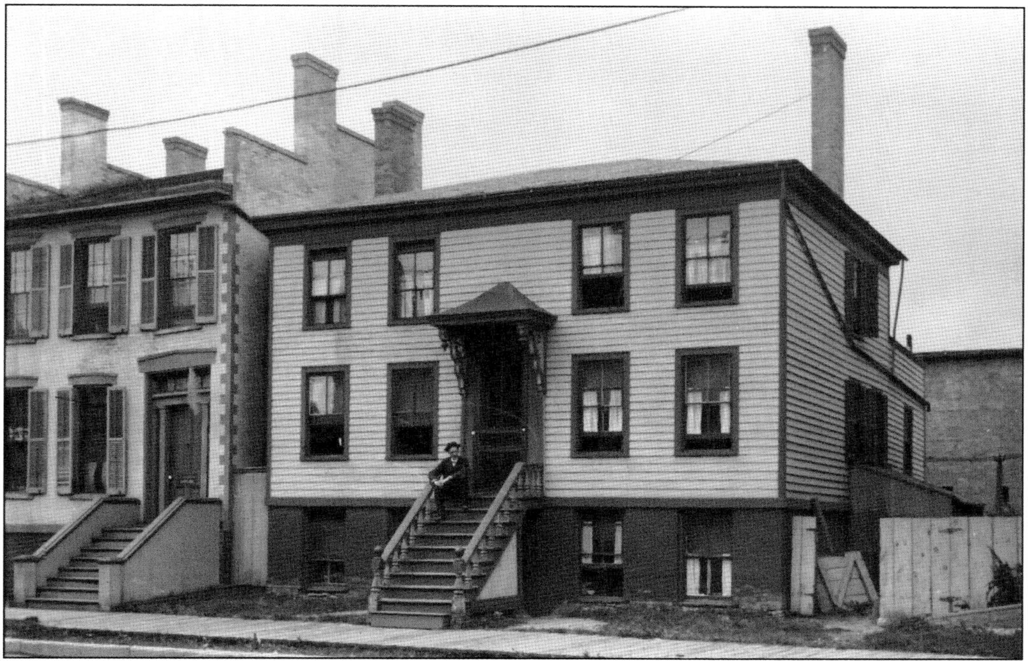

This home on the north side of Fifth Street between Wisconsin and College Avenues was the birthplace and early childhood home of Paul P. Harris, founder of Rotary International, one of the world's first service organizations. An unidentified person is sitting on the steps. The building was torn down in November 1956.

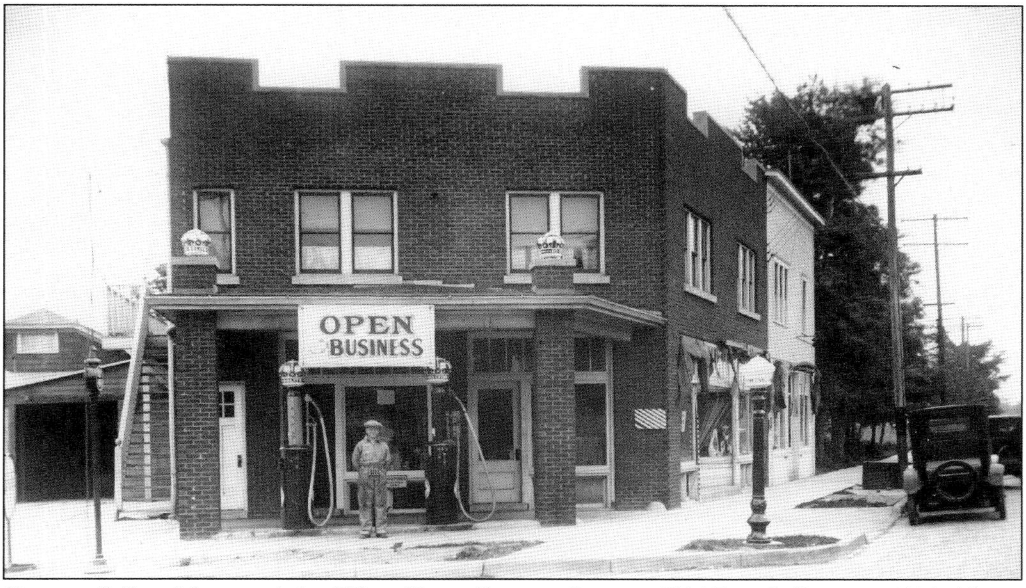

Gustave F. Spoehl opened the White Front Grocery Store at 1704 Rapids Drive in 1916. Above is the west side of this building in the 1920s, where two Red Crown gas pumps were located. Spoehl remained at this location for a number of years before moving to 720 Goold Street, where he operated the Spoehl Grocery Store until retiring in 1963. The young man in front of the store is unidentified.

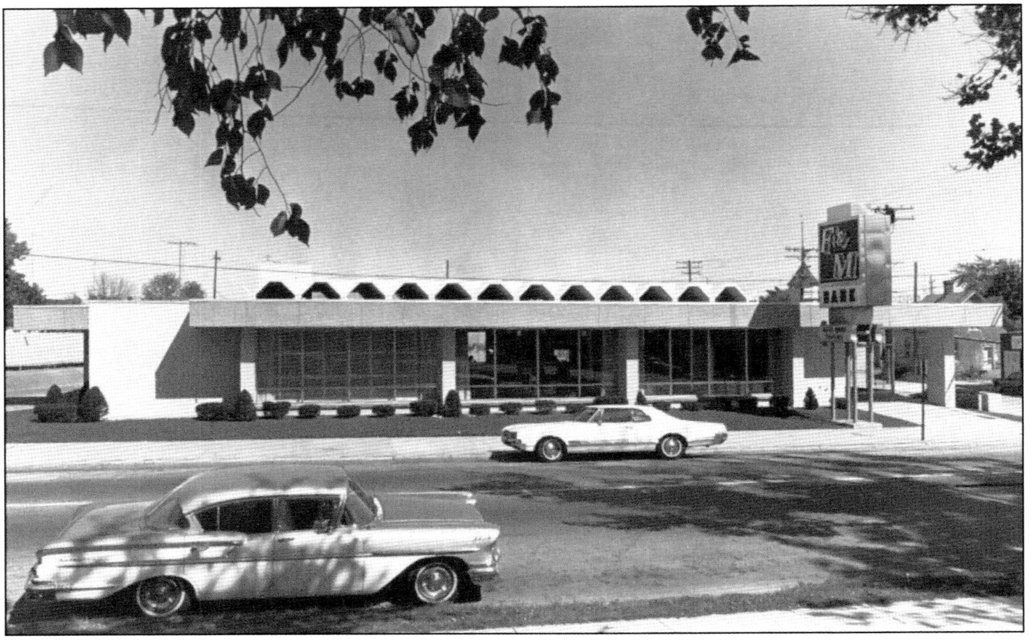

Farmers and Merchants Bank was chartered in 1915 and operated under that name through the 1970s. Originally, the bank was located at 1012 State Street. Their new bank building at West Street and Milwaukee Avenue, pictured above in 1966, was completed and open for business on Monday, April 12, 1959.

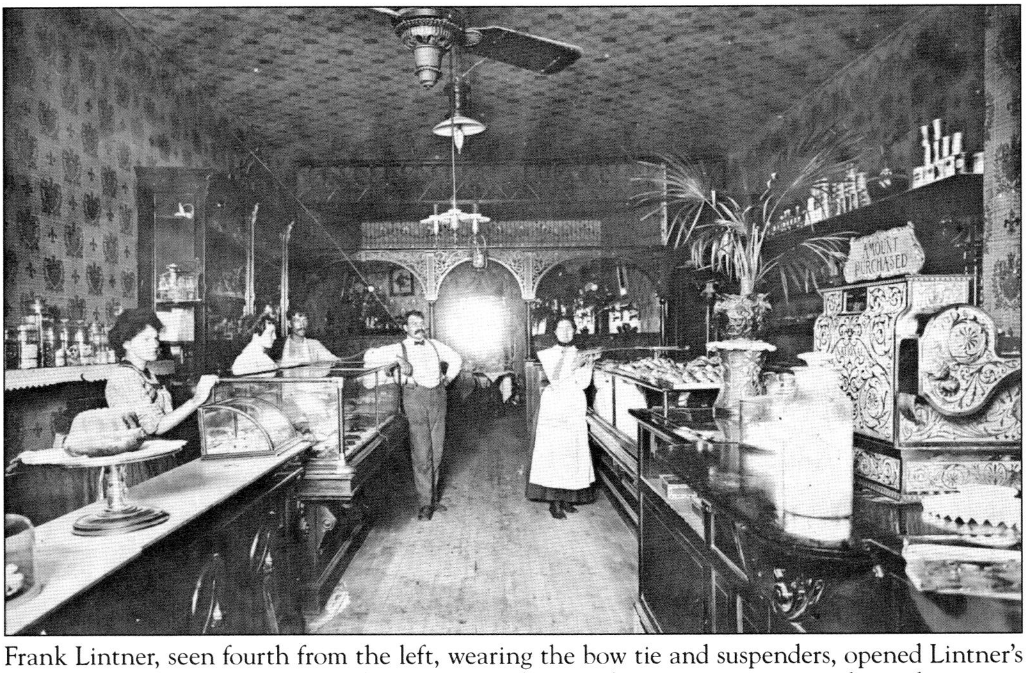

Frank Lintner, seen fourth from the left, wearing the bow tie and suspenders, opened Lintner's Bakery and Restaurant at 313 Sixth Street around 1895. This 1911 interior view shows the seating area for the restaurant in the far back of the store. Lintner's Bakery was closed sometime in the early 1920s. All others pictured are unidentified.

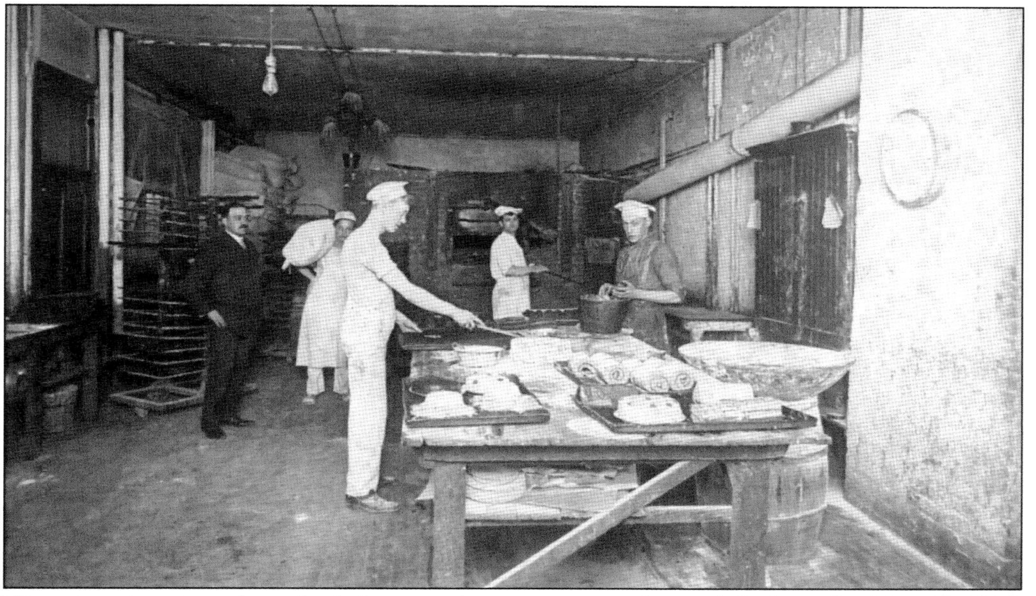

These interior views show the bakery production rooms at Lintner's Bakery. On May 15, 1906, State of Wisconsin bakery inspectors reviewed Lintner's Bakery, storerooms, shipping rooms, and materials, and pronounced everything to be in first-class condition. Frank Lintner was also the founder of the Texas Wisconsin Oil Company and, upon his death in 1966, left about $500,000 to the Sisters of St. Rita for the construction of a home for elderly men. This money was used in 1970, to begin construction of St. Monica's Home for Senior Citizens on a 42-acre site on Green Bay Road at Three Mile Road. A public subscription campaign was also conducted to complete the financing of the 102-bed facility.

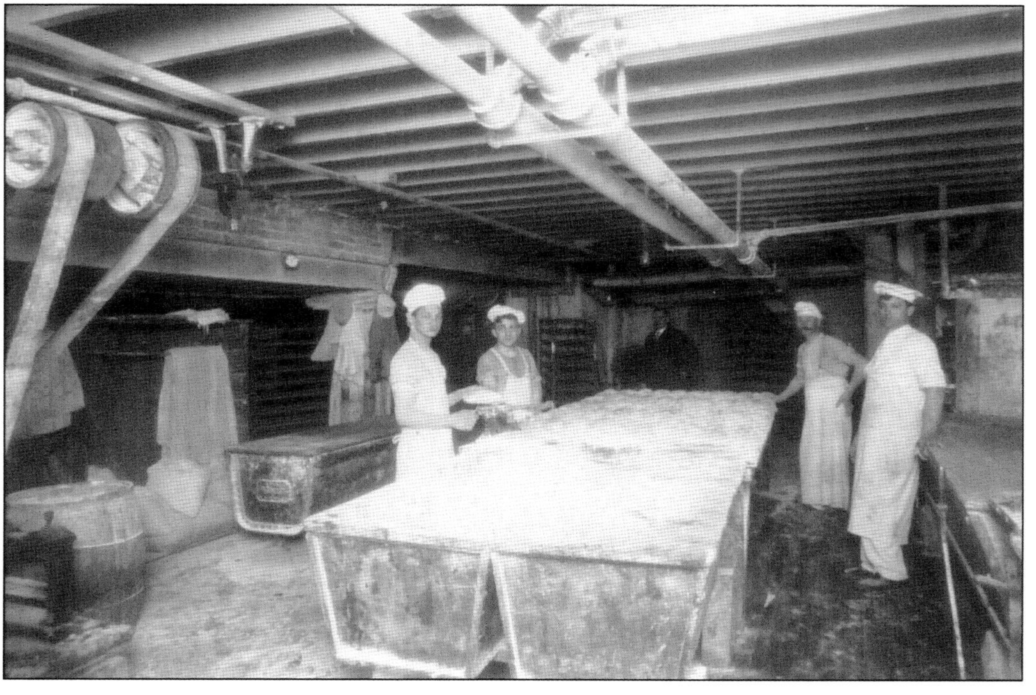

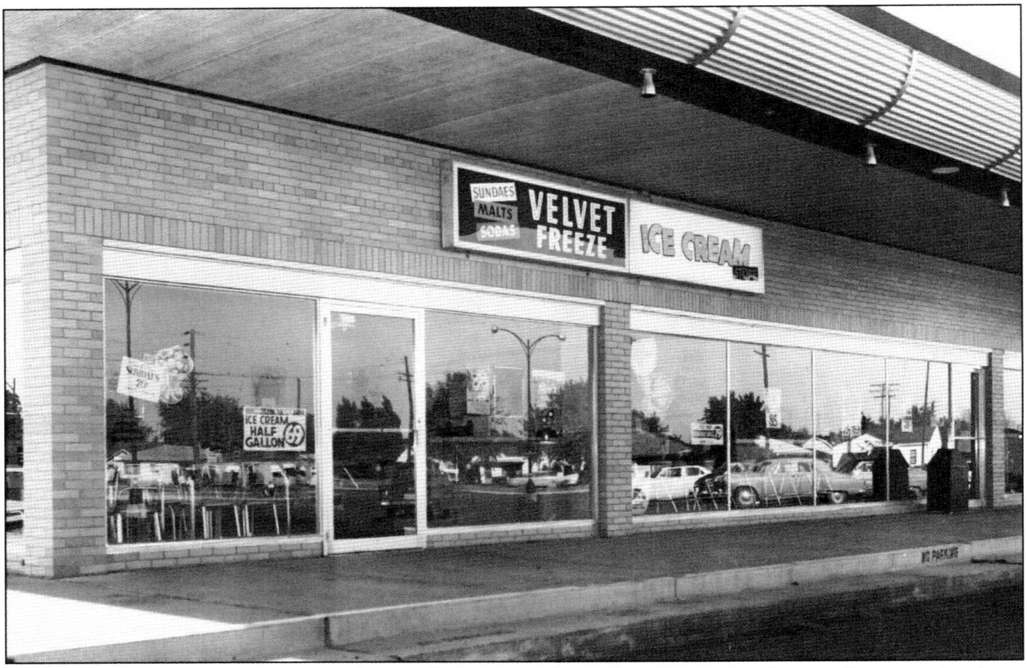

One of the first stores to open at Elmwood Plaza was the Velvet Freeze Ice Cream Store; a subsidiary of the Tompkins Ice Cream Company of St. Louis, Missouri. Opening in August 1956, the store featured one of the largest ice cream soda fountains in the entire Racine area.

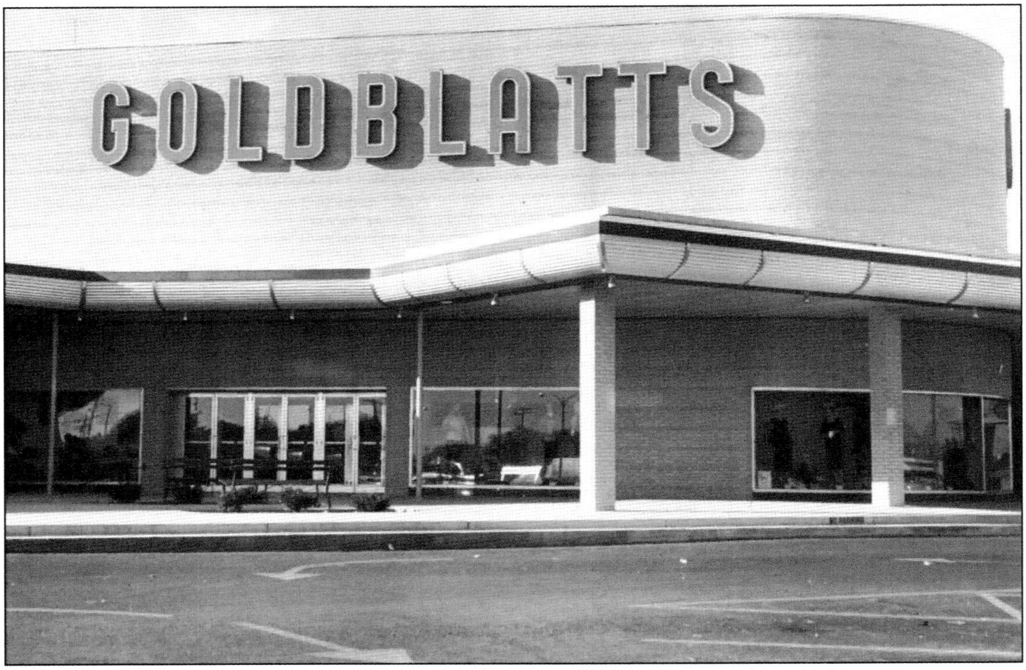

Goldblatt's Department Store opened with a huge gala celebration on August 22, 1956, six weeks prior to Elmwood Plaza's official grand opening. It was Goldblatt's first store outside of Illinois. This department store, Goldblatt's 18th, occupied two floors of about 50,000 square feet each.

The North Side Dairy was located on the northwest corner of Douglas Avenue at Rapids Drive. Operating from his home at 1311 Rapids Drive, Fred Krenske began selling milk to his neighbors around 1908. He would buy the milk from local farmers. In 1910, this building was constructed and Krenske's North Side Dairy opened. The business continued until 1935, when the Great Depression and continuing union problems with his drivers caused Fred to close.

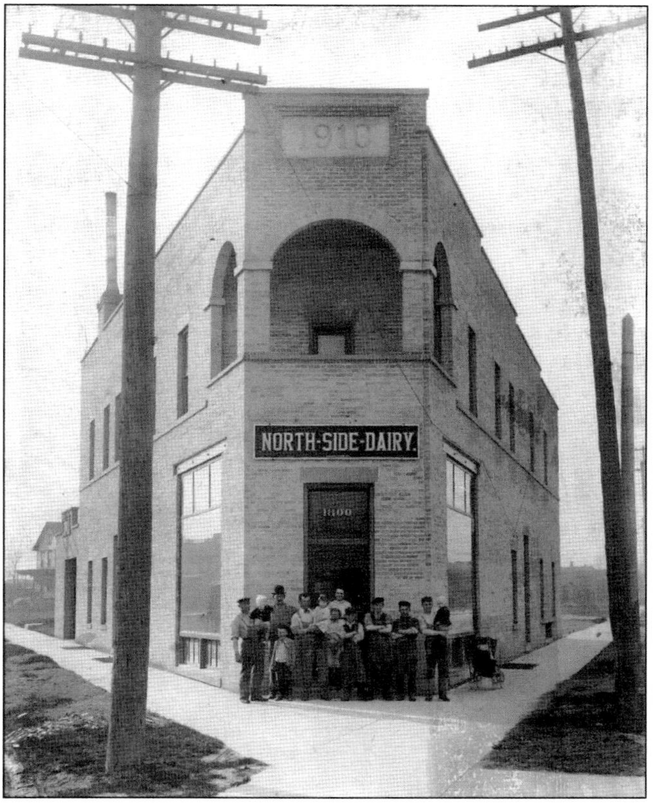

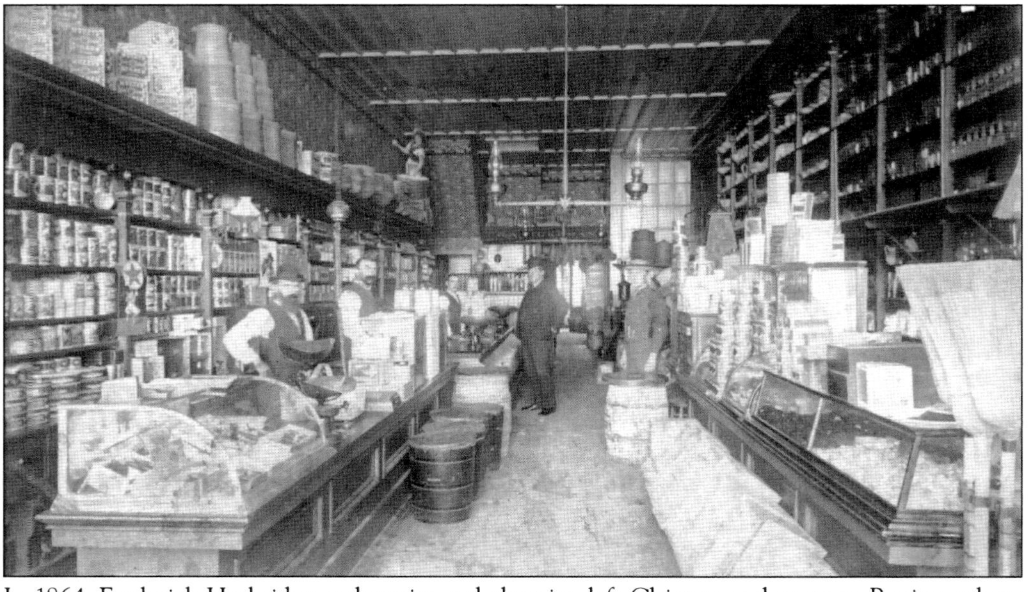

In 1864, Frederick Harbridge, a druggist and chemist, left Chicago and came to Racine, where he found employment at a drug store located at 148 Main Street. Around 1869, he purchased the business and added groceries. This is an interior view of F. Harbridge Grocery and Drug Store in the late 1800s.

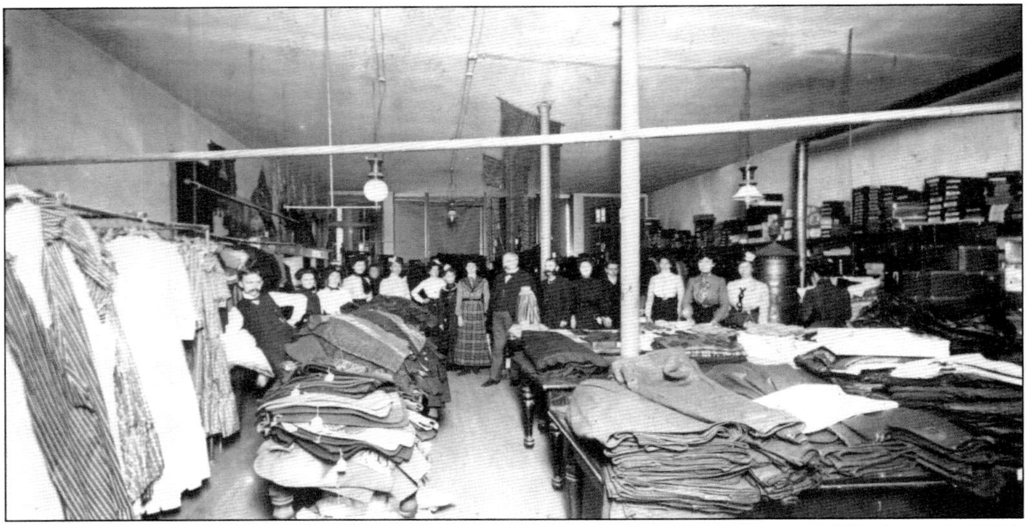

Harnett Dry Goods, above, was located at 507–509 Monument Square from 1897 through 1906, when it went out of business. They prided themselves on having the largest and best stock of merchandise ever for sale in Racine and prices as low as those found in Milwaukee or Chicago. Thomas L. Harnett, owner, is the large man pictured at center, just to the right of the woman wearing the plaid skirt.

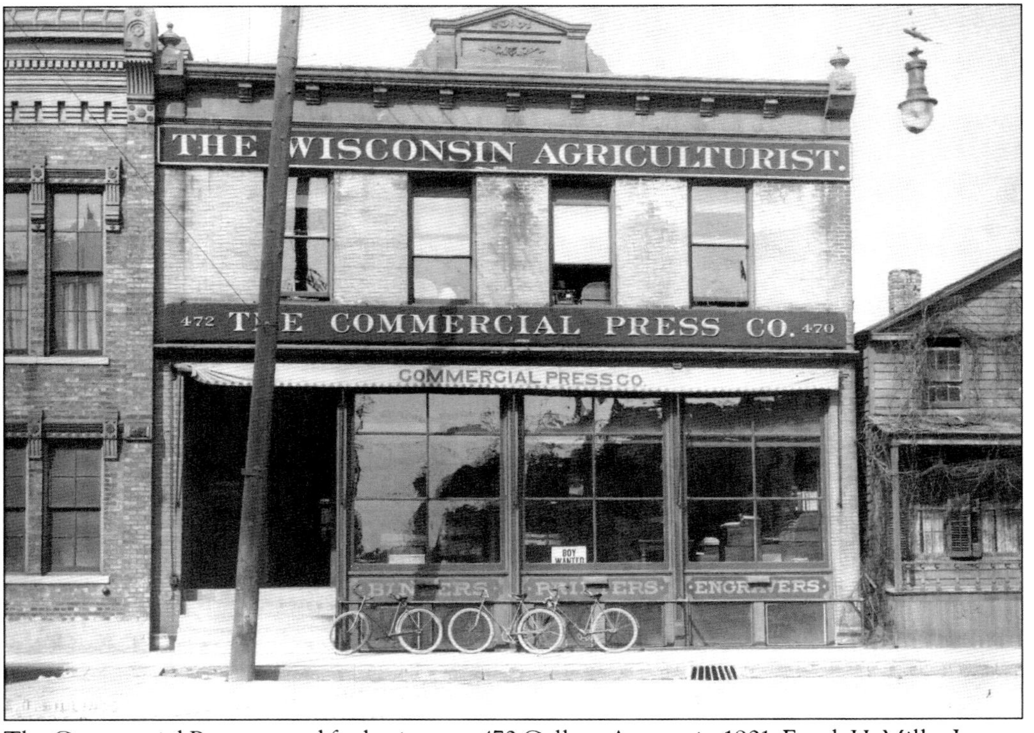

The Commercial Press opened for business at 470 College Avenue in 1901. Frank H. Miller Jr., was president of the firm until his death in 1968. In August 1969, Raymond C. Hauschel purchased the firm. Union Savings and Loan, next-door at 468 College Avenue, bought the building in 1973 and razed it for additional parking space in August 1975.

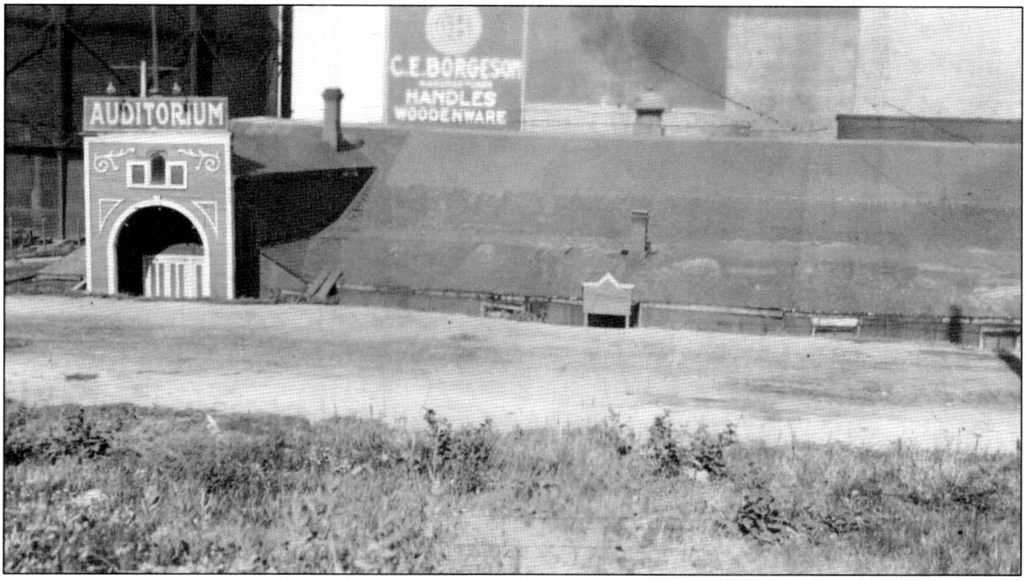

A fire destroyed the Lakeside Auditorium, pictured above, on December 13, 1919. Prizefights, roller polo games, bicycle races, and political and social events were held in the sprawling one-story building on the southeast corner of Third Street and Lake Avenue. The loss of Racine's only large meeting hall lent added urgency to a fundraiser underway to build Memorial Hall.

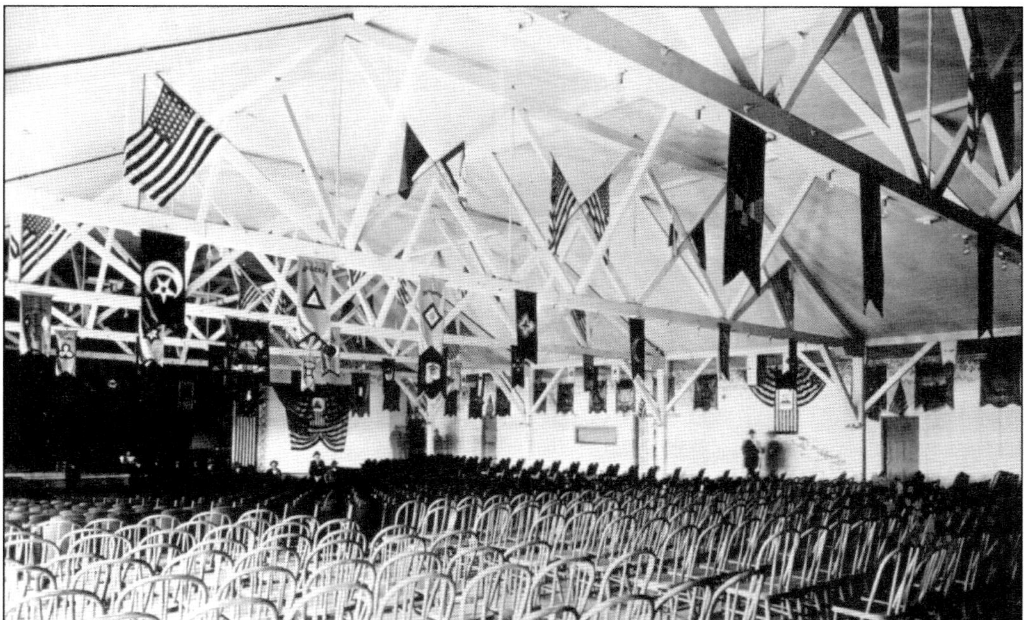

The Lakeside Auditorium, built in 1884, had a huge seating capacity, as illustrated above. The first auto shows in Racine were held there, and many prominent national politicians spoke at the venue, including Presidents Theodore Roosevelt and William Howard Taft, and Secretary of State William Jennings Bryan. Racine's Horlick roller polo team won the national title on the Lakeside rink by defeating the Hartford, Connecticut, team in 1900.

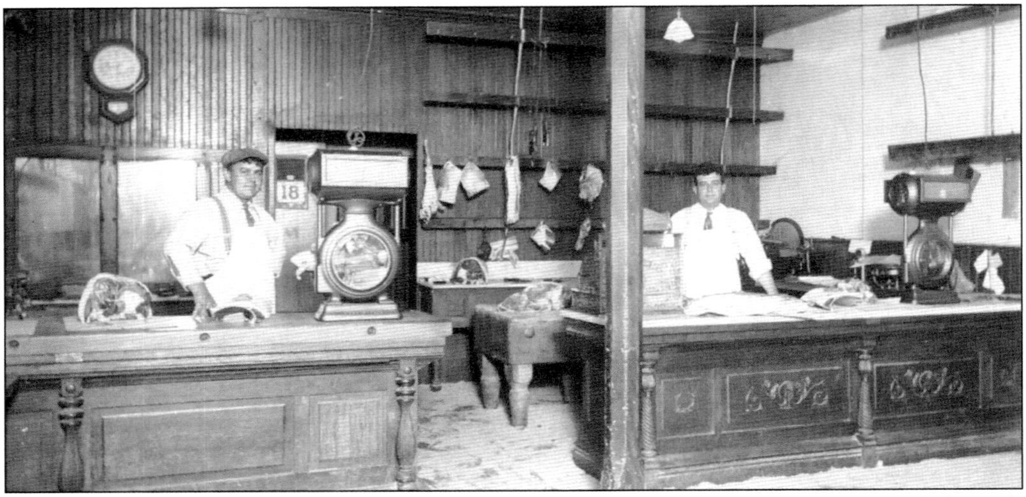

The meat and fish market of Hanson & Schweitzer, located at 417 Sixth Street, passed through a good many hands over the years. E. Jones opened the first meat market here in 1882 and was bought out by Bolton and Hanson in 1896. H.L. Hanson & Son bought it in the fall of 1905. Then, Hanson & Schweitzer bought the market in 1906 and operated it until selling it to Bervin Larson in 1964. The Hanson & Schweitzer Market is pictured above around 1910, with the owners Charles Schweitzer (left), and George Hanson (right). Pictured below is a display of the different meats Hanson & Schweitzer sold at the time. In 1910, Hanson & Schweitzer added a fish department. In December 1924, they sold reindeer meat—imported directly from Alaska—to the people of Racine for the first time.

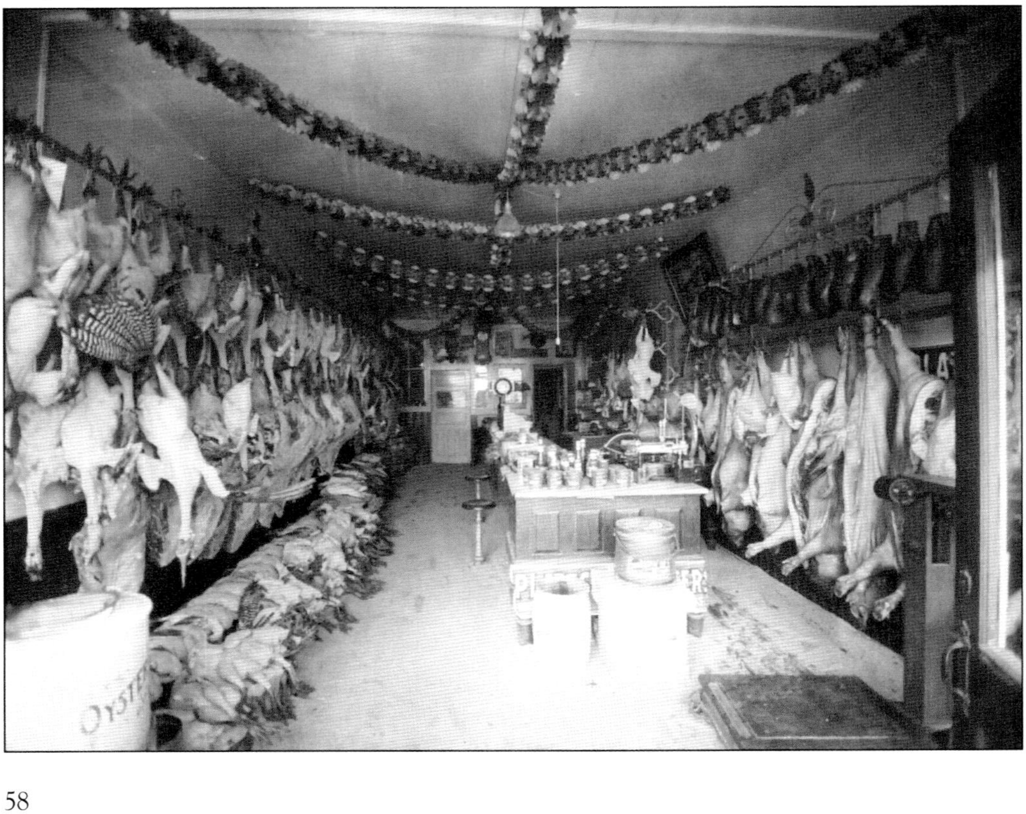

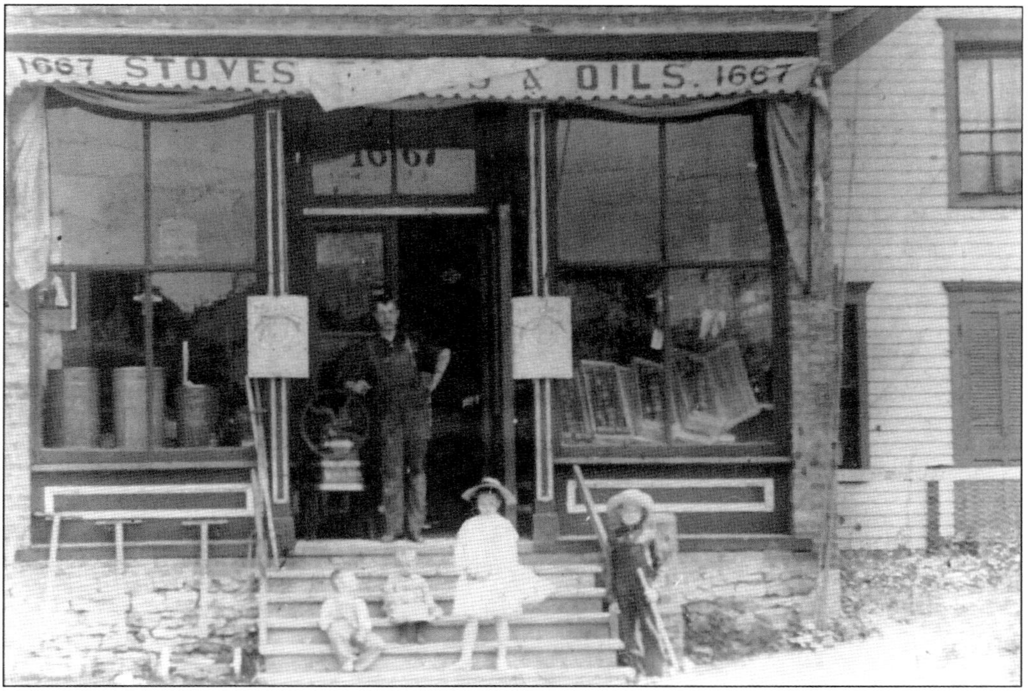

Prostrednik & Kroupa Hardware, pictured above and below, was located at 1667 Douglas Avenue from 1903 through about 1909. In addition to the usual items found for sale in today's hardware stores, they sold sleds, ice skates, roller skates, saving banks, punching bags, boxing gloves, bicycles, guns, gramophones, and sewing machines. In 1910, J. Prostrednik opened a hardware store specializing in bicycle repairs at 1234 Douglas Avenue.

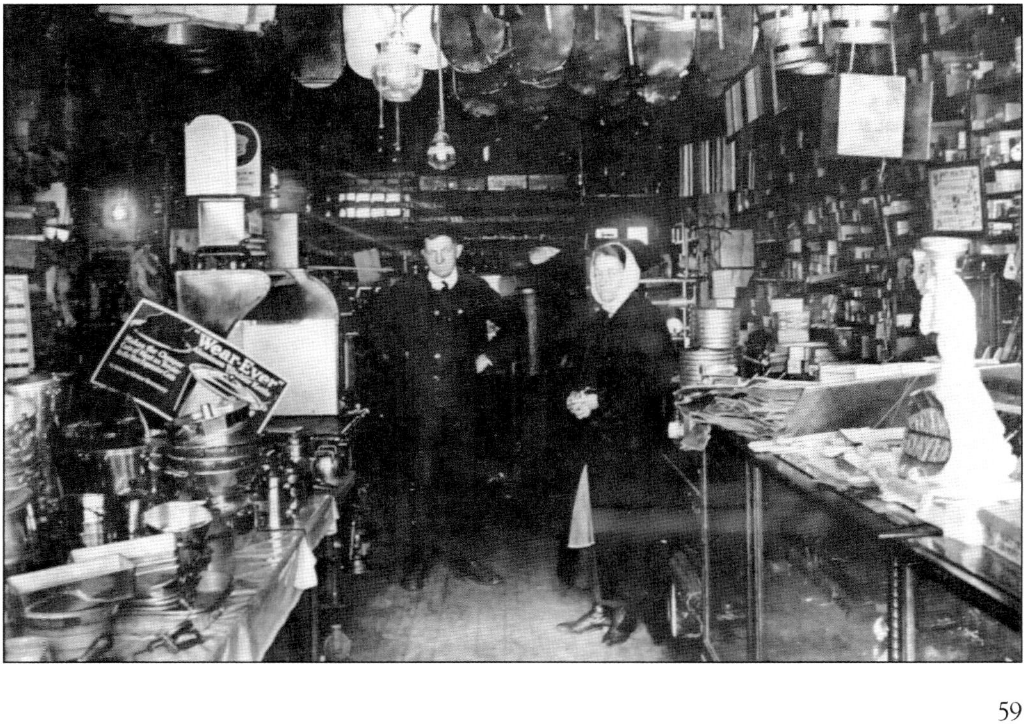

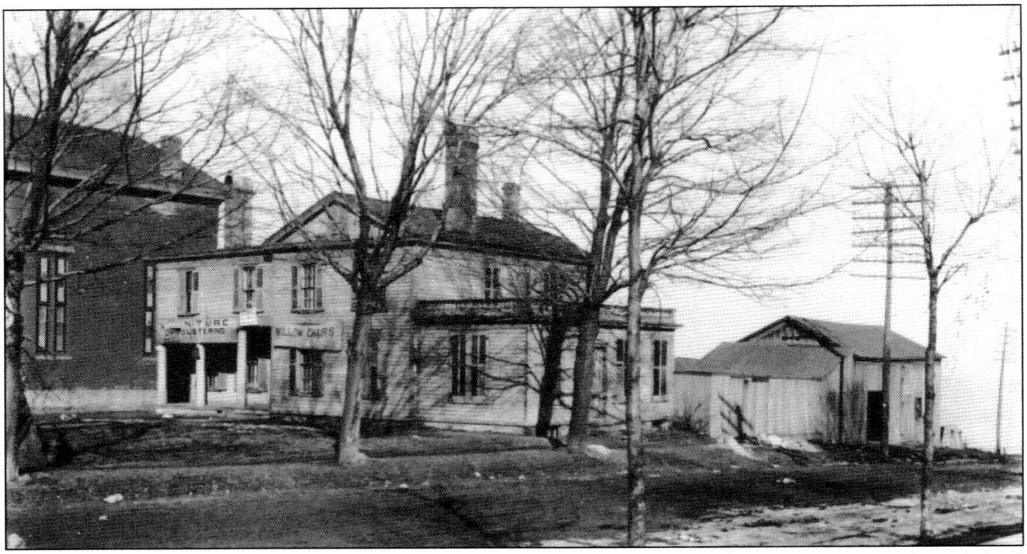

This house, located on the corner of Main and Sixth Streets, was built in 1840. It was demolished in 1891 to make room for Hotel Racine.

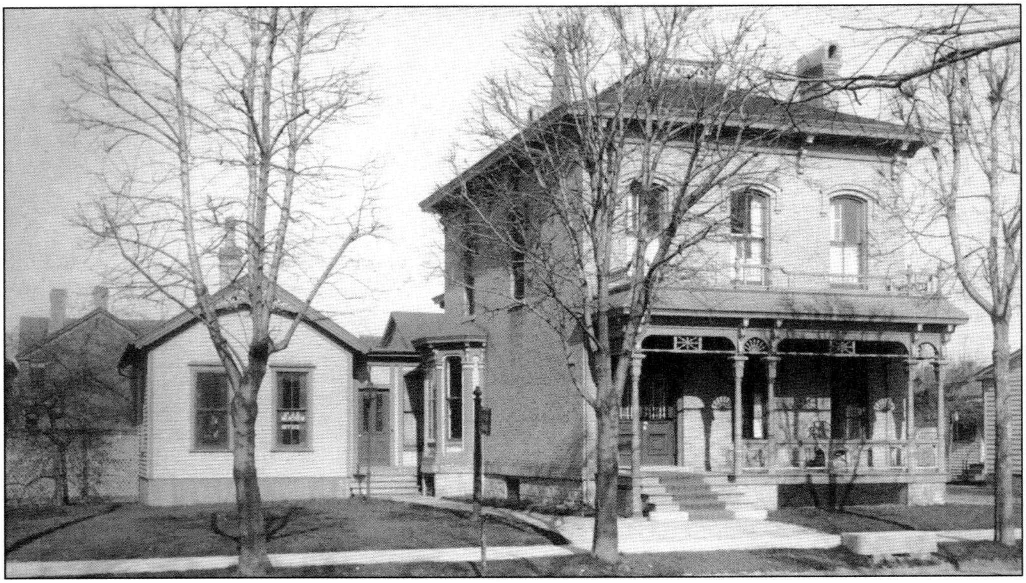

This house, once located at 734 College Avenue, was built prior to 1850. For a time, it was the home of Dr. John G. Meachem. Meachem served three terms as mayor of Racine in the 1870s and founded St. Luke's Hospital in 1871. The house was demolished in July 1951 by Ode Wrecking and Lumber Company, to clear the way for the new YWCA.

Five

MANUFACTURING

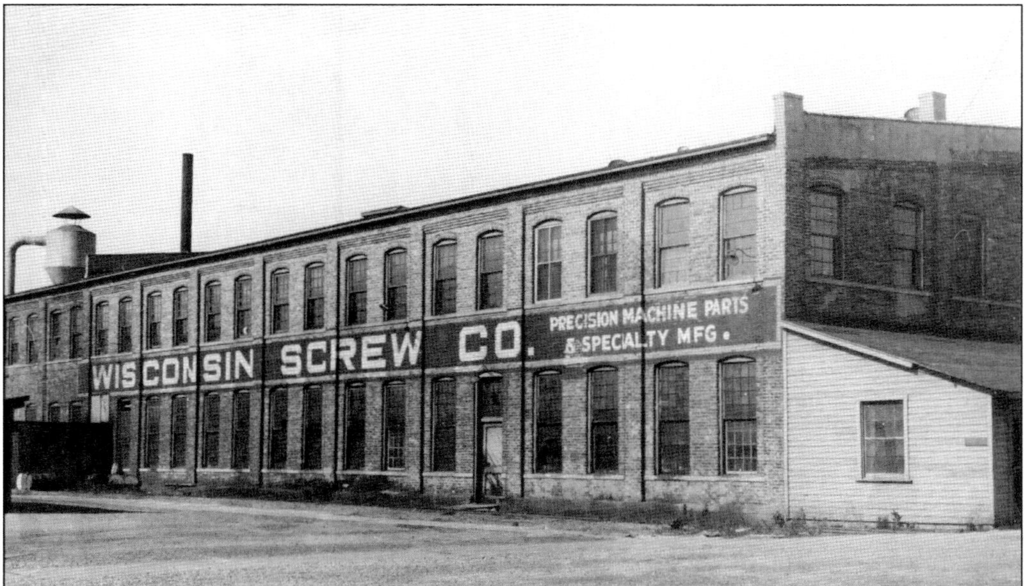

The Wisconsin Screw Company, once located at Twenty-first and Clark Streets, were makers of screw products since at least 1919. This structure burned down on April 28, 1957. The company intended to immediately rebuild, but its insurance carrier fought the claim for damages in court for almost five years. After the case was done in court, the company's owners filed for bankruptcy. The Wisconsin Screw Company was declared bankrupt in 1963.

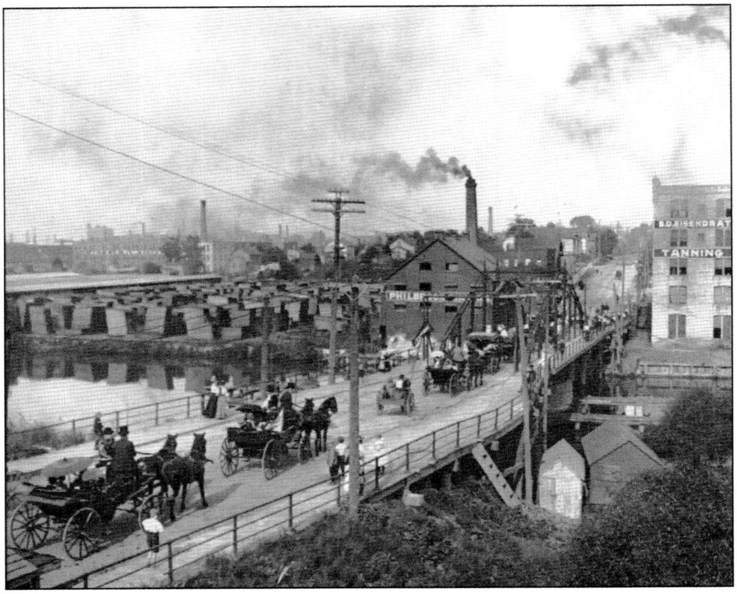

Looking east across the Sixth Street Bridge—toward downtown—around 1900, the B.D. Eisendrath Tanning Company is seen on the right. By 1903, this was one of the largest and most successful tanneries in Wisconsin. Across Sixth Street is the Philbrook Shoe Company. Founded in 1864, L.W. Philbrook took over the business from his father in 1882 and ran it until his health failed in 1904.

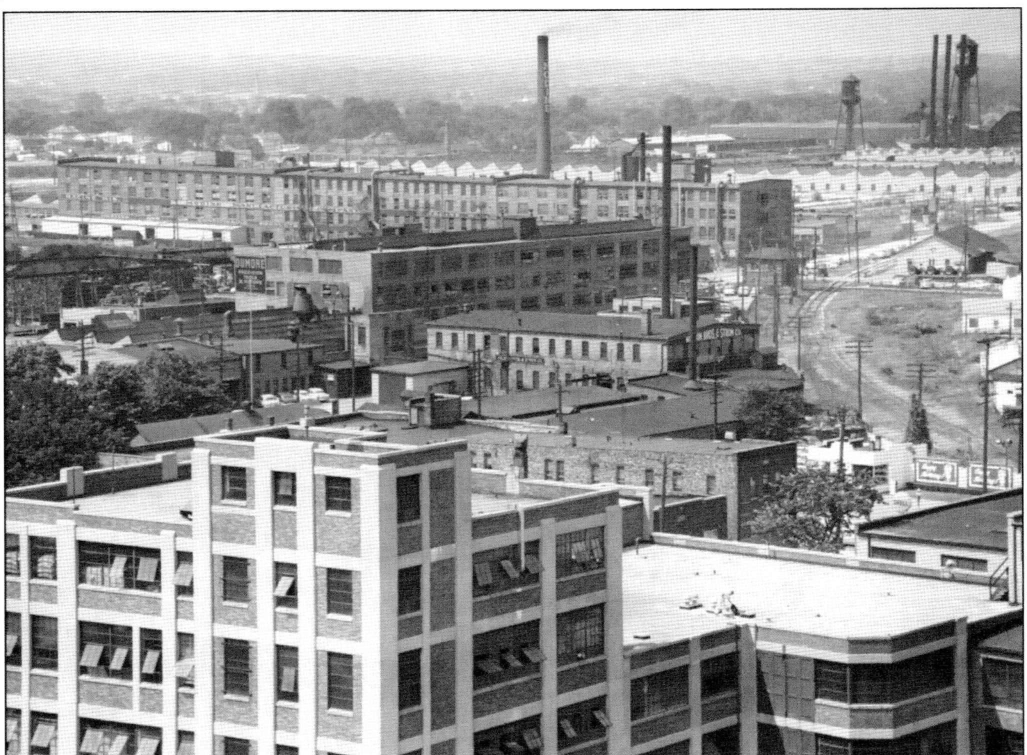

Much of southwestern Racine's industrial complex can be seen in this 1959 photograph. The large building spanning across the bottom is part of the S.C. Johnson campus at 1525 Howe Street. Above it, from front to back, are the Nelson Brothers & Strom Company, the Dumore Company, the Modine Manufacturing Company, and the Mitchell Motor factory—now the home of Massey-Ferguson, Inc.

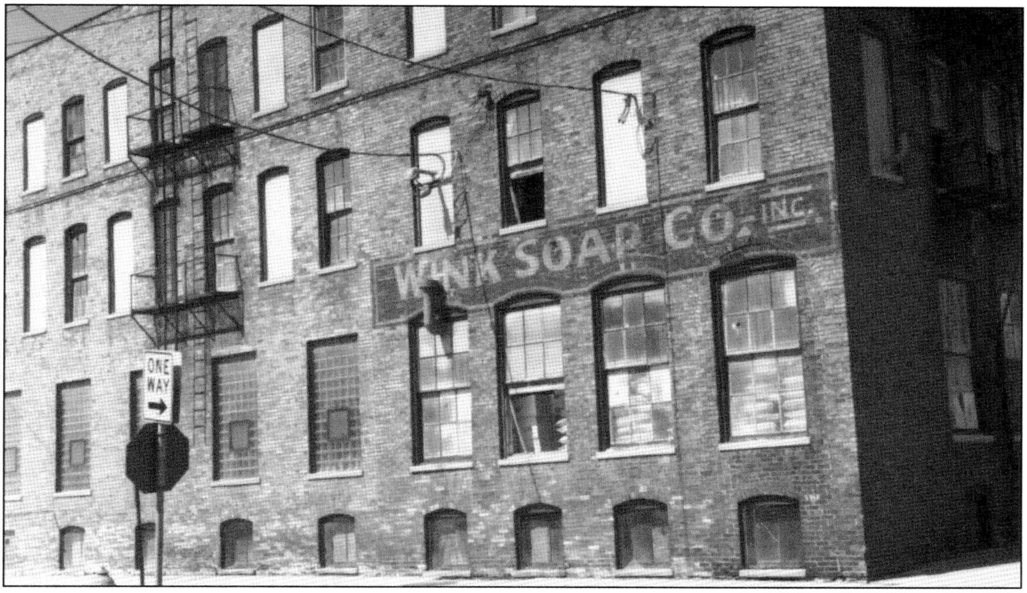

This historic "Cream City" brick building at 932–946 Garfield Street was constructed in 1900 and still stands today. From 1938 through 1980, it was the home of the Wink Soap Company; a manufacturer of soap and detergents for use in home and industry.

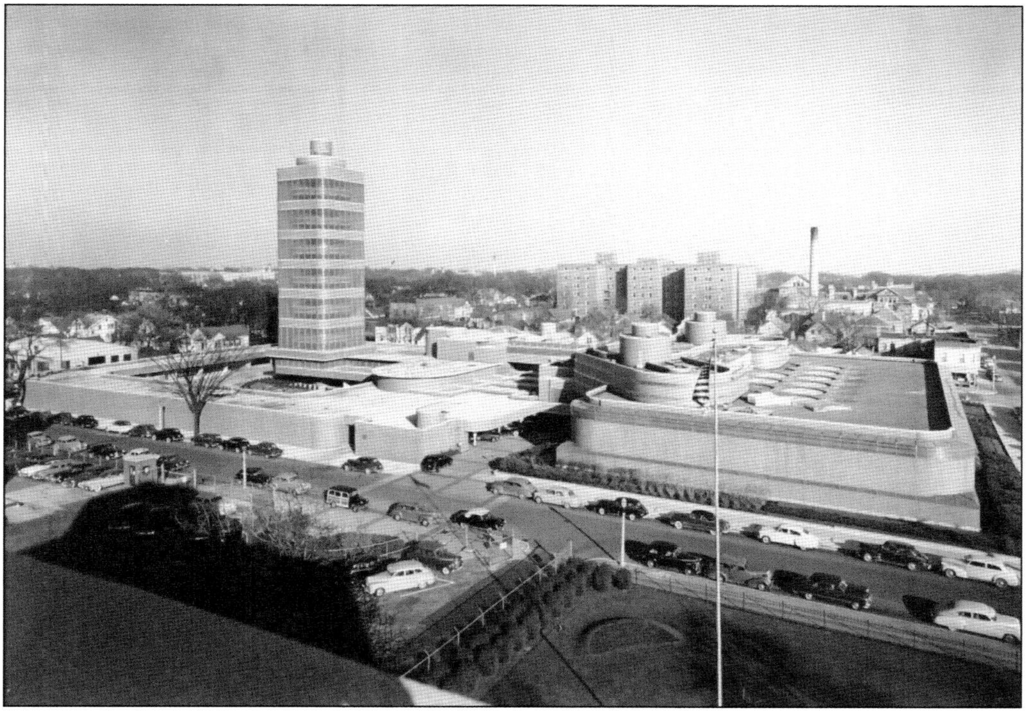

This aerial photograph of the S.C. Johnson campus at 1525 Howe Street was taken in the early 1950s. The campus is anchored by two Frank Lloyd Wright designed buildings; the 15-story Research Tower (left) and the Administration Building (right). Both are on the National Register of Historic Places. S.C. Johnson offers a variety of free tours of the campus.

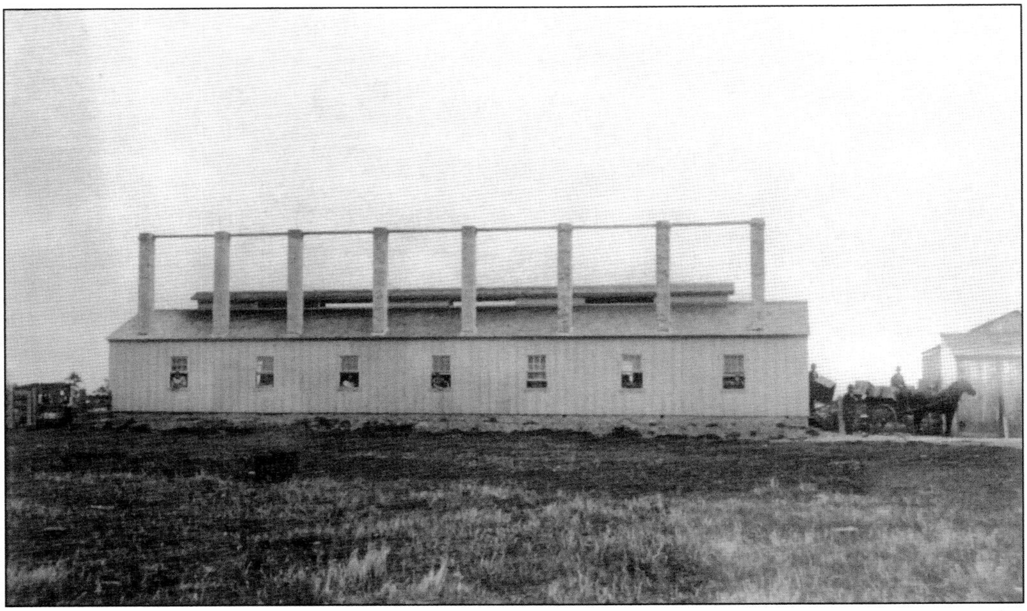

William Horlick came to Racine from England in 1869. In 1873, he began manufacturing "Horlick's Food," a prepared food for infants, invalids, and the aged. In 1875, the Horlick Food Company was incorporated and the plant pictured above was constructed. The old Horlick's Corporation campus still stands at this site on Northwestern Avenue.

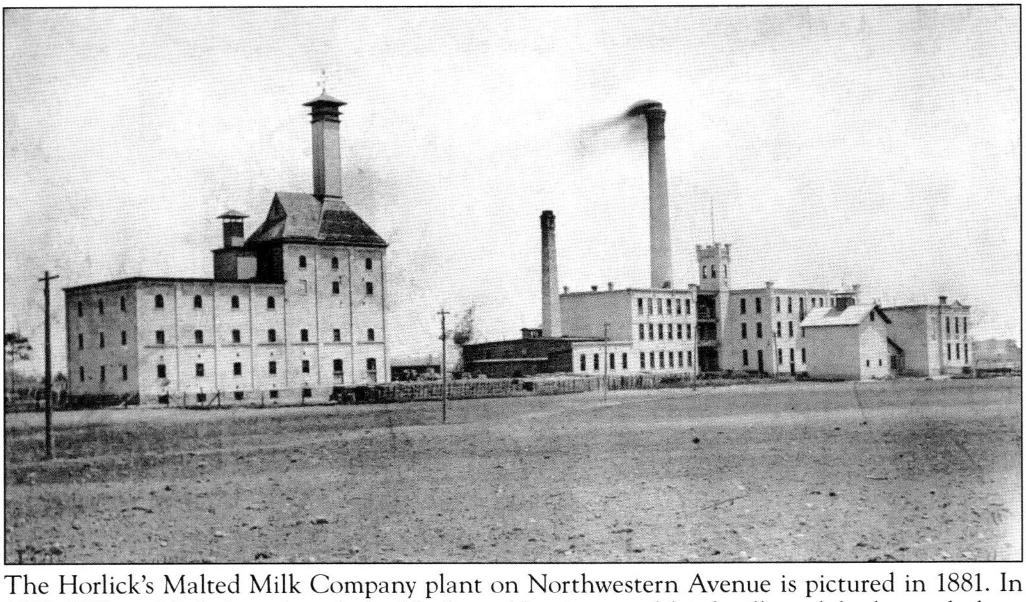

The Horlick's Malted Milk Company plant on Northwestern Avenue is pictured in 1881. In 1887, William Horlick perfected a highly digestible mixture of dried milk, malt barley, and wheat product, which was capable of keeping indefinitely in any climate. The product, called Horlick's Malted Milk, became an instant success.

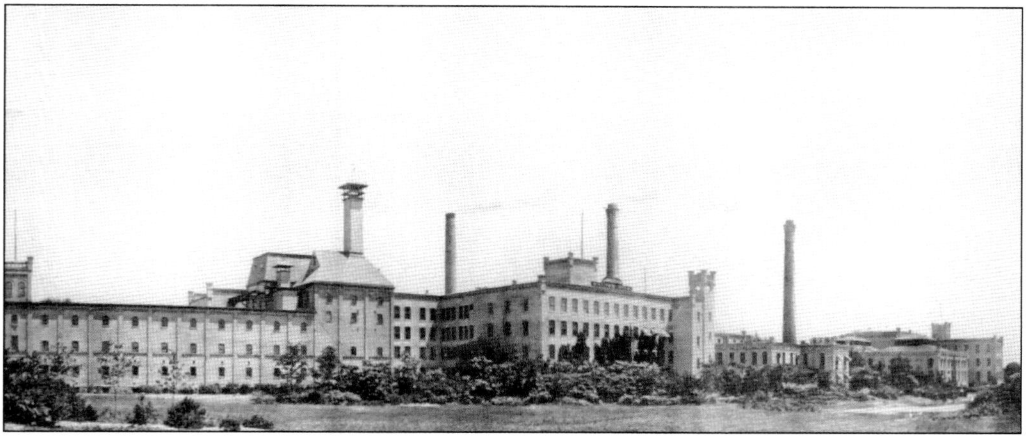

Because of its booming business, Horlick's Malted Milk Company quickly grew into a sprawling complex of buildings on Northwestern Avenue. A second plant was built there in 1902, and a third in 1905. A new milk house, the world's largest at that time, was constructed in 1915. By 1900, the firm had over 200 employees, and this grew to 500 by 1910. The company operated in Racine until 1975.

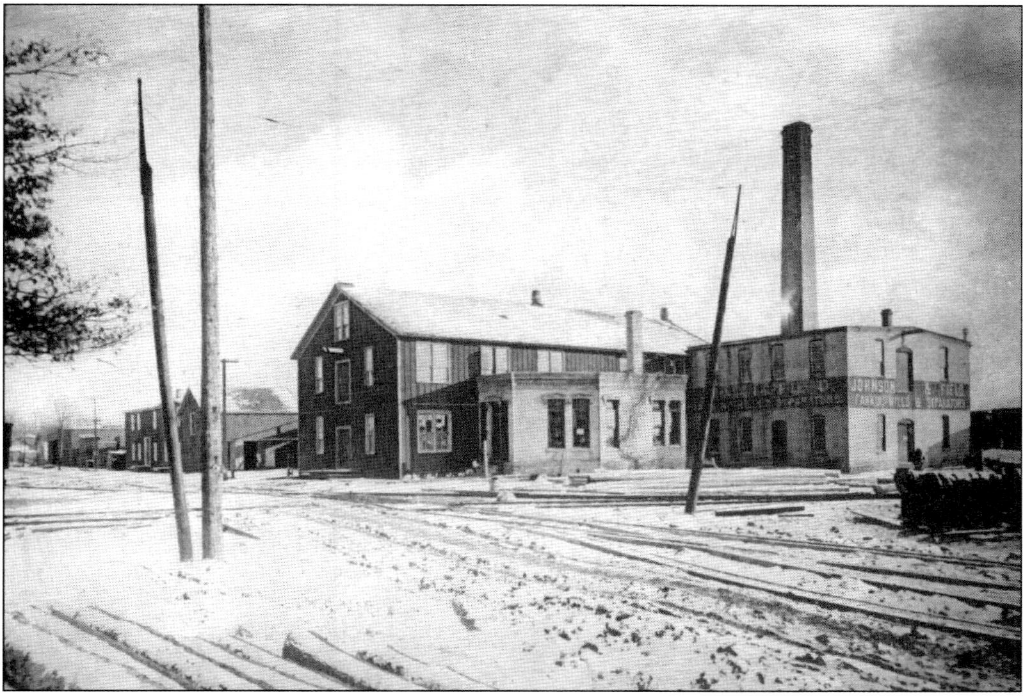

Johnson & Field commenced making fanning mills (a hand-cranked device used to separate grain from its stalk) in 1869. They also began making bicycles in the 1890s and gradually became a large wholesale dealer in bicycles and supplies. Their factory, above, was located on Seventeenth Street at the Chicago & North Western railroad tracks. It was destroyed by fire on September 21, 1916.

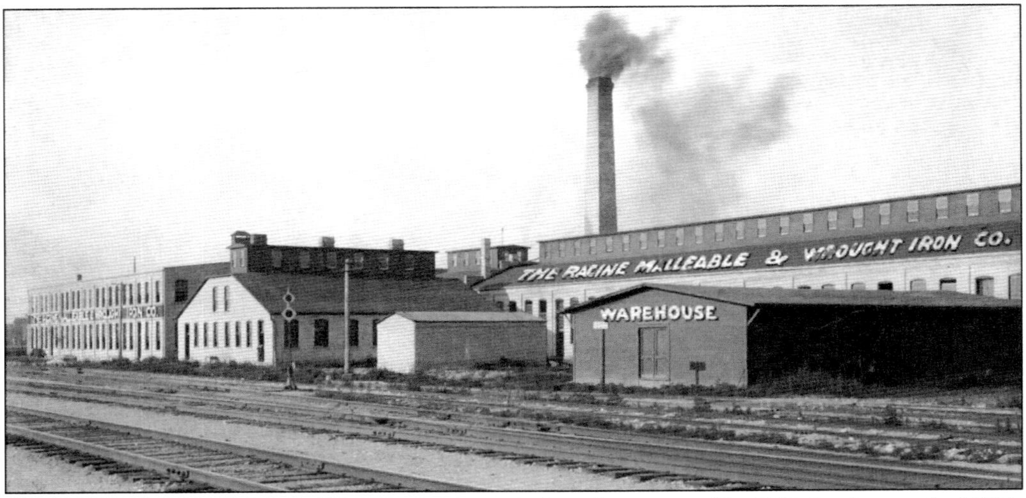

Few realize the importance of Racine as an early foundry center. By 1917, Racine ranked 37th among American cities, with 21 foundries employing nearly 3,000 men. In 1917, the Racine Malleable and Wrought Iron Company, above, manufactured malleable castings, wagon hardware, and hacksaws.

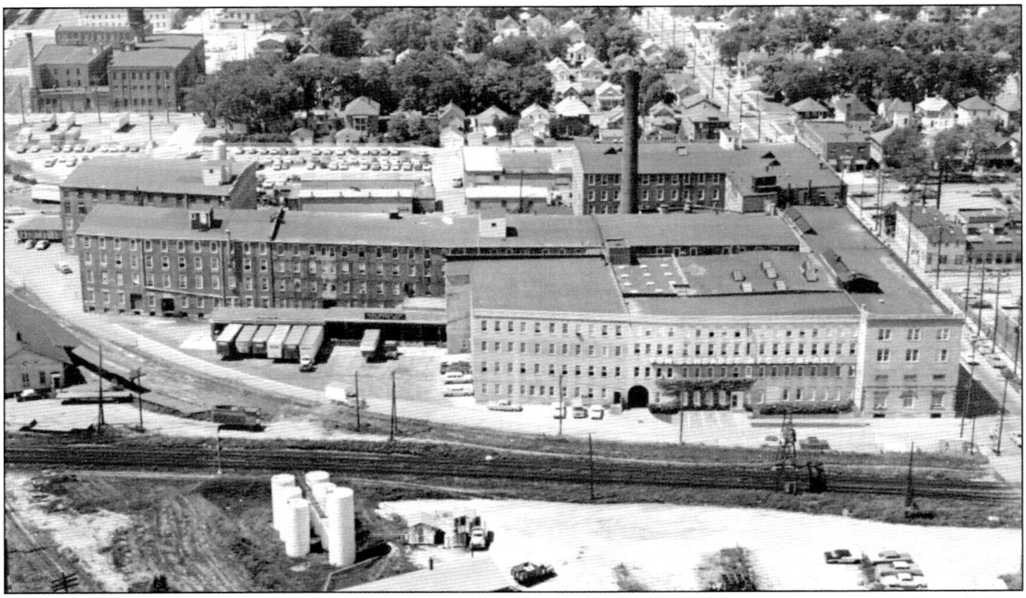

The Von Schrader Manufacturing Company, seen here in a 1966 aerial photograph, was founded in 1935 by Francis Von Schrader. Located at Sixteenth Street and Junction Avenue, they manufacture carpet and upholstery cleaning equipment for industrial clients and businesses worldwide.

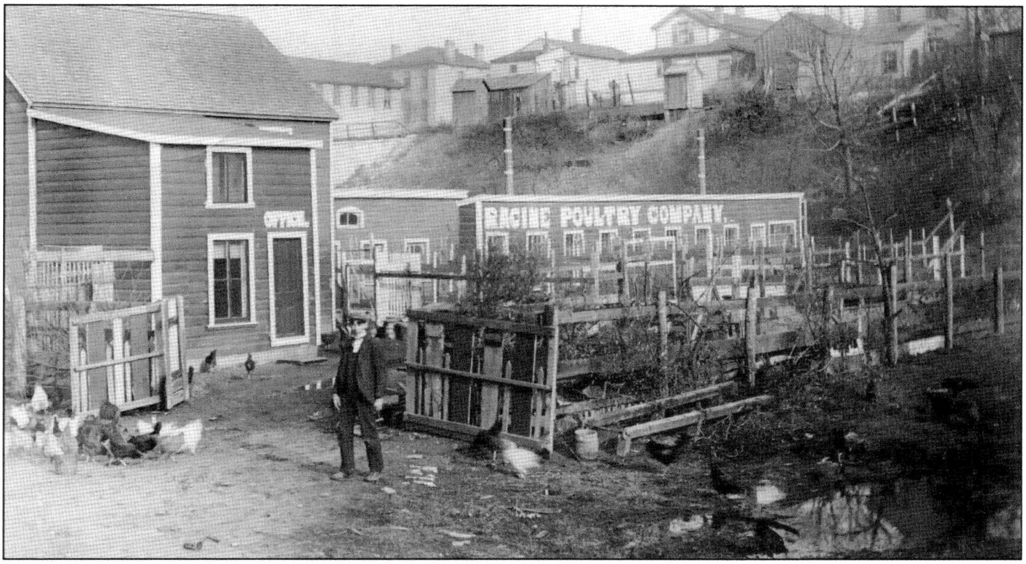

The Racine Poultry Company was a poultry farm in the city of Racine for a number of years around 1900. A November 1898 advertisement stated that the Racine Poultry Company, located at 800 State Street, had geese, ducks, turkeys, and chickens for sale at wholesale and retail prices. At the Racine Poultry, Pigeon, and Pet Show, held in January 1901 at the Lakeside Auditorium, the Racine Poultry Company entered several different breeds of chickens and won numerous first prizes. A November 1912 advertisement indicated that the Racine Poultry Company was now located at 519 Center Street; however, the exact location where these photographs were taken is unknown.

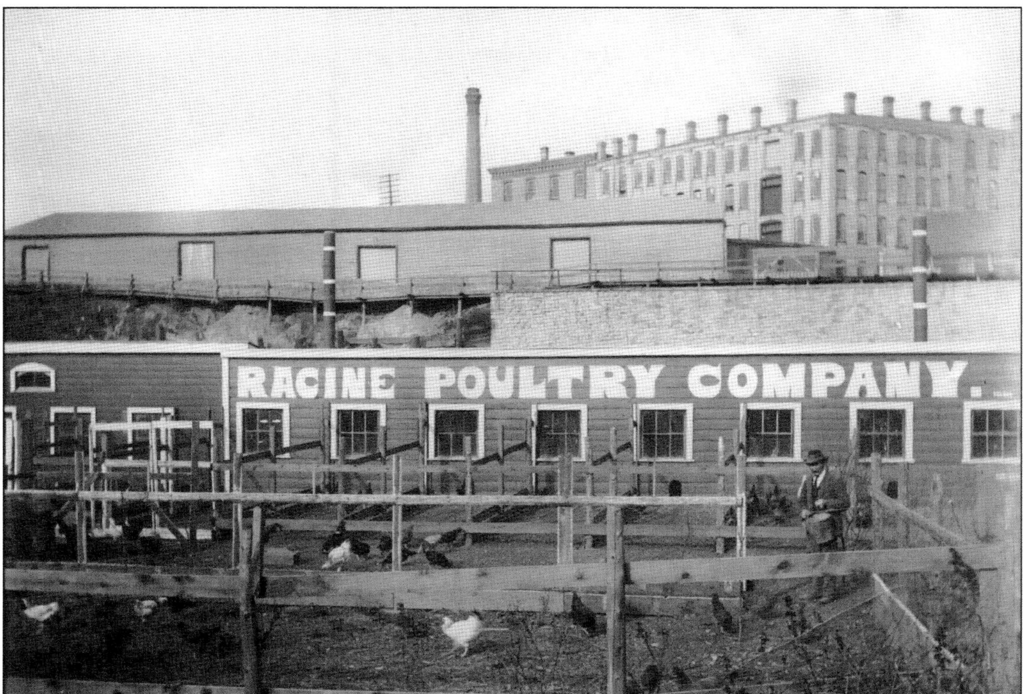

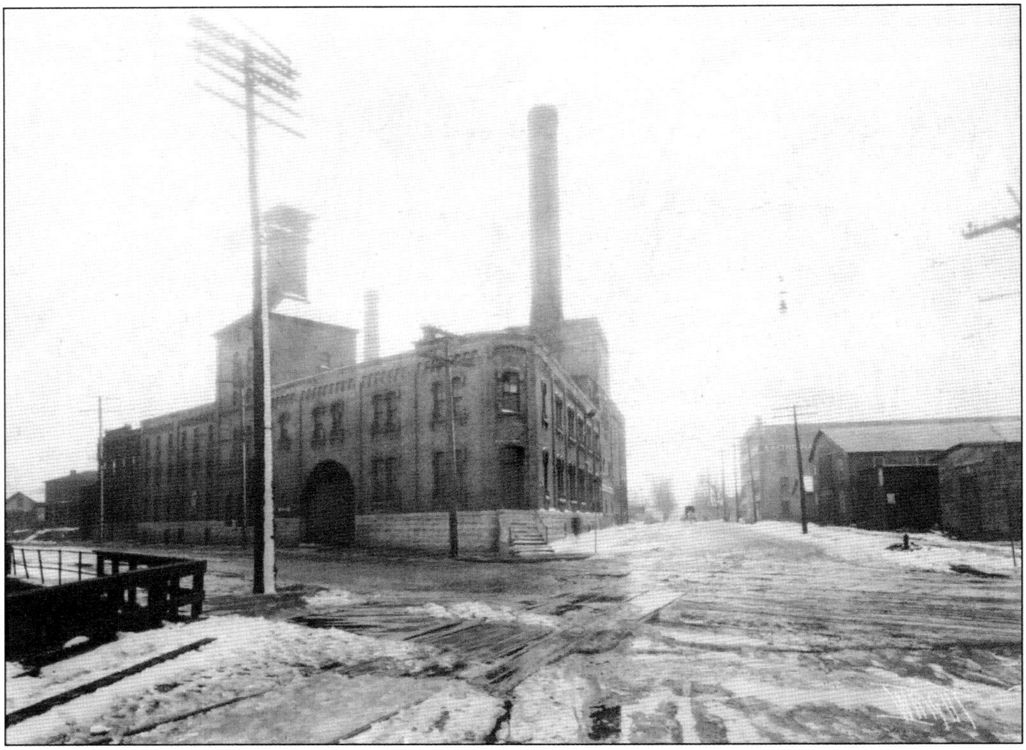

The Ernst Klinkert Brewery Company stood on the southwest corner of Washington Avenue and Eighth Street. It began operations in 1881 and was the largest Racine brewery that has ever existed. Most of the beer was sold in the Racine and Kenosha area. Klinkert purchased many taverns in Racine and leased them to persons who would only sell his beer.

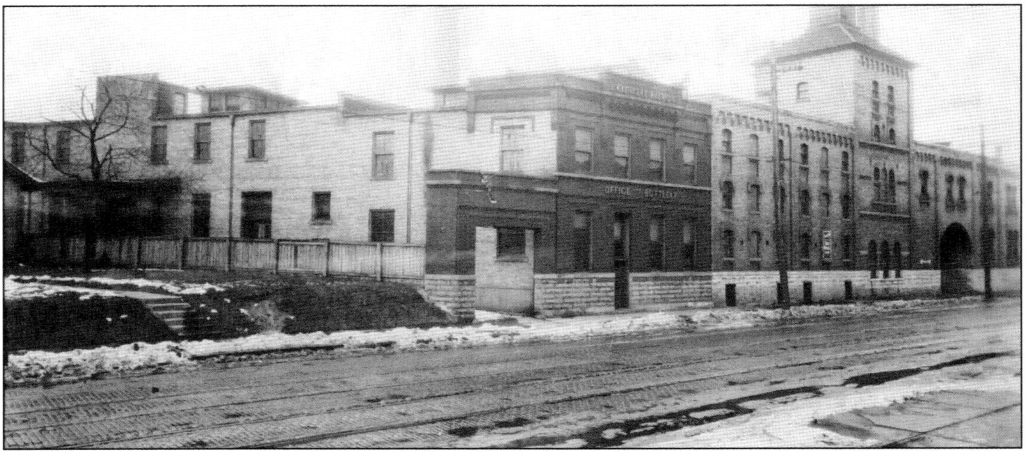

Looking northward from about Ninth Street, the Ernst Klinkert Brewery Company brick buildings—built in 1886—sprawl along Washington Avenue from Eighth Street. The brewery closed in 1920, when Prohibition caused the company to shut down. For a short time during Prohibition, Klinkert manufactured near beer in the plant, but the buildings were eventually abandoned and most were razed in 1931.

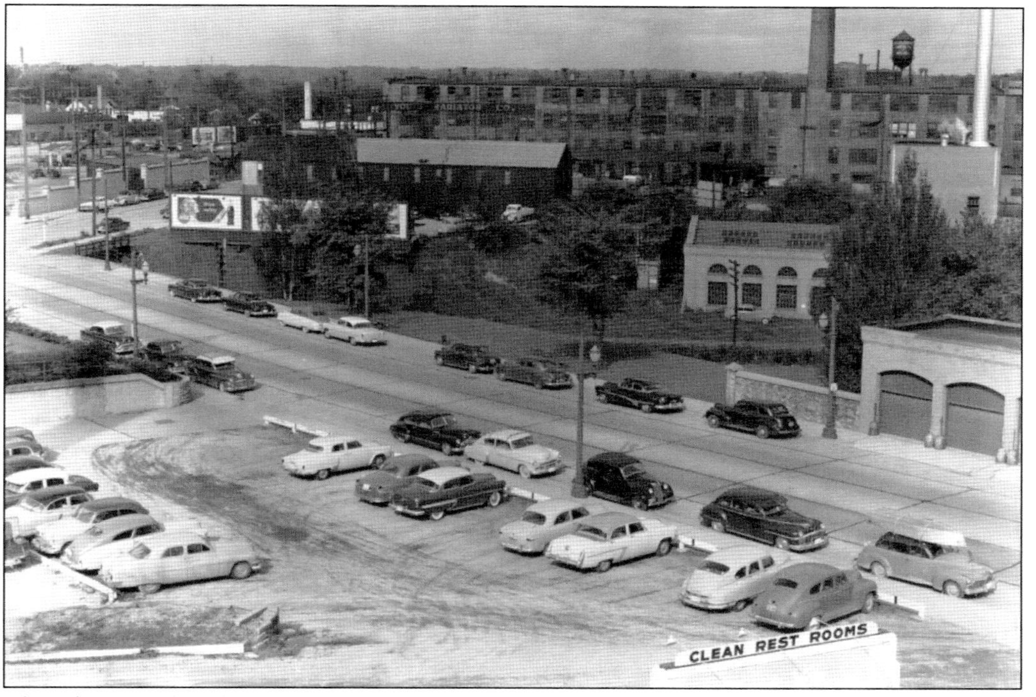

This photograph, taken in the early 1950s, looks southwest from behind Racine's city hall. Its parking lot is in the foreground, and the Young Radiator plant is seen spanning across most of the horizon. Both this Young Radiator factory and its predecessor at this location, the Racine Manufacturing Company factory, burned down in spectacular fires.

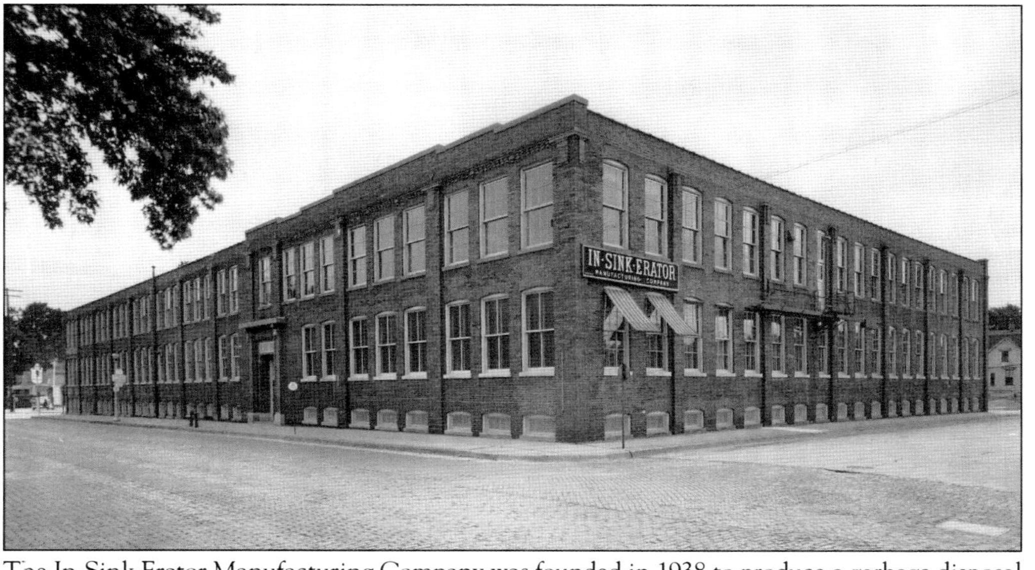

The In-Sink-Erator Manufacturing Company was founded in 1938 to produce a garbage disposal unit invented by John Hammes. In-Sink-Erator purchased the pictured building at 1225 Fourteenth Street from the Dumore Company in 1949. They occupied it until late 1962, when they built and moved into their current home at 4700 Twenty-first Street. In-Sink-Erator sold this building to Qualheim, Inc. in 1963.

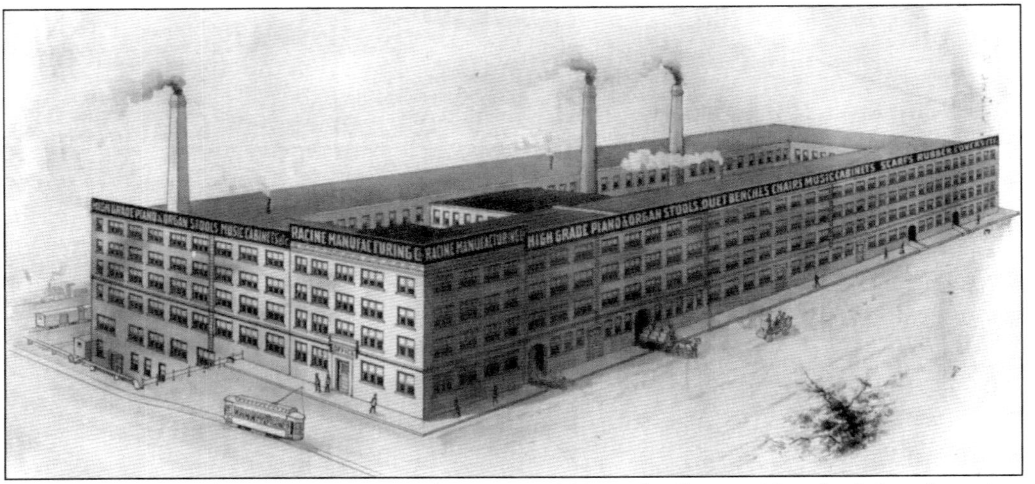

The Racine Manufacturing Company began in 1902 as the Racine Novelty Manufacturing Company. The company quickly grew and, by 1907, had two large factories in Racine. Factory No. 1, pictured above, was at Sixth and Marquette Street. It burned down on December 13, 1909, and was immediately rebuilt.

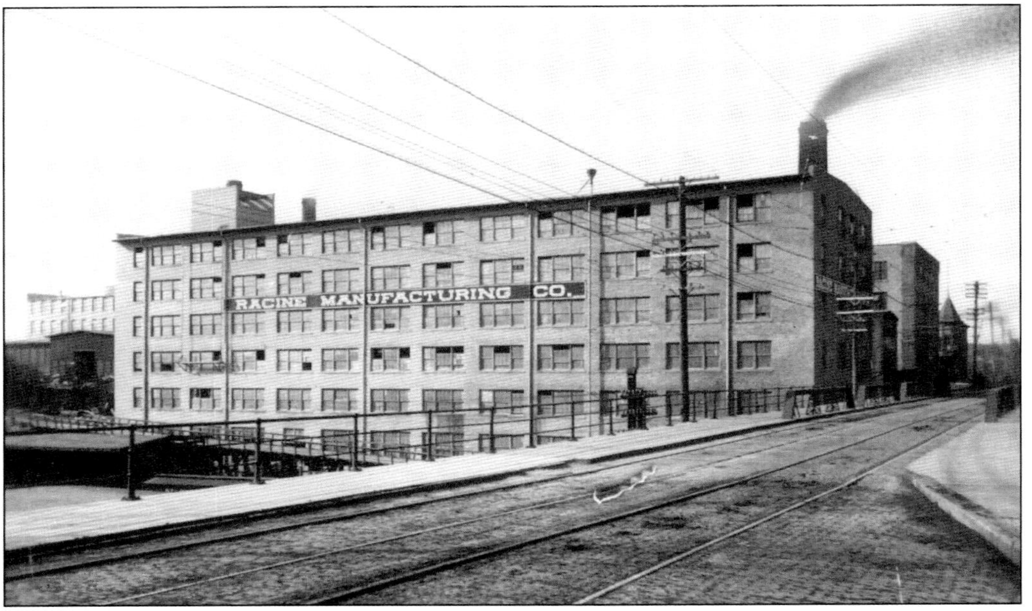

In 1910, the Racine Novelty Manufacturing Company changed its name to the Racine Manufacturing Company, and by 1916 it was a major producer of automobile bodies. Its bodies were used on Stearns-Knight, Moline-Knight, Kissel, Auburn, Case, Jordan, Haynes, Standard Steel, and Grant automobiles; as well as on Yellow Taxicabs in Chicago, and Black and White Taxicabs in New York.

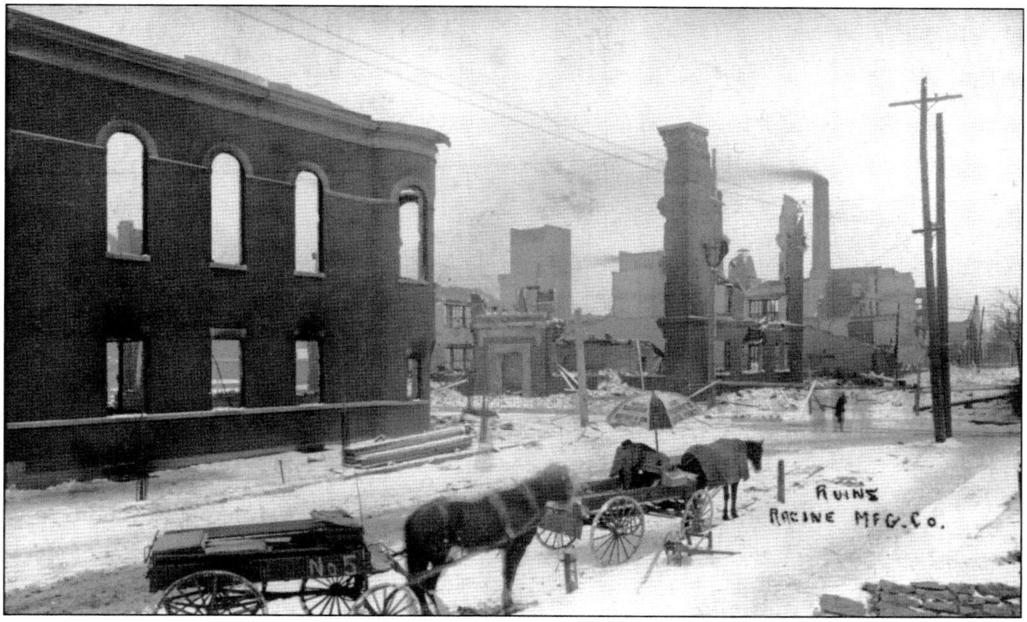

On December 12, 1909, six buildings of the Racine Manufacturing Company at Marquette and West Sixth Streets were destroyed by fire, along with Danish Brotherhood Hall, several residences and the Mitchell & Lewis Company warehouse. The ruins of Danish Brotherhood Hall, erected in 1904, are seen in the foreground on the left.

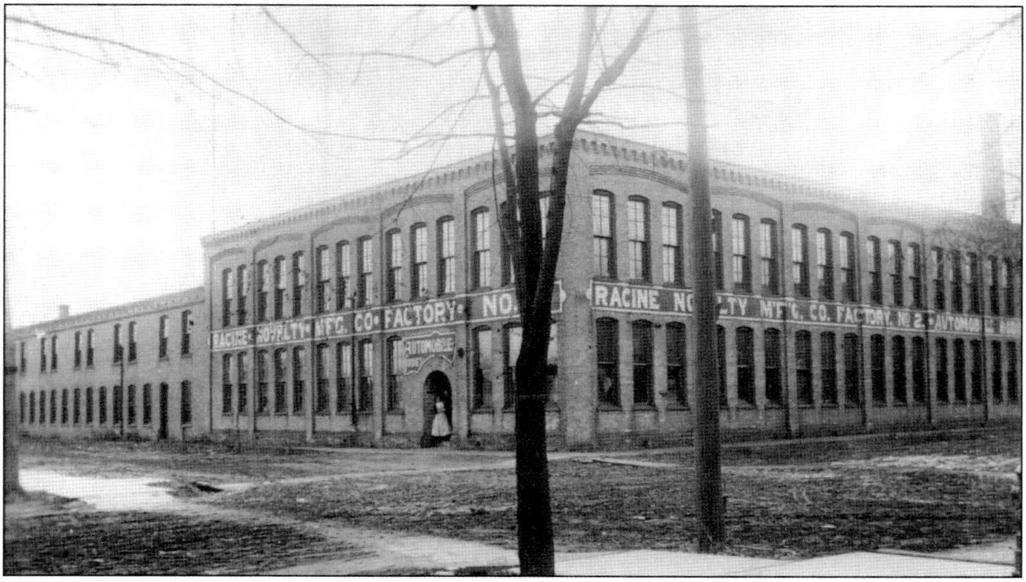

Picture above is the Racine Novelty Manufacturing Company's Factory No. 2, located at Clark and Fifteenth Streets in the early 1900s.

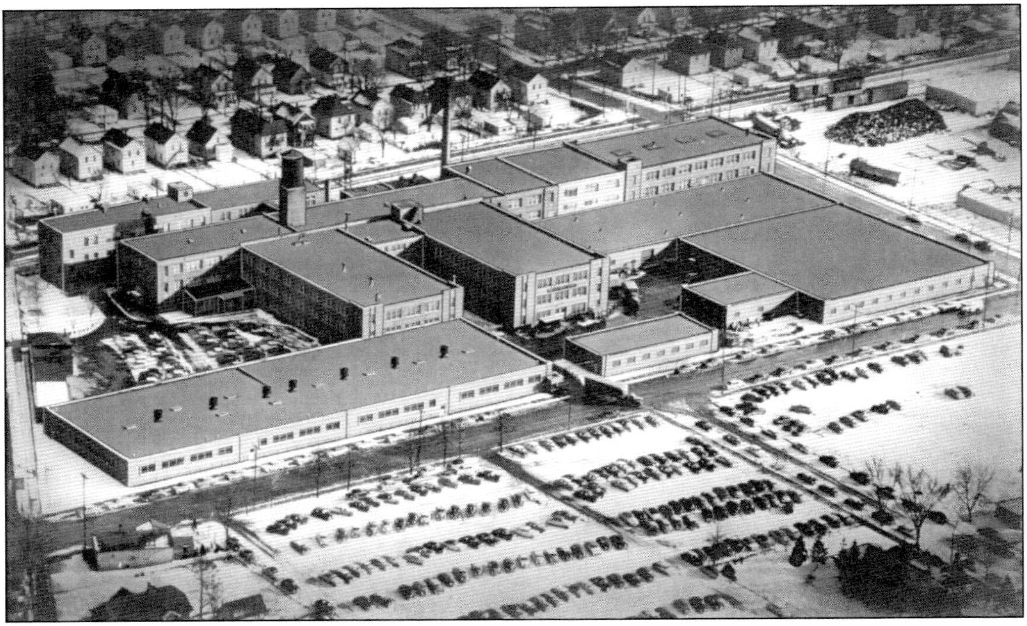

The Hamilton Beach Company campus, pictured here around 1955, spanned Memorial Drive from Rapids Drive to West High Street. In 1910, Chester Beach and L.H. Hamilton joined forces to establish a company for the manufacture of electric motors. Its development of the fractional horsepower "universal" motor was the backbone of the company's growth and success.

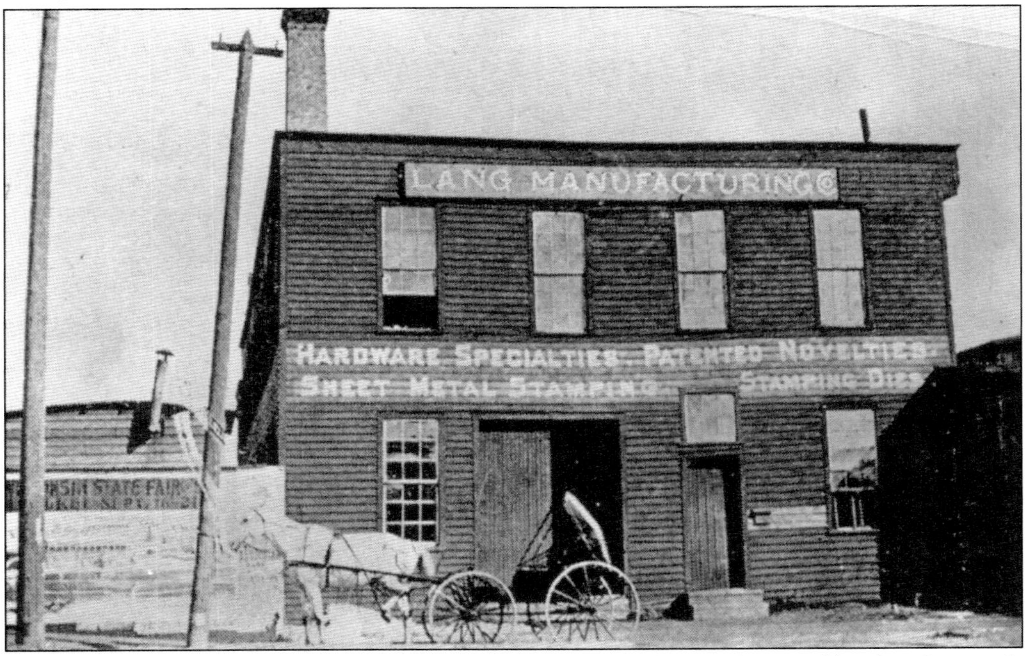

In 1895, Robert B. Lang started a manufacturing business in a factory (pictured here) at Sixteenth Street and Junction Avenue. In 1901, a large, two-story brick factory was built at the corner of Holborn and Eighteenth Streets to accommodate the increased business. This factory, however, was built without toilets because there were no sewers for them to be hooked up to.

Six

TRANSPORTATION

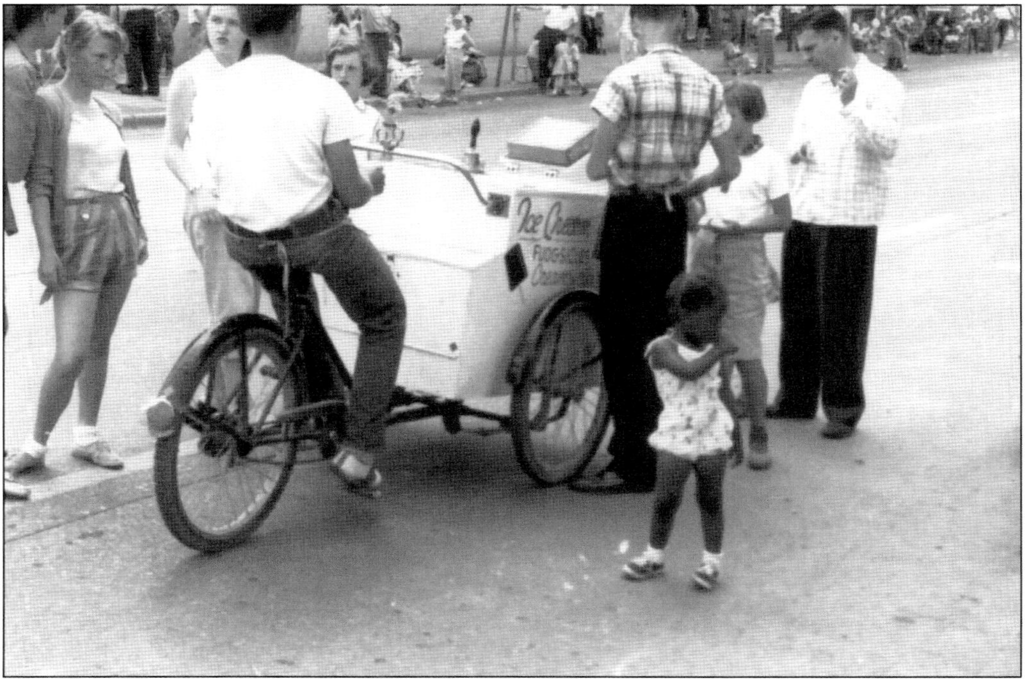

Ice cream vendors riding bicycles, such as the one pictured above, are a common sight riding through neighborhoods in Racine on nice summer nights and along parade routes. Bells, such as the one visible on the icebox above, are rung as they peddle about to attract the attention of potential customers.

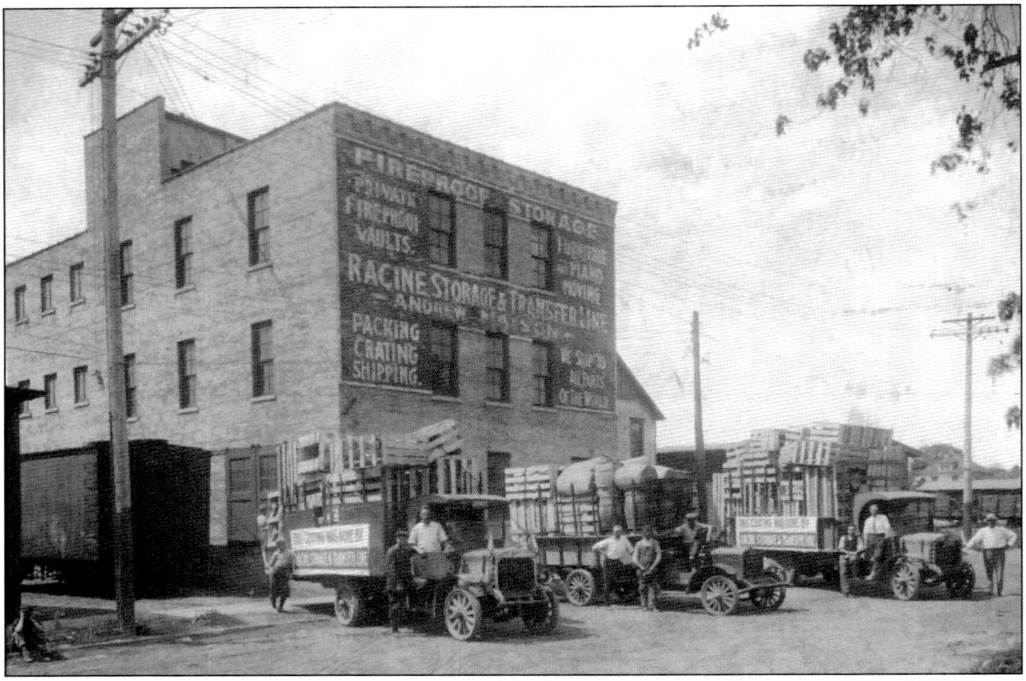

Racine Storage and Transfer Company opened for business in around 1918 at 1327–1331 Liberty Street, as seen above. In 1944, it moved to a warehouse at 1010 State Street. In 1961, Racine Storage & Transfer Company relocated to a building owned by the J.I. Case Company at 815 Eighth Street. The company filed for bankruptcy on January 12, 1965.

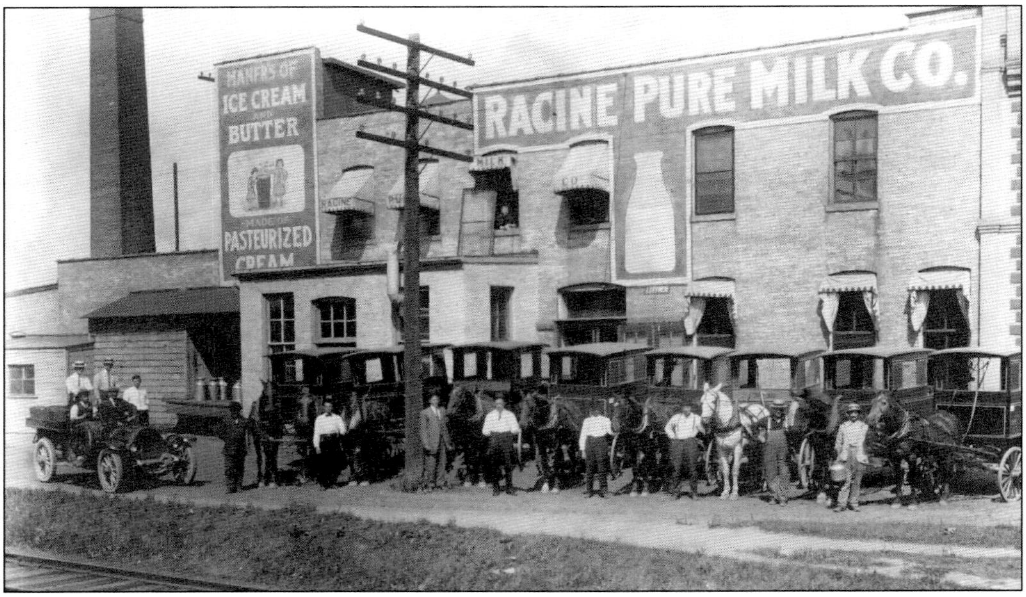

A group of investors organized the Racine Pure Milk Company during the summer of 1903. Its purpose was to build a sanitary milk plant to furnish pasteurized milk, cream, and butter to Racine area residents. In August 1903, a committee chose 1010 Thirteenth Street as the site for its new dairy, and building commenced immediately.

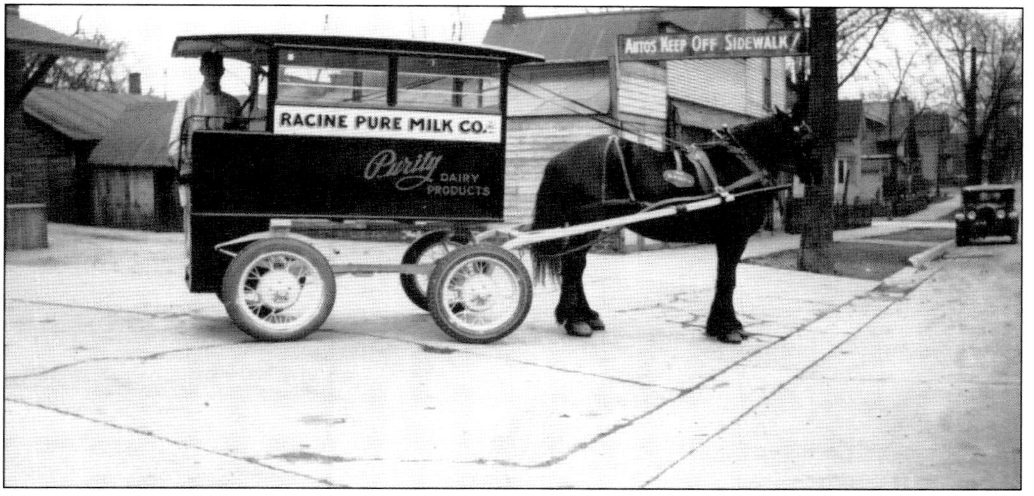

The Racine Pure Milk Company began operations in December 1903, with four milk routes. It soon grew to become Racine's largest dairy. On March 2, 1929, it was taken over by the Borden Company. The old name was retained until around 1940, when all its products began bearing the Borden brand name.

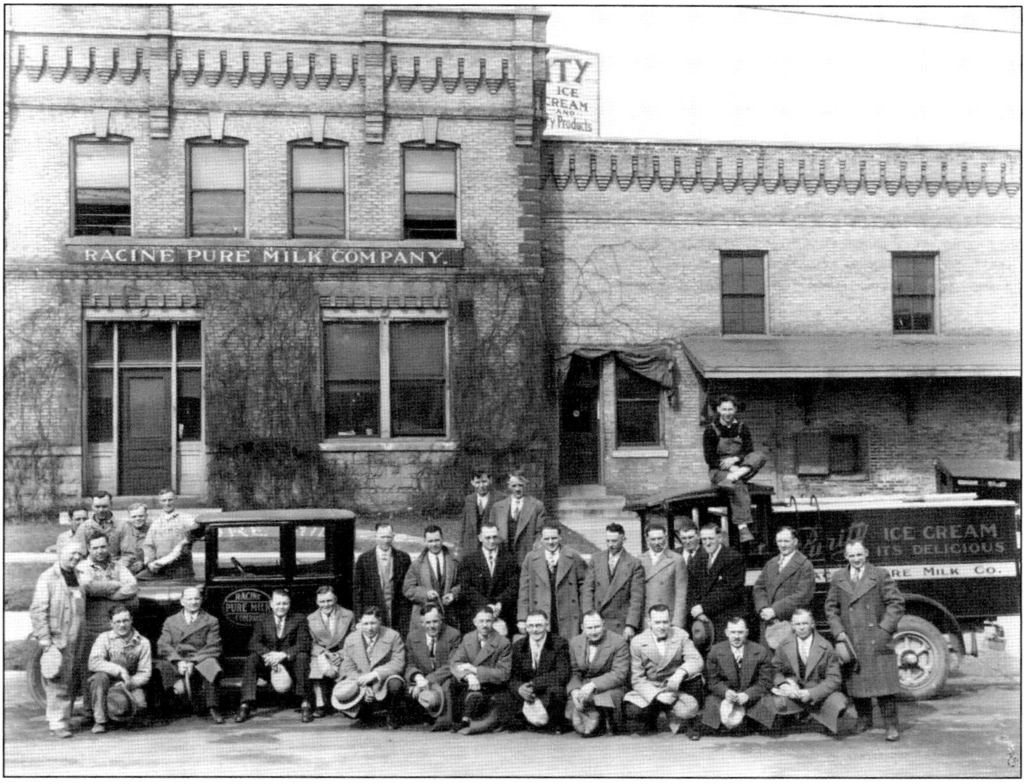

From its very beginning, the Racine Pure Milk Company used newspaper advertising to tout the benefits of pasteurized milk; stating that it is not foul with germs like the average, common milk. In 1904, it sold its milk in sealed glass bottles for 5¢ a quart delivered. Also in 1904, three flavors of ice cream were made and sold for 35¢ a quart: vanilla, chocolate, and pistachio.

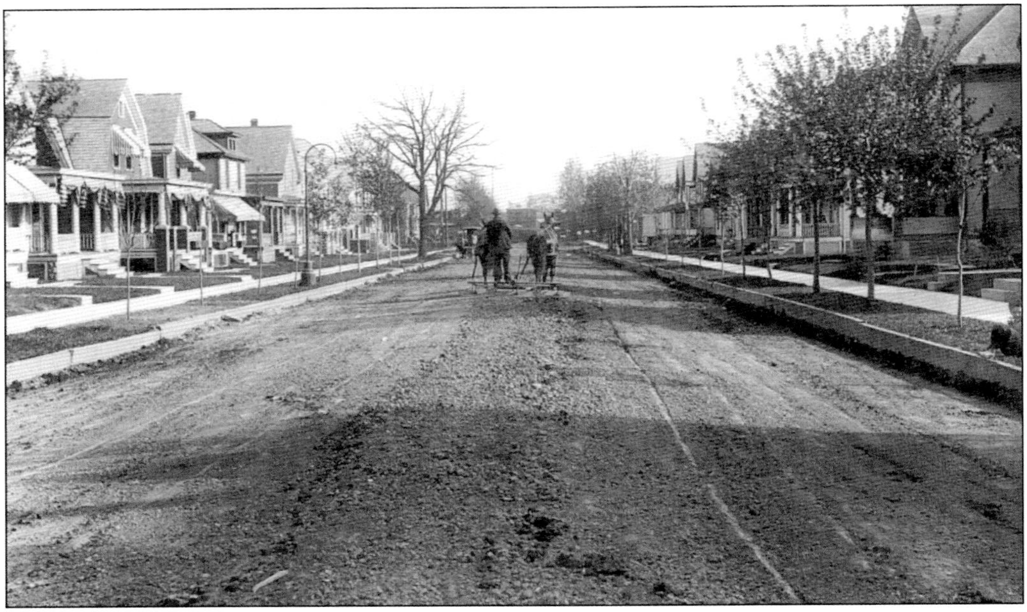

Pictured above is a Case H&L Road Drag, in operation on Boyd Avenue during the 1910s. This system was used to smoothen out the dirt streets of Racine in the 1910s. Tipping the blades (visible below) backwards causes the Drag to cut; the lever being at the operator's hand, he can adjust the blades to make them cut more or less. Also, the operator can tip the blades until they distribute or dump the load into the chuckholes or depressions in the road. Moving the blades forward causes the Drag to break or smash clods of dirt. It also packs them together until the street has a nice and smooth bonded surface. It was recommended that six operations or passes be made on the street to put it in the very best condition.

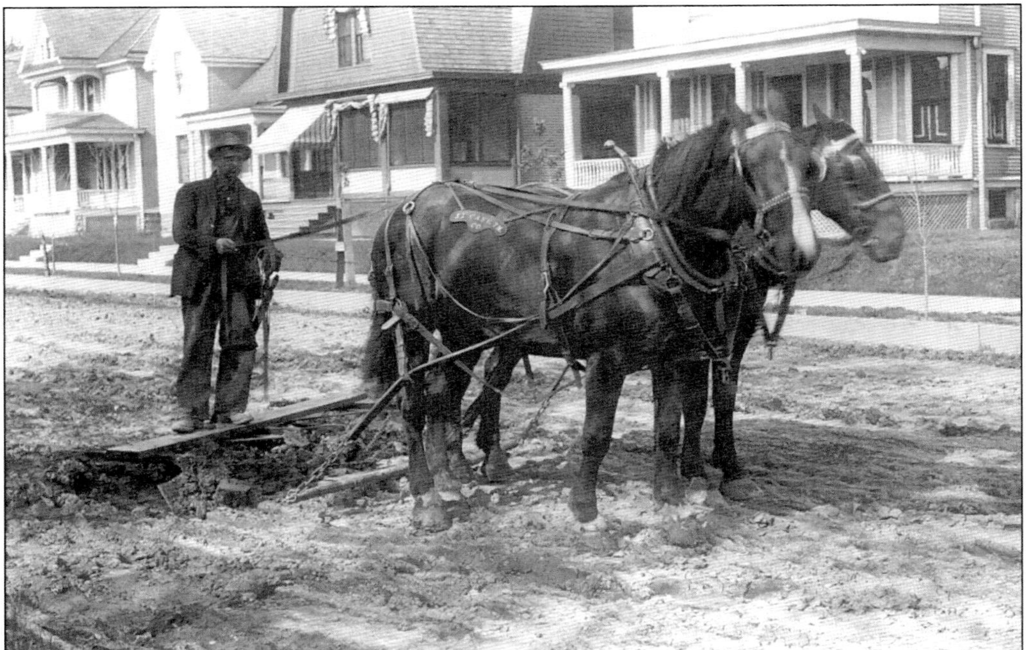

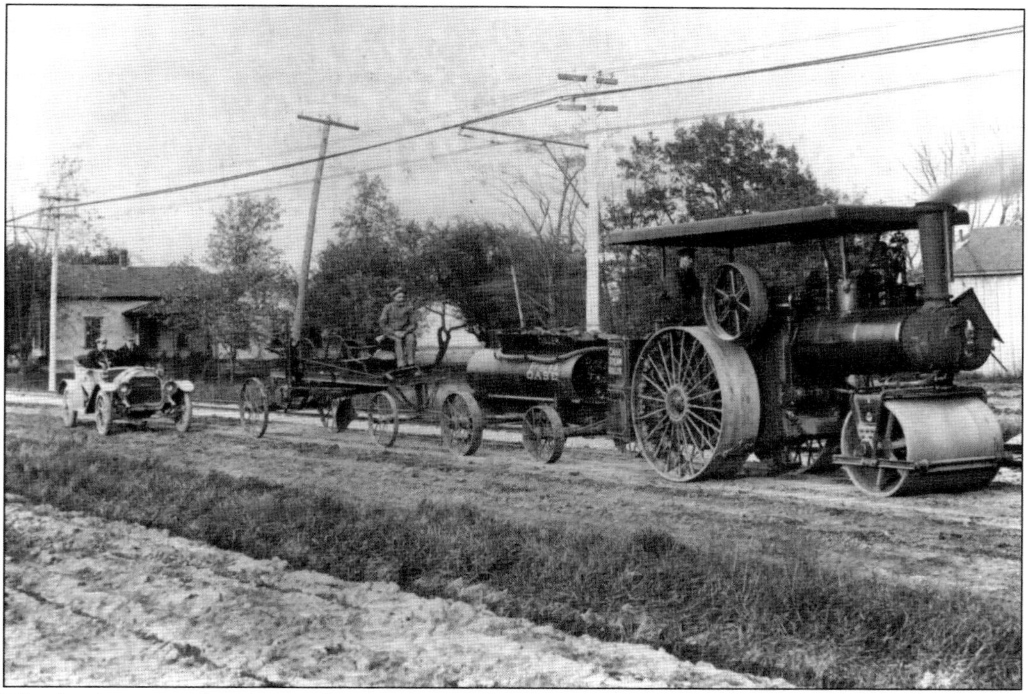

The development of mechanized equipment used to smooth out dirt streets made the job much quicker and easier. Left to right are a Case automobile, grader, water tender, and a Case steamroller.

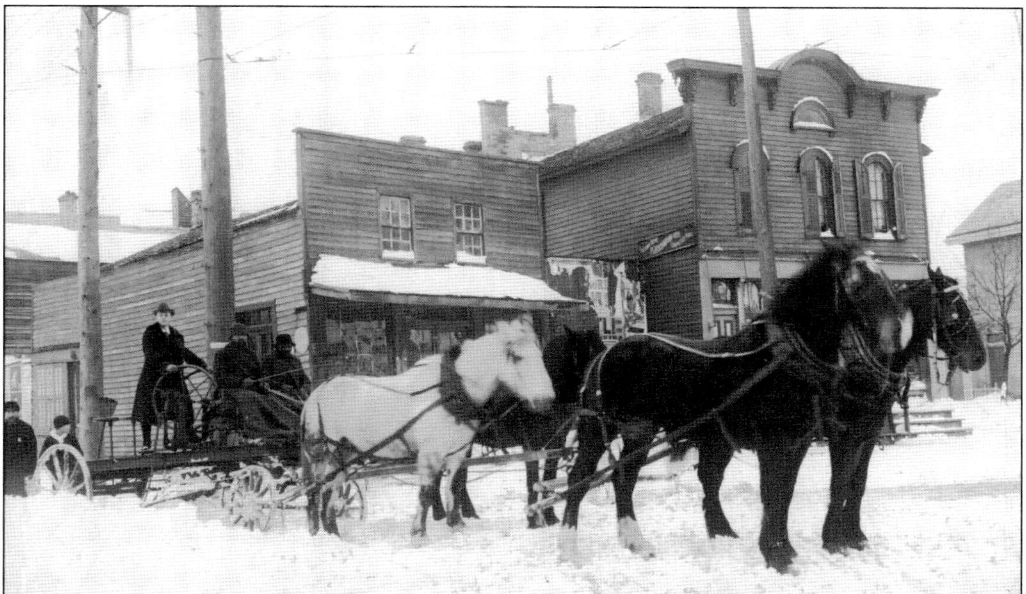

Jackson I. Case and crew are operating a grader to remove the snow from the streetcar tracks on Sixth Street at Grand Avenue about 1898. At that time, Jackson I. Case, visible standing on the wagon, was owner of the electric trolley car system in Racine. The two west-facing buildings on Grand Avenue are the Hartweg Grocery Store, left, and Keupfer Bakery, right.

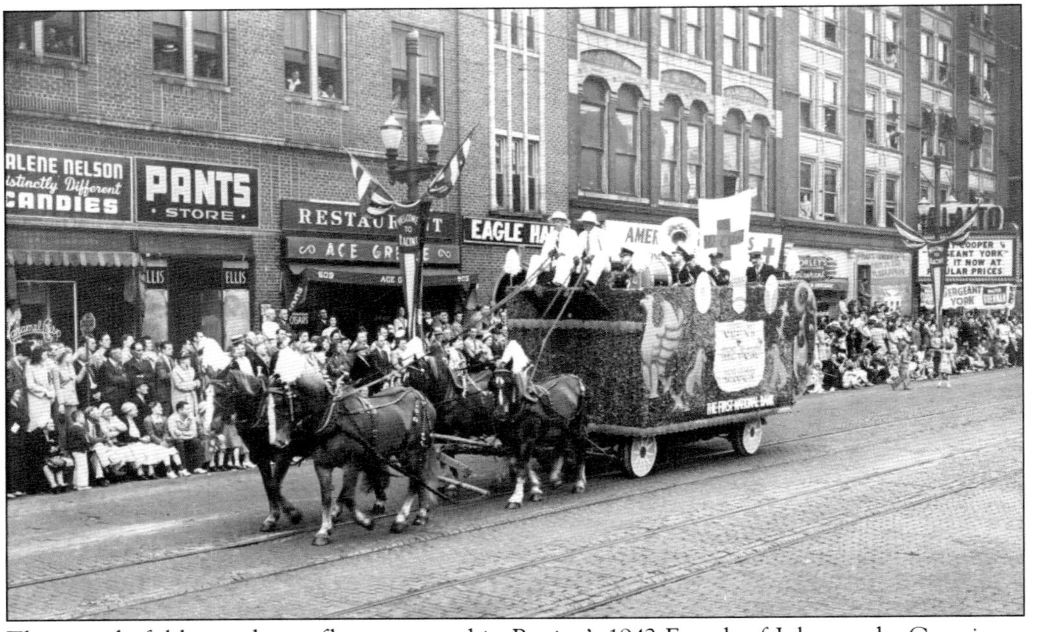

This wonderful horse-drawn float appeared in Racine's 1942 Fourth of July parade. Carrying a band, the float's patriotic message, "Get on the Bond Wagon," was a play on words in support of the US War Savings Bond drive. *Sergeant York*, starring Gary Cooper, played at the Rialto from July 3 through July 9 in 1942.

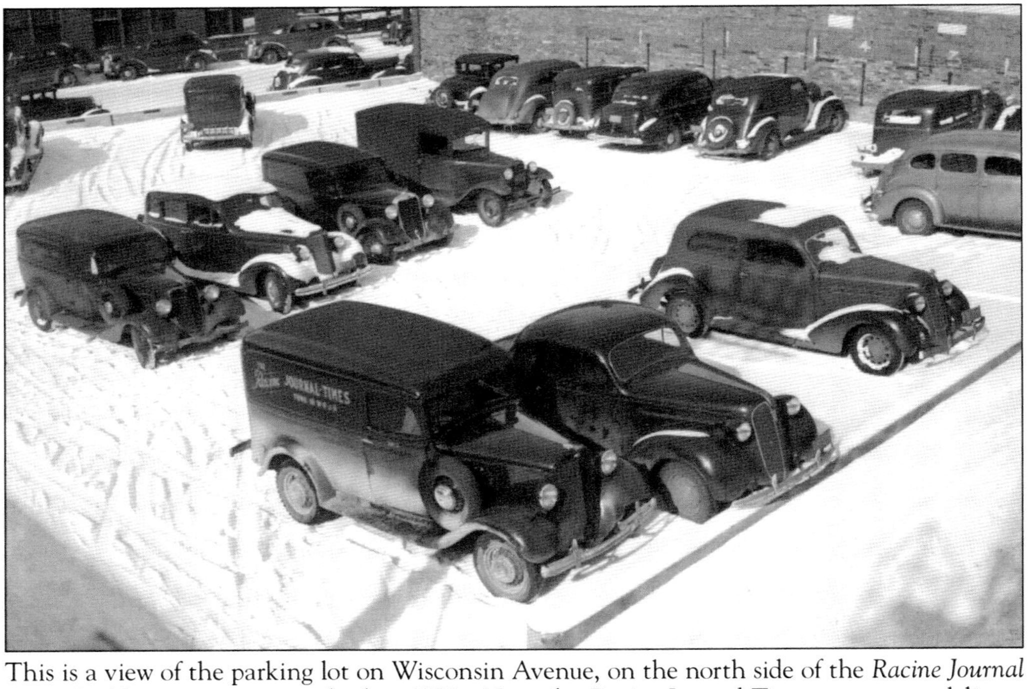

This is a view of the parking lot on Wisconsin Avenue, on the north side of the *Racine Journal Times* building, sometime in the late 1930s. Note the *Racine Journal Times* newspaper delivery trucks parked in the lot. All of the buildings seen in this photograph have since been torn down—mostly for additional parking.

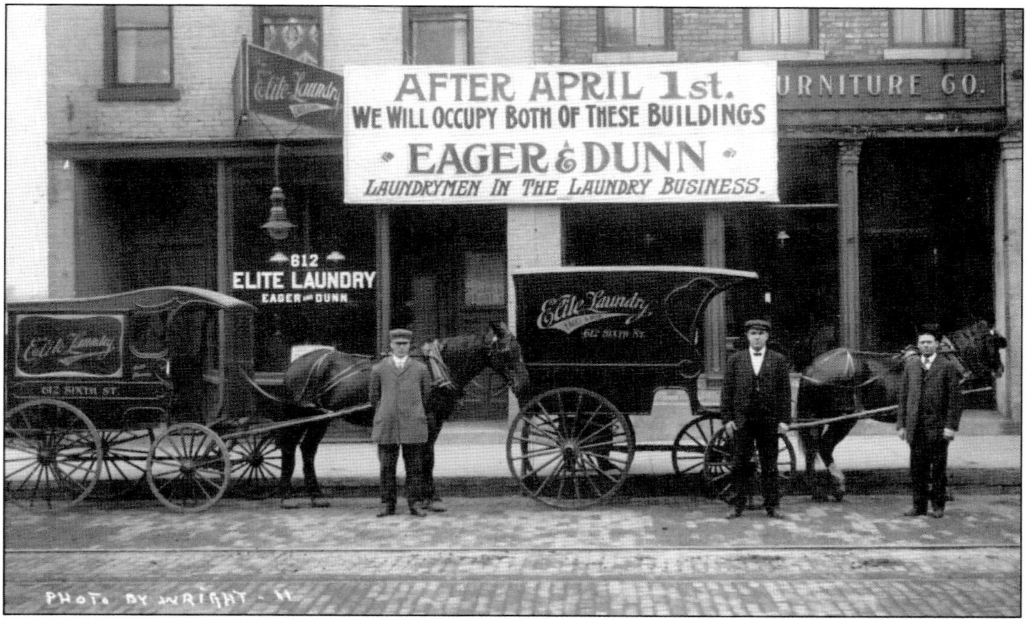

Elite Laundry, located at 612 Sixth Street, opened for business Wednesday, July 5, 1905. A.E. Anderson and S.H. Chapman were the original proprietors. In May 1909, John Eager and Bert Dunn purchased the Elite Laundry. On April 21, 1919, John Eager bought the interest of Bert Dunn in the Elite Laundry, now located at 931 Carroll Street, and became the sole owner.

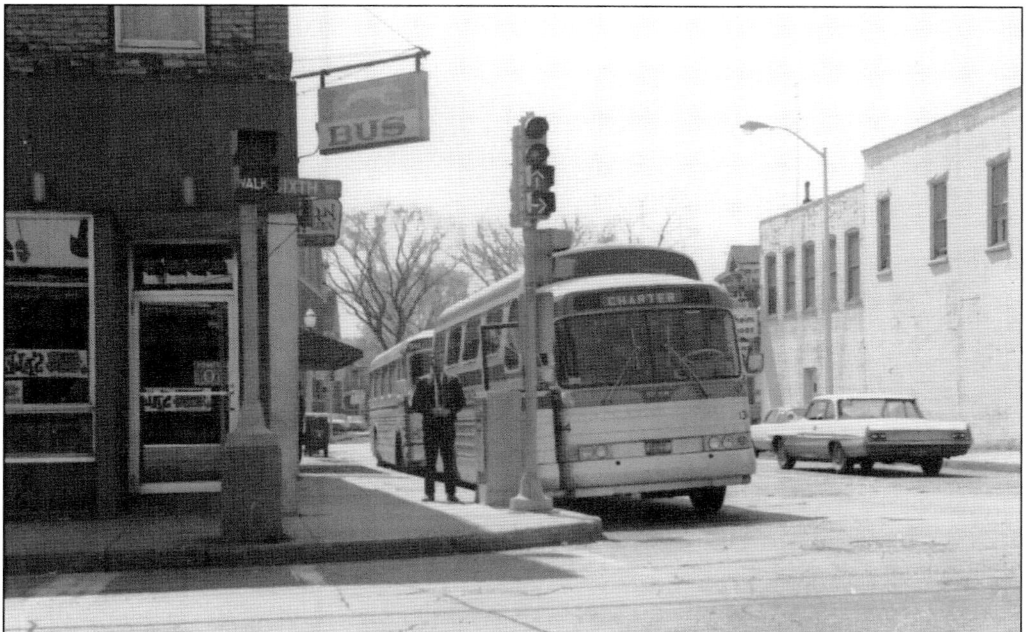

The Greyhound Bus Depot, pictured at its location at the corner of Sixth Street and College Avenue, was a popular place. Originally, the depot was at 523 Main Street. By 1944, Greyhound buses traveled directly to 298 communities throughout Wisconsin, and were linked to more than 6,500 destinations nationwide.

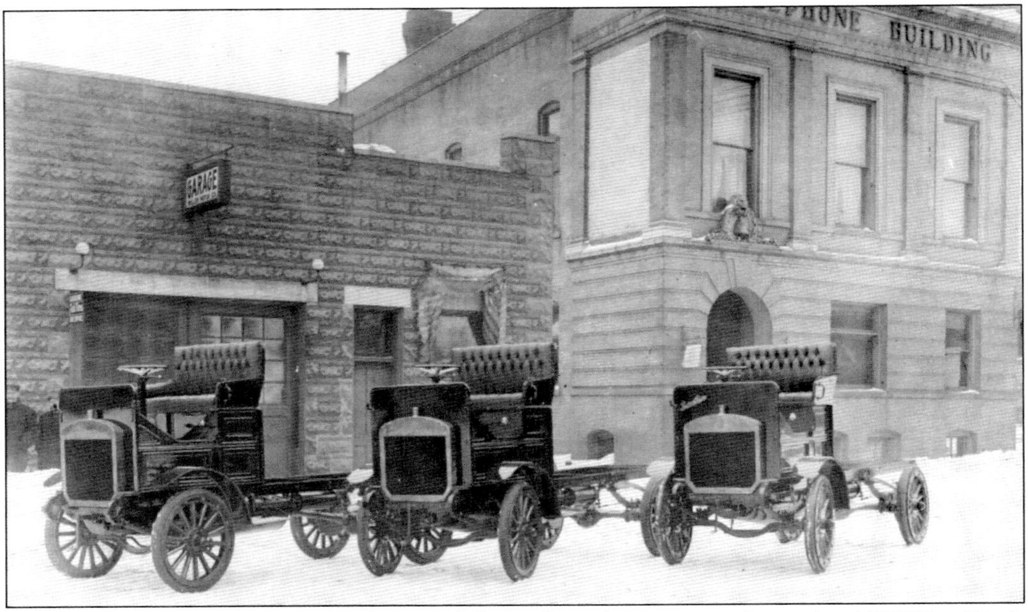

Piggins Brothers, manufacturers of automobiles and gasoline engines, located at 1113 West Sixth Street, built their first truck in 1911. The truck was so well received that the Piggins Motor Truck Company was incorporated on March 5, 1912. Pictured above are three Piggins truck chassis. Business went elsewhere when the Piggins Motor Truck Company proved unable to keep up with initial orders, and the company was declared bankrupt in August 1914.

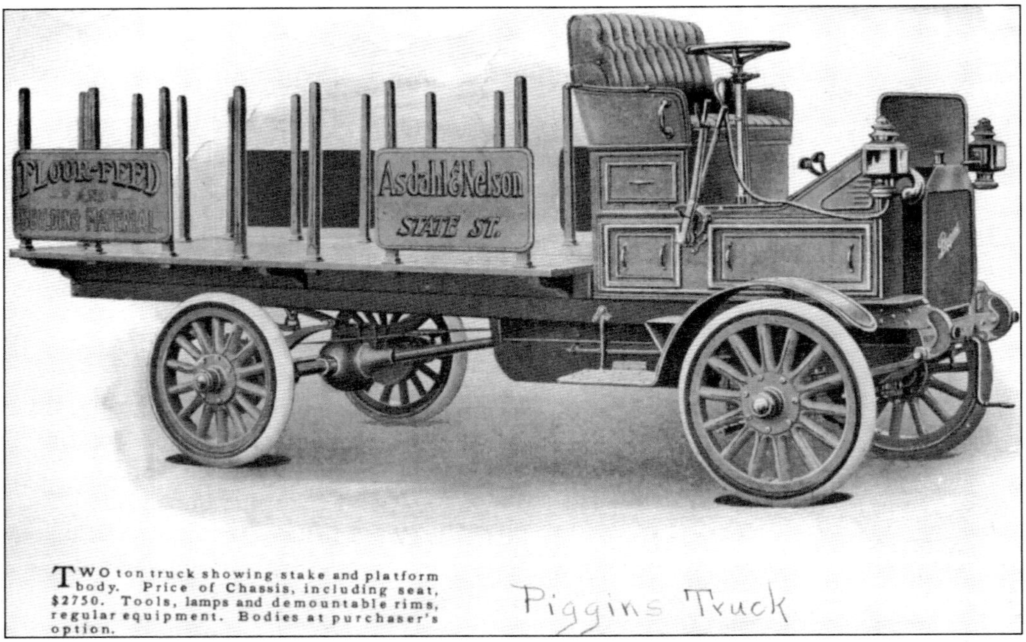

The pulling power of the Piggins truck was proved in June 1913. A one-ton Piggins truck was hauling a load of furniture to Sausalito, California, when it came upon a truck loaded with pianos stuck in axle deep mud. The little Piggins truck simply waded through the mud before easily freeing the stuck truck.

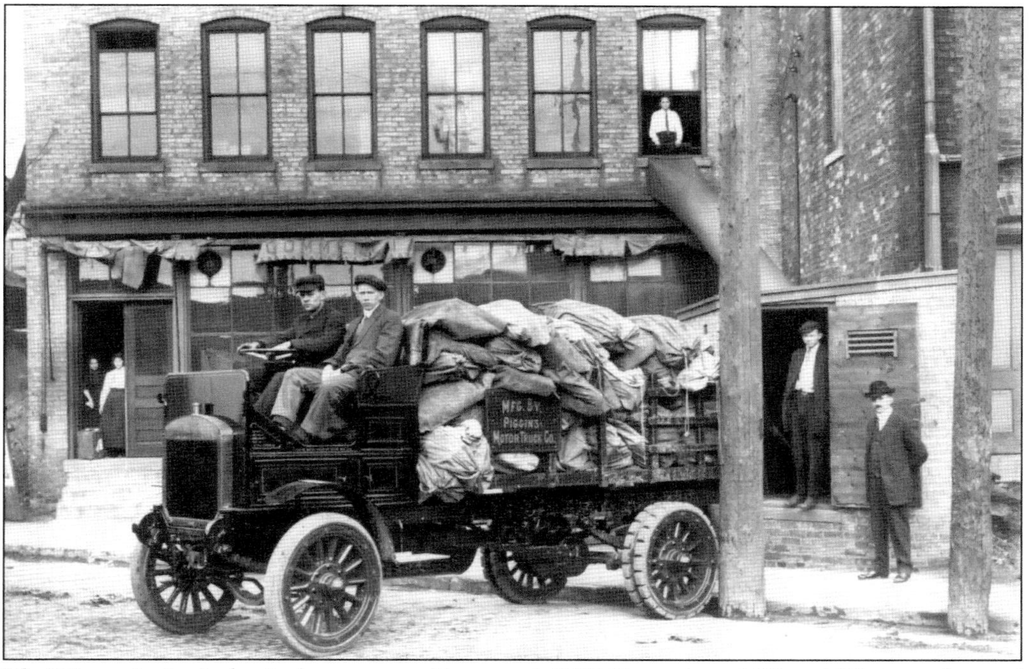

The Wisconsin Agriculturist first appeared January 1, 1877. From about 1921 to 1931, it was located here on the second floor at 472 College Avenue. After that, it moved to two other locations in Racine before finally moving to Madison in 1976. This Piggins truck is being loaded on the Water Street side of the building.

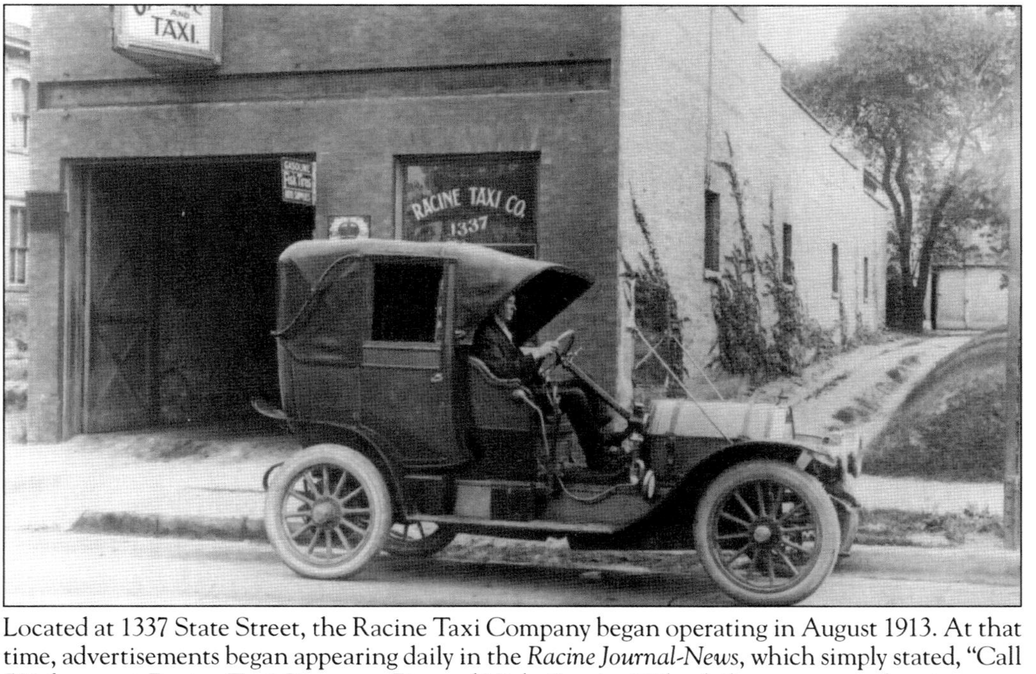

Located at 1337 State Street, the Racine Taxi Company began operating in August 1913. At that time, advertisements began appearing daily in the *Racine Journal-News*, which simply stated, "Call 500 for a taxi. Racine Taxi Company. Day and Night Service." The daily newspaper advertisements stopped in the summer of 1915.

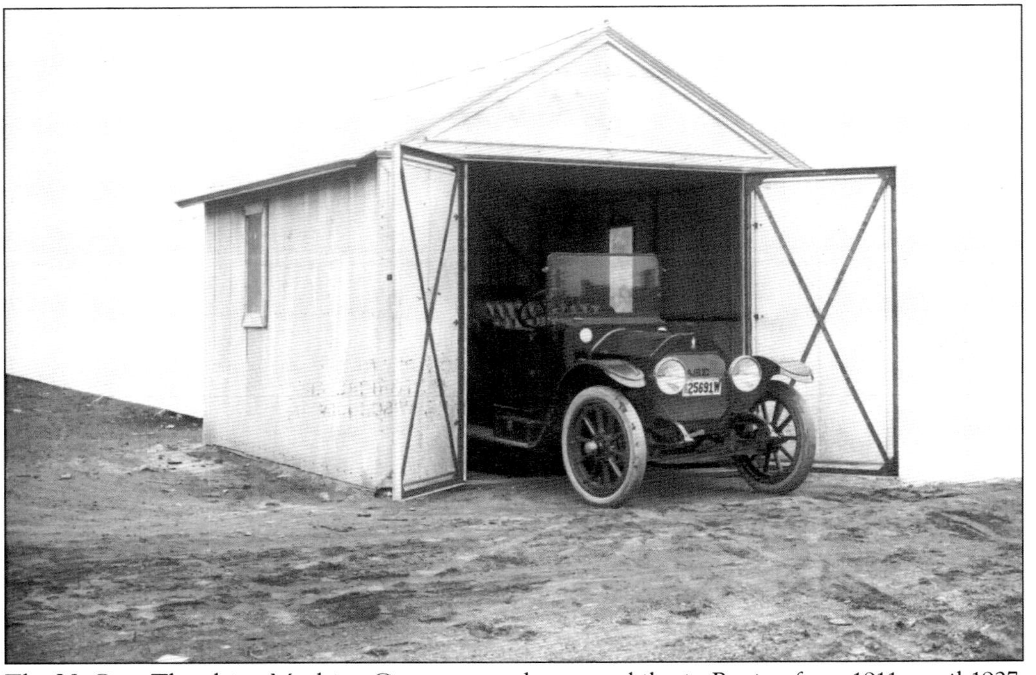

The J.I. Case Threshing Machine Company made automobiles in Racine from 1911, until 1927. Parked in the pictured collapsible, galvanized-iron garage is a 1914 Case automobile. These unique collapsible garages were made and sold by the Mohr-Jones Hardware Company. They were made in the company's sheet metal shop at the corner of Eleventh Street and the St. Paul railroad tracks.

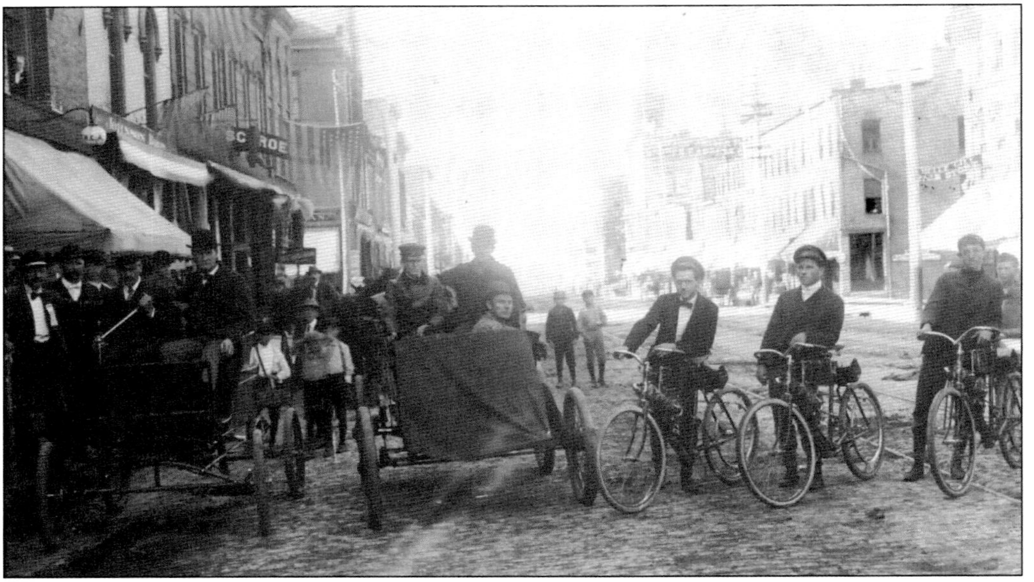

Racine's first automobile race started in front of Grand Union Tea Company on Main Street, south of Fourth Street, at 11:00 a.m., August 16, 1900. A.J. Horlick drove a Locomobile, left, and Robert W. Hindley raced in a Winton, right. Since Horlick's car broke down, Hindley won the race by arriving at Western Union Junction, now Sturtevant, sometime in mid-afternoon.

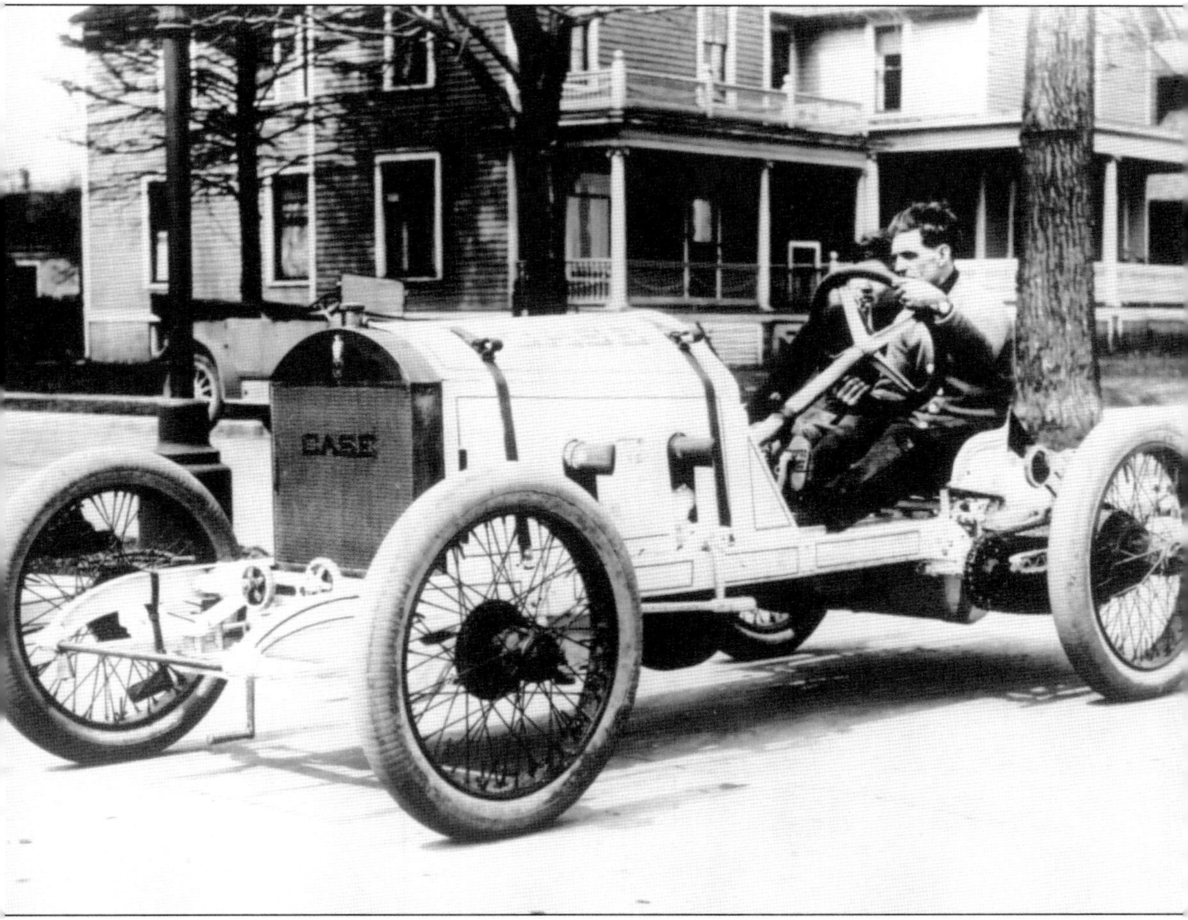

Seated at the wheel of this J.I. Case racecar is William "Wild Bill" Endicott. As a member of the J.I. Case Race Car Team in 1912, he was part of a racing exhibition put on in downtown Racine on Thursday night, August 29, 1912. Between 6,000 and 8,000 people gathered on both sides of Main Street, from Sixth to Fourteenth Streets, to witness five high-horsepower Case race cars run up and down Main Street—at speeds up to 80 miles per hour—in an exhibition of speed and power. Main Street was blocked off from 6:45 p.m. to 7:15 p.m. for this event. Police were stationed at every intersection and patrolled both sides of Main Street during the exhibition to make sure that there was no danger of accidents.

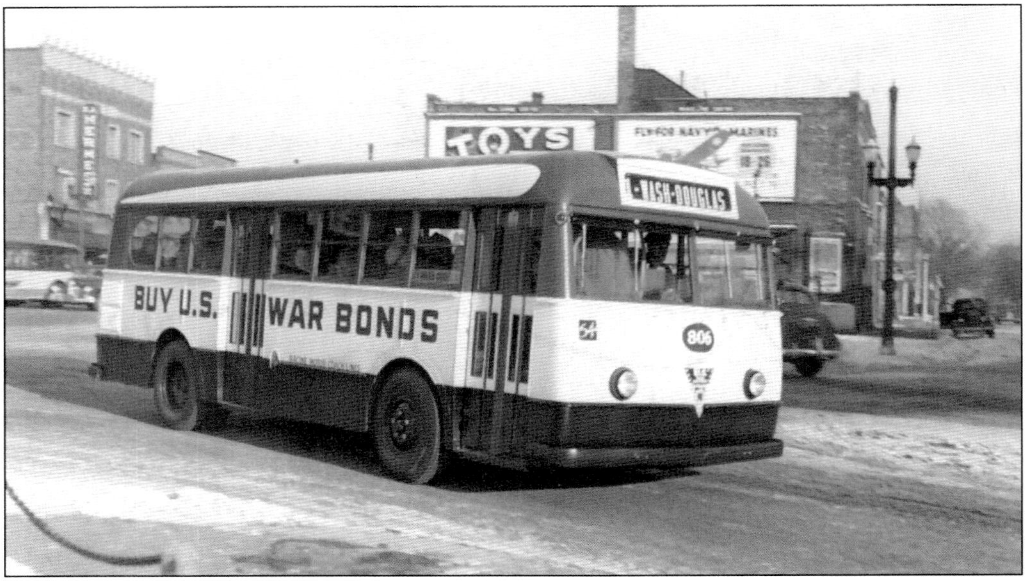

In 1939, the Milwaukee Electric Railway and Transport Company—owners and operators of Racine's transportation system of buses and streetcars—decided to sell or abandon the entire system due to unprofitability. The system was first offered to the City of Racine for $200,000; however its purchase was quickly turned down by the city council. Then, on January 1, 1940, Henry P. Bruner of Chicago assumed ownership of the system and began operating it as the Racine Motor Coach Lines. Notable changes made by Bruner during its first year of operation were the abandonment of streetcars, modernization of the fleet of buses, and the inauguration of new and more efficient routing of the buses. Pictured are two of the first advertisements to appear on Racine Motor Coach Lines buses: "Buy U.S. War Bonds" in 1942, and "Why Jaywalk Yourself to Death?" in 1947.

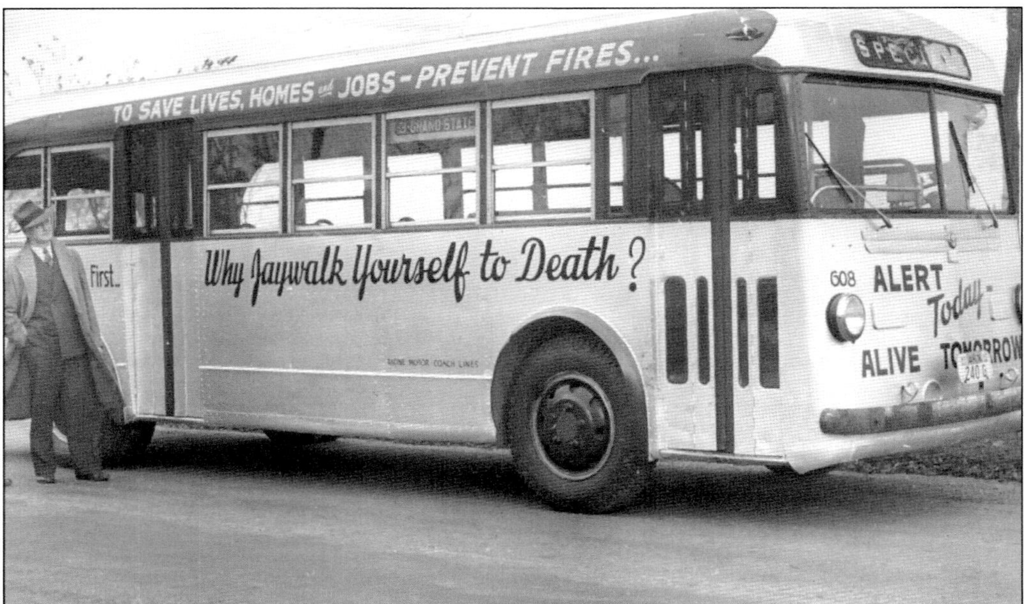

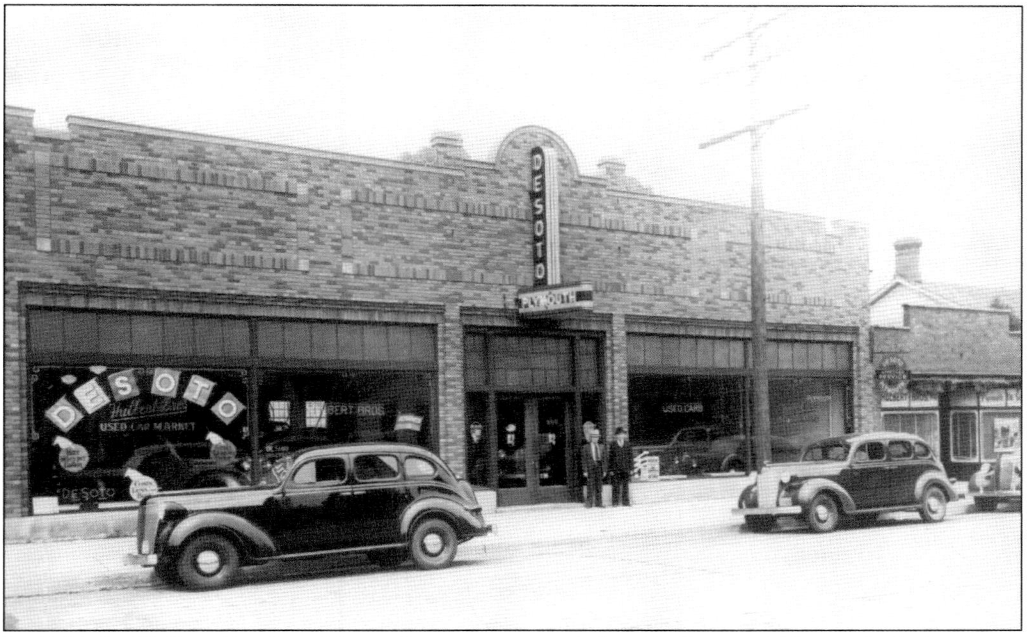

In 1925, the Hulbert Brothers Motor Company opened their DeSoto and Plymouth dealership at 1014 Herrick Avenue. They moved to 1000 South Lafayette Avenue in 1955. Then, in February 1962, the Hulbert Brothers Motor Company relinquished its Plymouth franchise and became Hulbert-Stauffacher Ford.

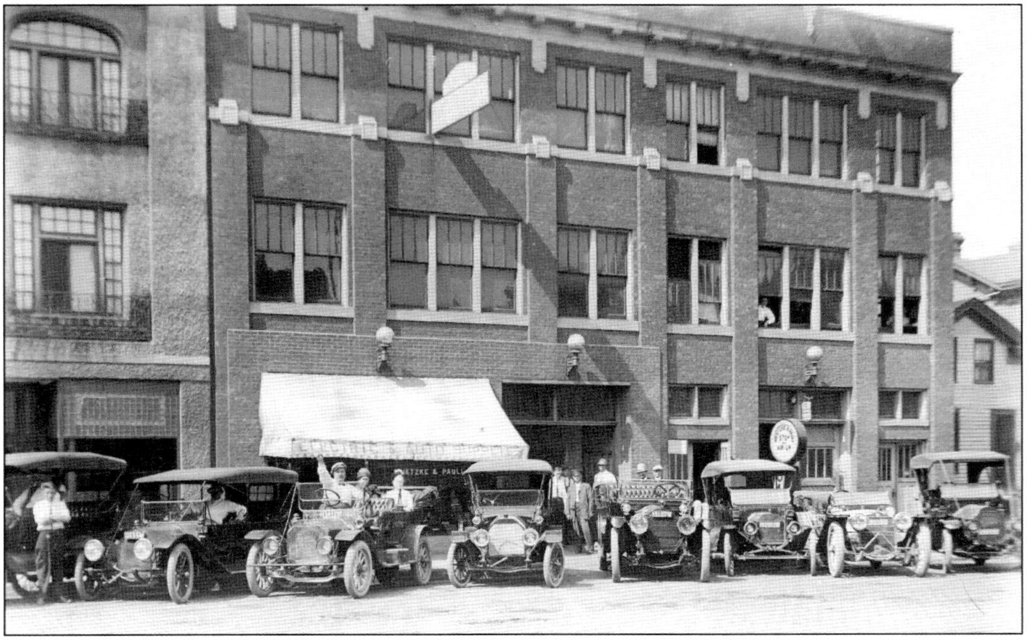

Charles Brietzke was Racine's first auto dealer. He started selling Mitchell automobiles in 1903, when the company began production in Racine. Around 1906, he opened a garage at 518–522 College Avenue. Several years later, he built at 510–512 College Avenue. His other business interest, the Brietzke-Pauli Electric Supply Company, shared space with the auto dealership.

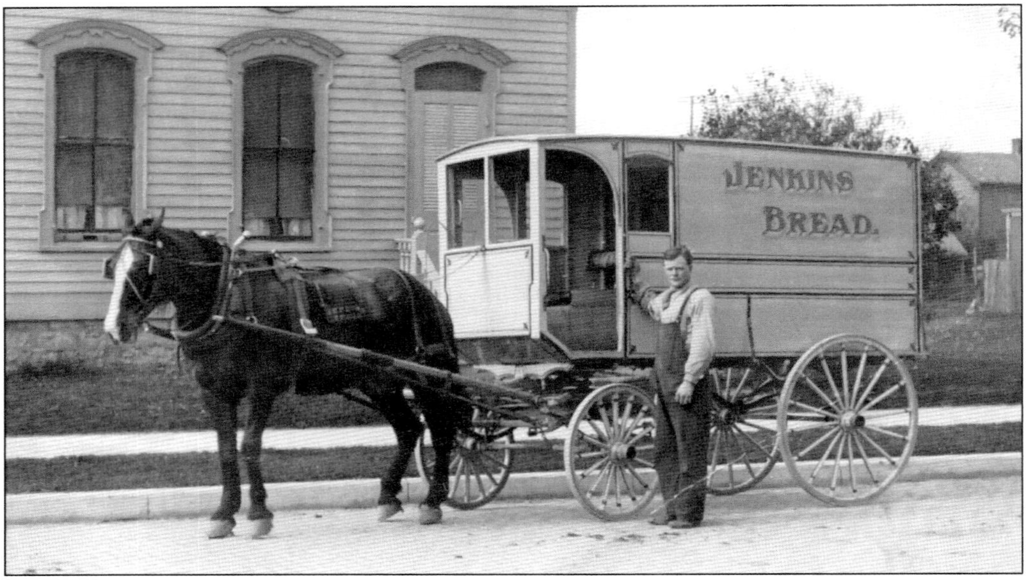

Jenkins Bread was an on again, off again bakery business in the early 1900s, operated by J.R. Jenkins out of his home at 1239 North Wisconsin Street. In 1906 and 1907, Jenkins bread and rolls were sold at Peter Slot's Grocery Store, at 1200 State Street. After reentering the bakery business in July 1916, Jenkins Bread advertised rapid automobile delivery service.

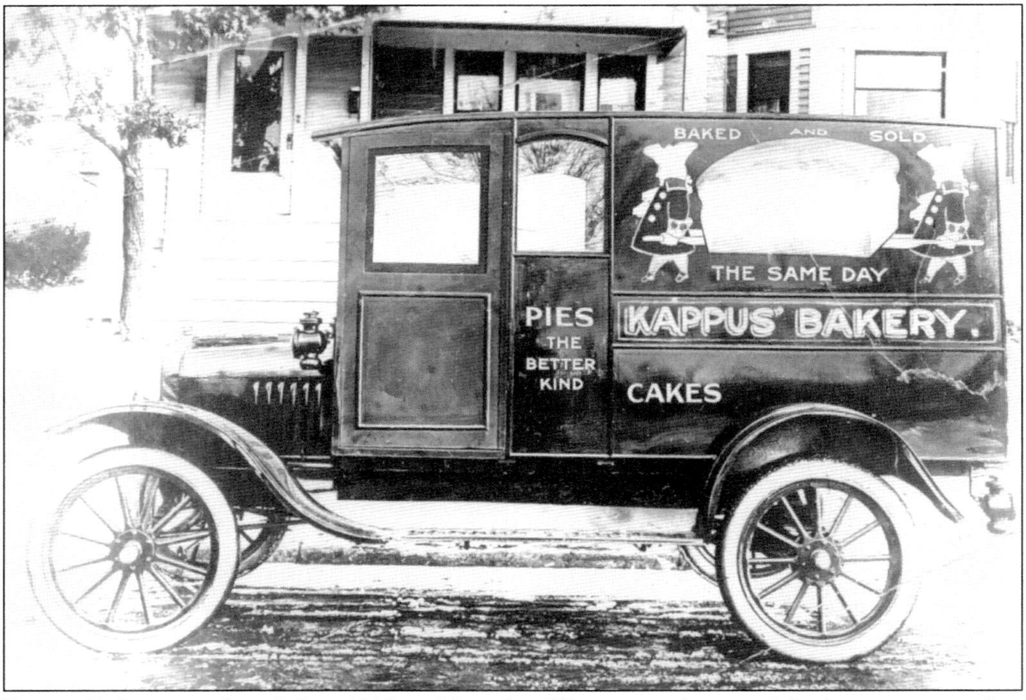

Kappus Bakery was founded in 1915, in Kenosha, Wisconsin. A second facility was opened in Racine in 1922, at 1601 Sixteenth Street. In 1968, the Chicago-based New Process Baking Company acquired the family-owned Kappus Bakery Company. After the acquisition, only sandwich buns were produced at the Racine plant. The Racine plant was closed in April 1977.

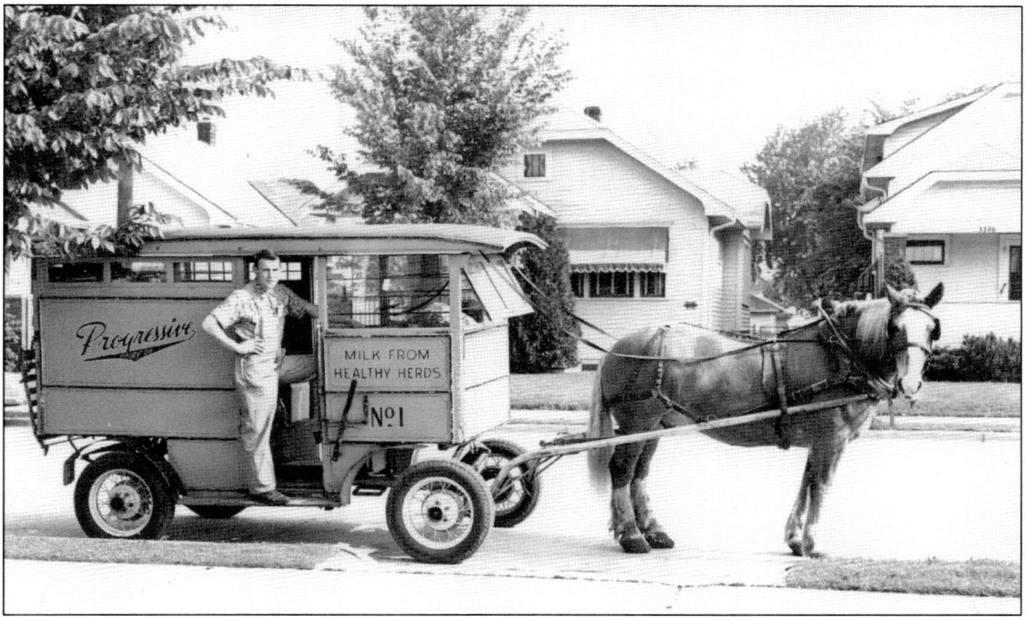

Racine's Progressive Dairy Co. started business in 1912 as the Gifford Brothers Sanitary Dairy. Its first delivery wagon was handmade and had a load capacity of 360 gallons of milk. The above photograph was taken in June 1952, in the 3700 block of Sixteenth Street. It was the last month that the Progressive Dairy Co. used a horse-drawn wagon to deliver milk.

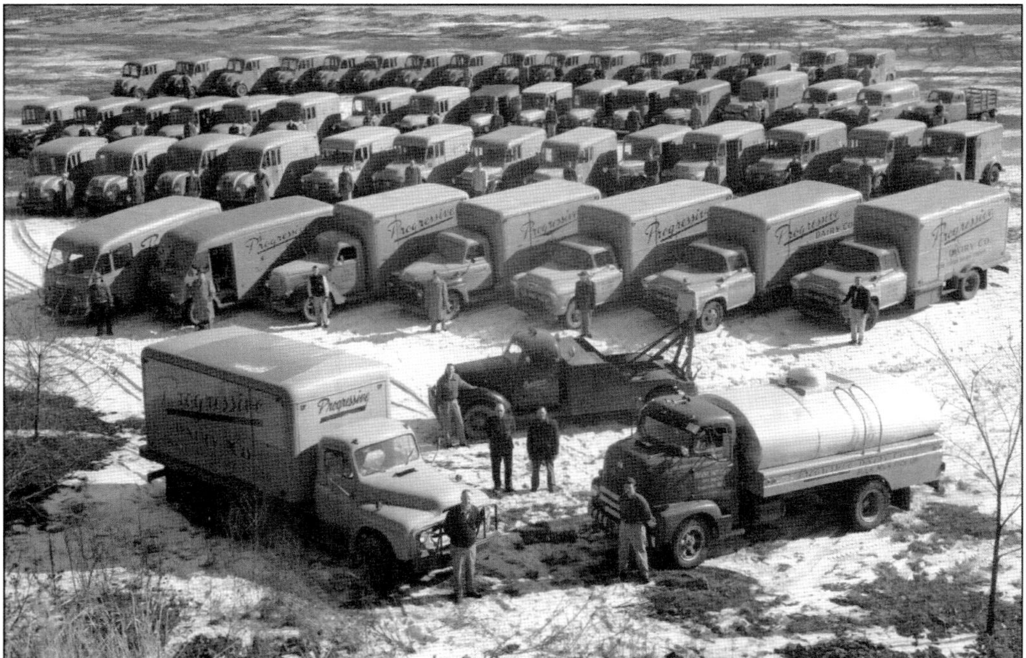

This publicity photograph for Racine's Progressive Dairy Co. was taken at Pershing Park in 1956. Numbering 56 vehicles, this fleet symbolized the growth of the Progressive Dairy Co. during its first 44 years of operation.

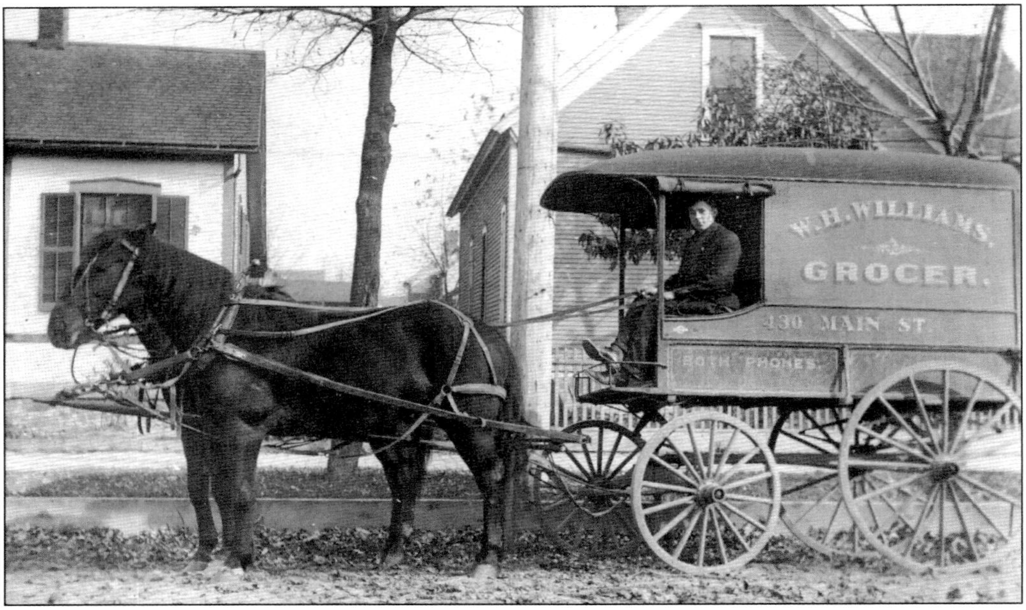

The Williams Grocery Store was established at 430 Main Street in the summer of 1866 by R.W. Wickham and W.H. Williams. The firm name then was Wickham & Williams. W.H. Williams's son, William O. Williams, eventually took over the business, and he remained with it until he liquidated it and retired on July 1, 1941.

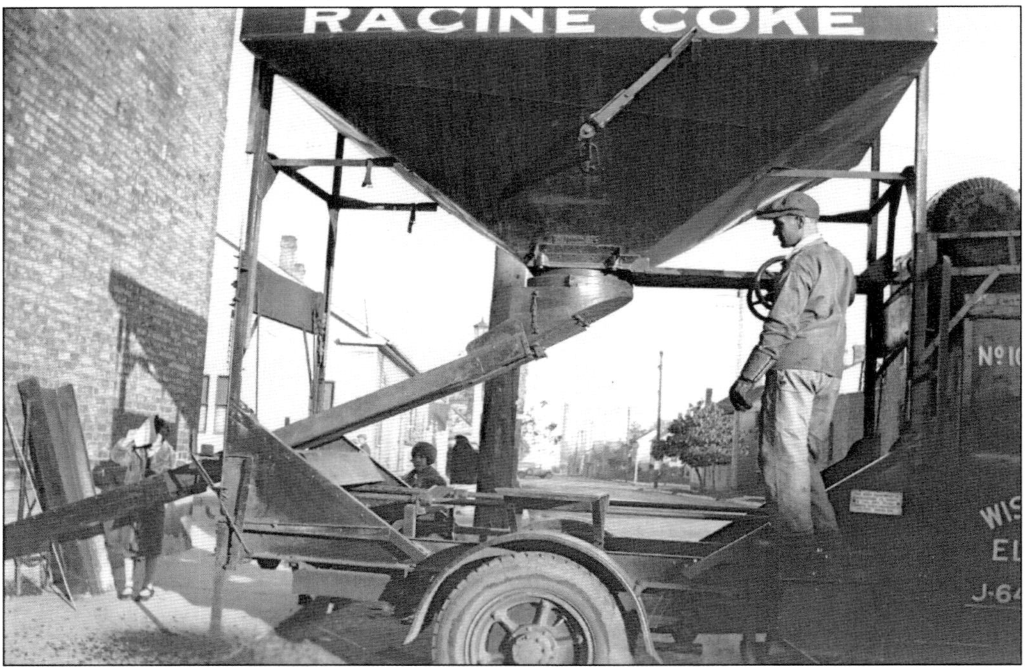

Established in 1905, Racine Coke was made from the best eastern coal by the Wisconsin Gas & Electric Company. The gas, sulfur, dirt, and impurities were removed leaving a fuel high in carbon, and low in ash. Deliveries of Racine Coke were a common sight in Racine until after 1950, when natural gas became available.

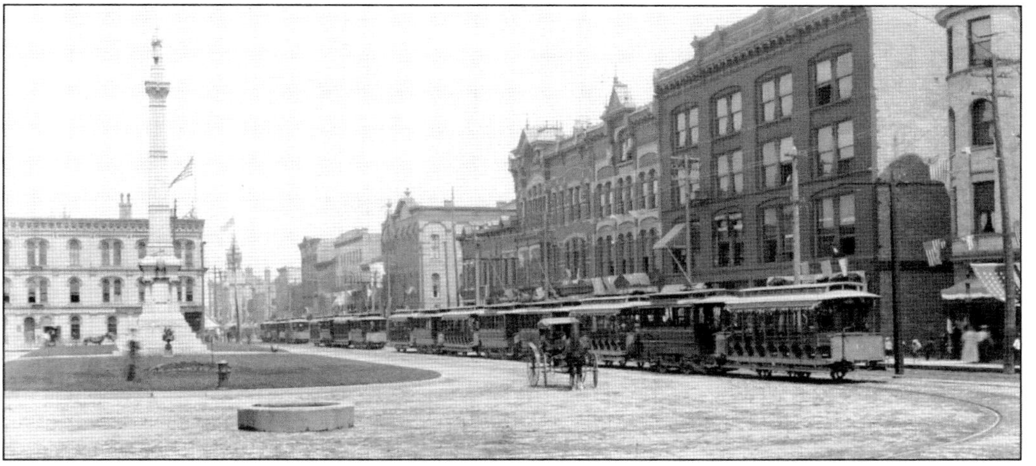

In this 1901 photograph, electric streetcars are lined up all along the east side of Monument Square. The first electric streetcars clanged along Racine streets in 1892, replacing the horse-drawn cars that had been in operation since 1883. The last electric streetcar rolled into the Goold Street barns on September 30, 1940.

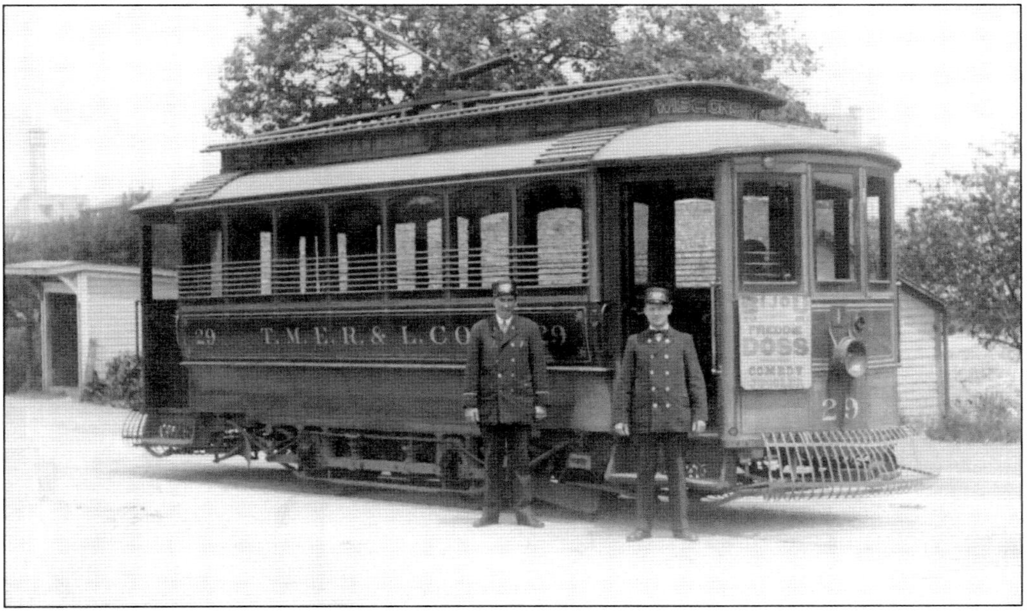

Racine streetcar No. 29, owned and operated by the Milwaukee Electric Railway and Light Company, (TMER&L) in 1910. The advertisement on the front indicates that Freddie Doss, comedy juggler, would be performing at the Bijou on June 6. One of his best stunts involved balancing his stovepipe hat and a cigar on the tip of his toe and flinging them into the air. The hat would land on his head, and the cigar in his mouth.

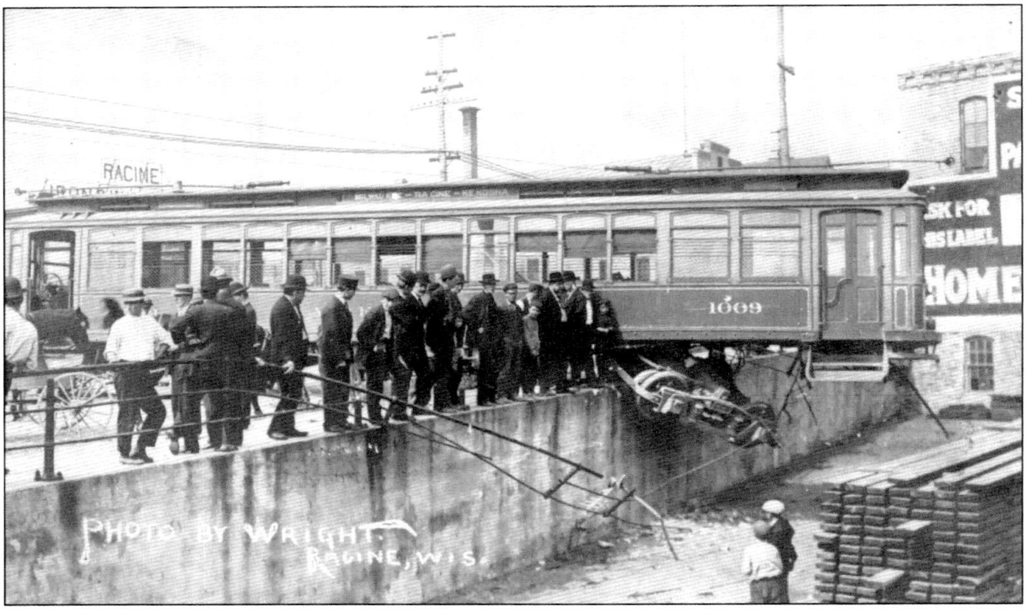

Accidents involving streetcars in Racine were quite common, as were complaints about them traveling too fast. Mostly, these accidents involved the striking of a pedestrian or a moving vehicle such as a horse-drawn carriage or an automobile. In this scene from the early 1900s, a Milwaukee-Racine-Kenosha Interurban has jumped the tracks on Douglas Avenue, north of State Street.

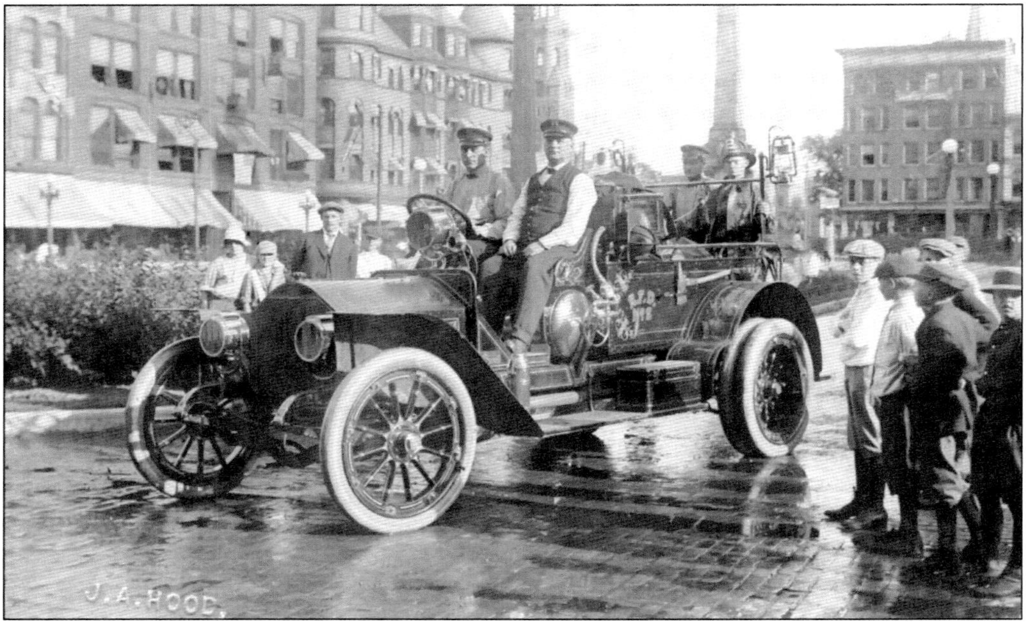

In April 1911, Company No. 2 took delivery of the Racine Fire Department's first motorized fire truck: an American La France combination chemical and hose truck. Showing off their new fire truck on Monument Square is Jack Stripple, driver, with John McCarthy in the front passenger seat. In the rear are Carl Holm, left, and Harry Yoakum, right.

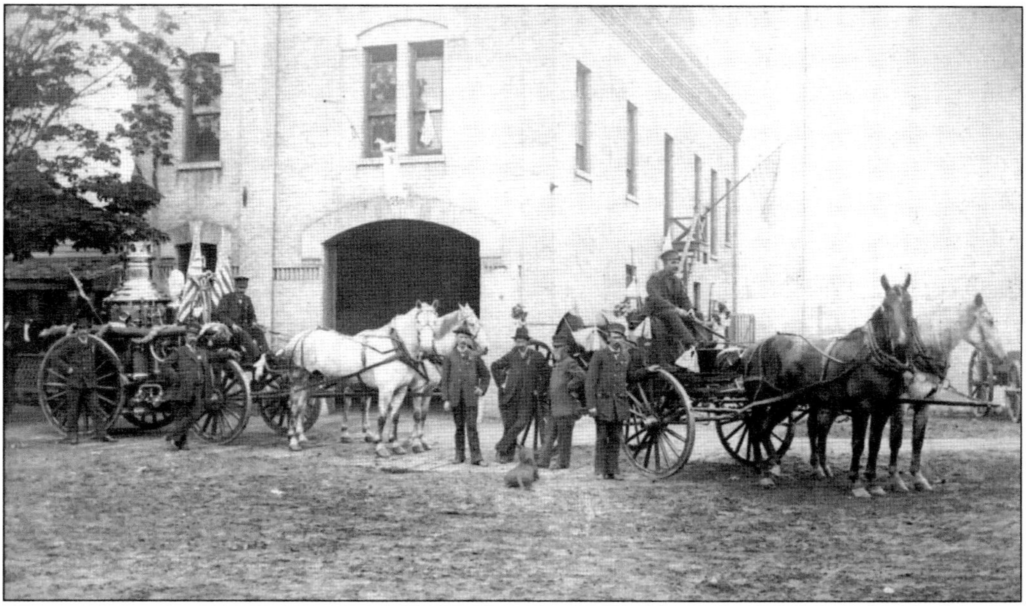

Located at 700 Sixth Street, Firehouse No. 3 was built in 1882. From 1882 through 1918, it housed the pictured horse-drawn steamer and hose cart. Later, it housed motorized fire apparatus, including Racine's first full-time Rescue Squad. The building was officially closed on December 31, 1967, and is now the Firehouse 3 Museum, an educational experience open by appointment only.

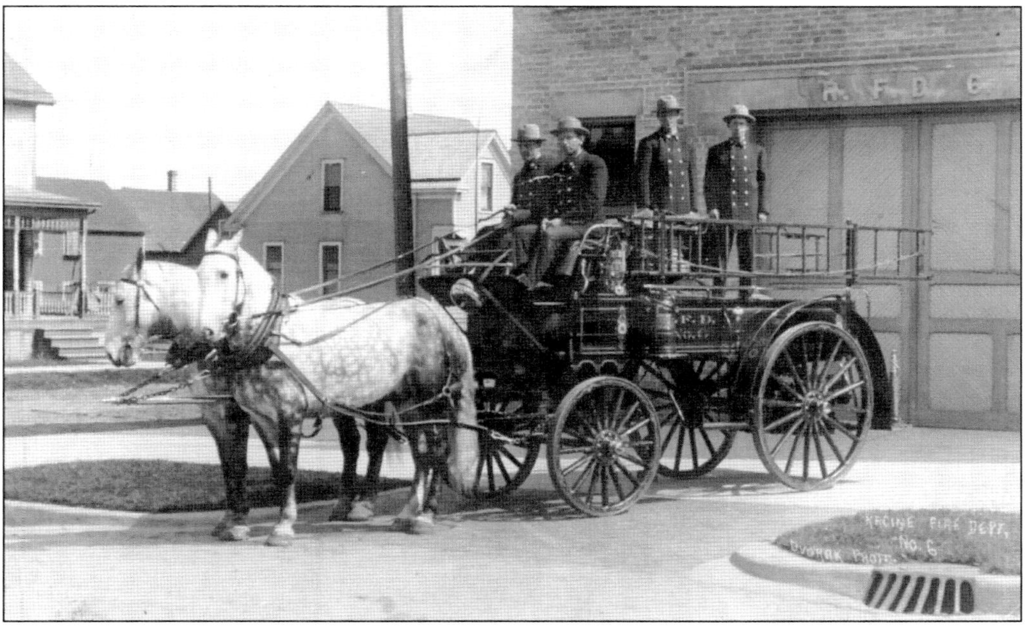

Construction of Firehouse No. 6, located at 2101 Sixteenth Street, was completed in February 1908; however it was not operational until some months later. The two new wagons purchased for the station had not yet arrived, and no other equipment was available for use.

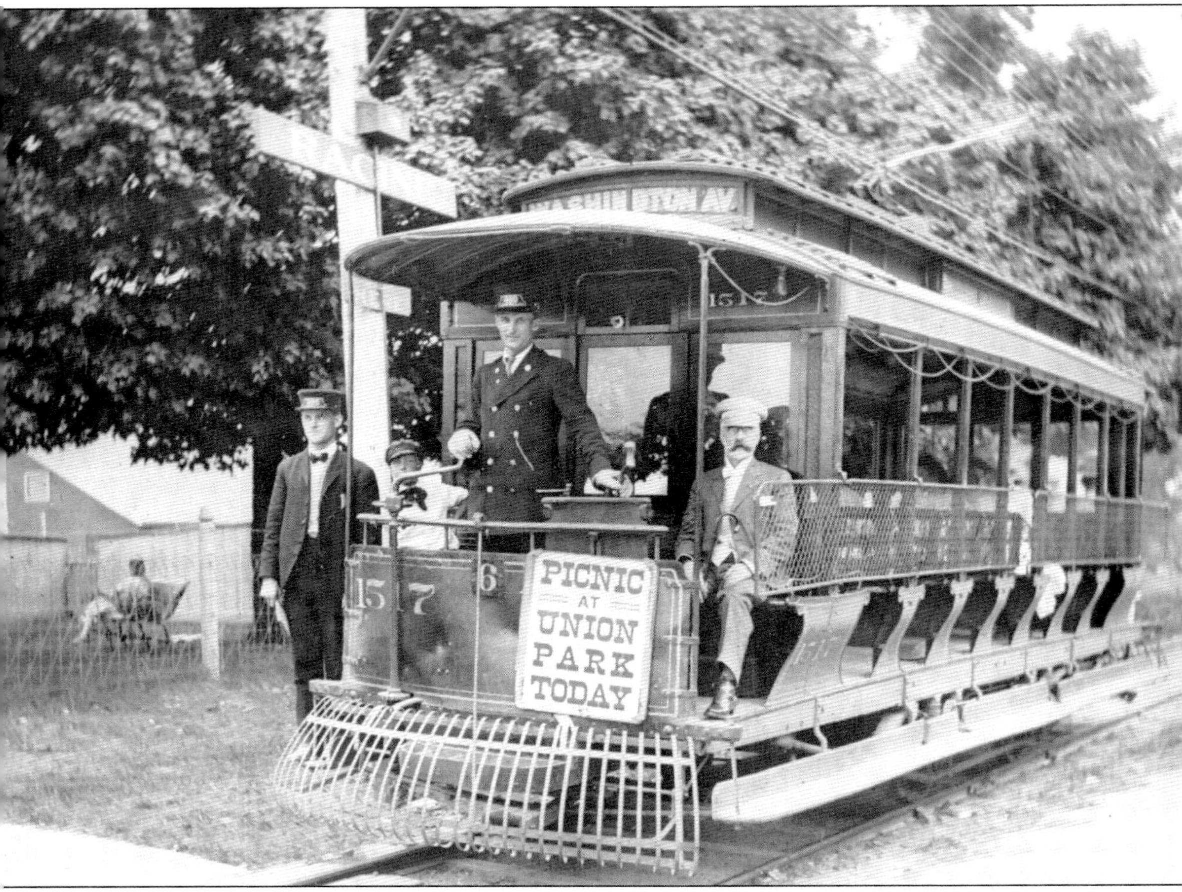

Pictured at the far right of this Milwaukee Electric Railway & Light Company streetcar's cab is John I. Beggs, the company's general manager. This was the company that operated the streetcars in Racine. Although there were many picnics at Union Park every summer, the advertisement at front proclaiming "Picnic at Union Park Today" is most likely in reference to the annual Labor Day picnic staged there in the early 1900s by Racine's Trades and Labor Council. Union Park was a privately owned commercial venture at the time. In the fall of 1920, the park was purchased by the City of Racine specifically to be developed into a badly needed playground on the north side. In 1921, the City of Racine spent $2,000 cleaning up, trimming trees, removing old buildings, and remodeling the old hall. Today, it is known as Douglas Park.

Seven

EDUCATION AND SCHOOLS

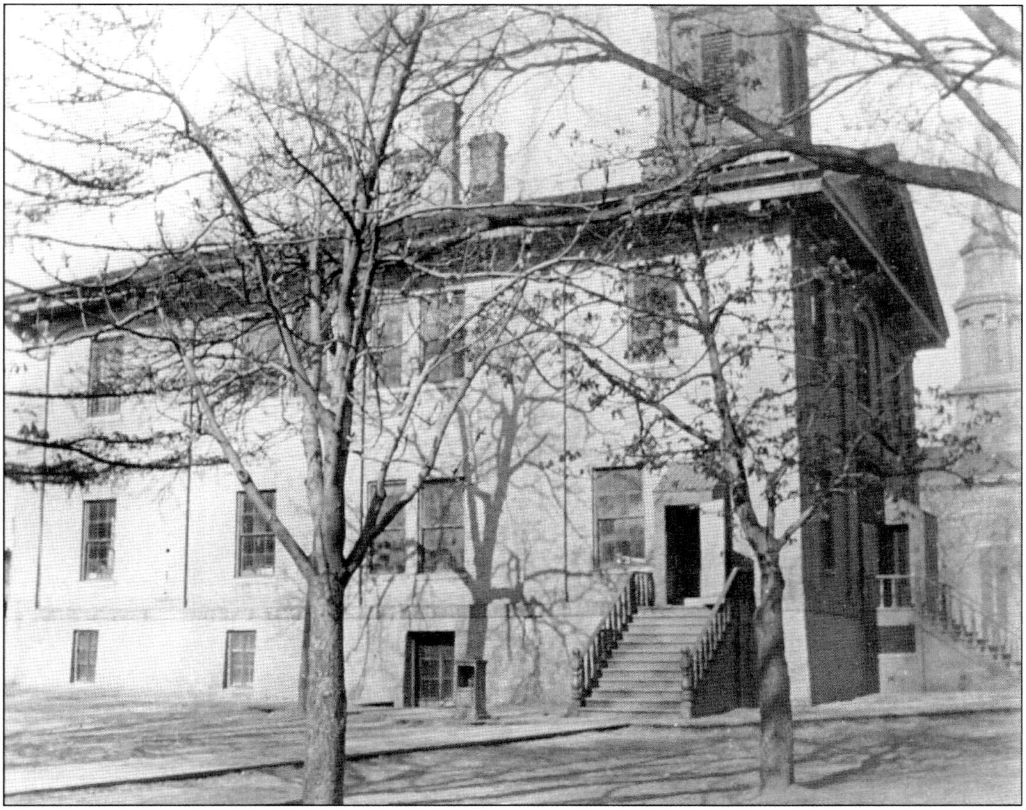

Racine's first high school was built in 1853 on the south side of Seventh Street, and midway between Wisconsin Avenue and Center Street. At the time, it was considered to be one of the best schools in the state. On December 24, 1857, the school graduated 10 seniors. They were the first high school graduating class in the history of the state of Wisconsin.

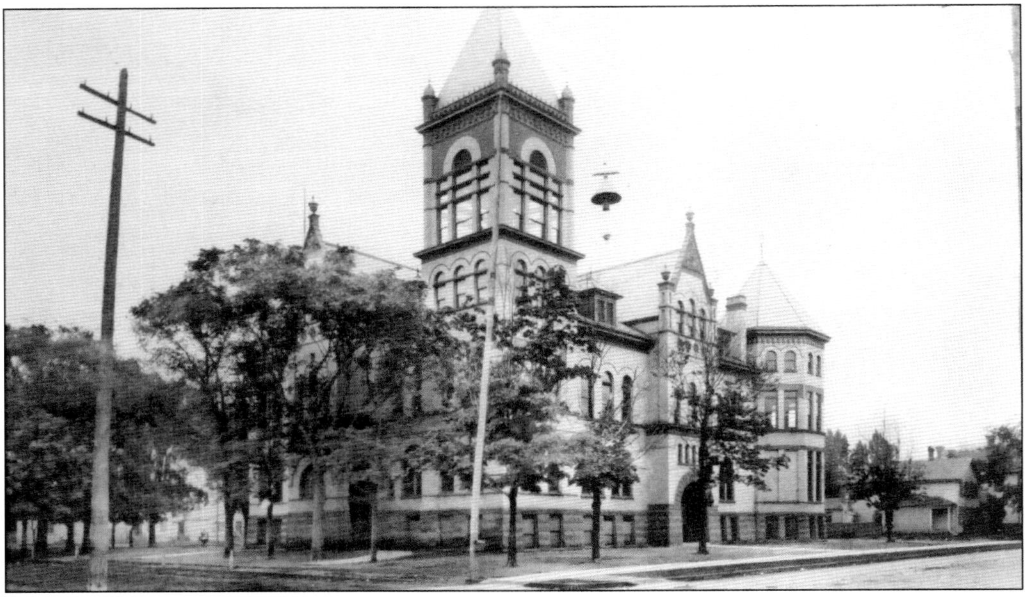

Racine's second high school was built in 1895, on the southeast corner of Seventh and Center Streets. The old Racine High School, seen in the background on the left, became the Second Ward School, an elementary school. The Second Ward School quickly became overcrowded. In 1900, to relieve overcrowding, 100 primary school students attended school in the basement of the new Racine High School.

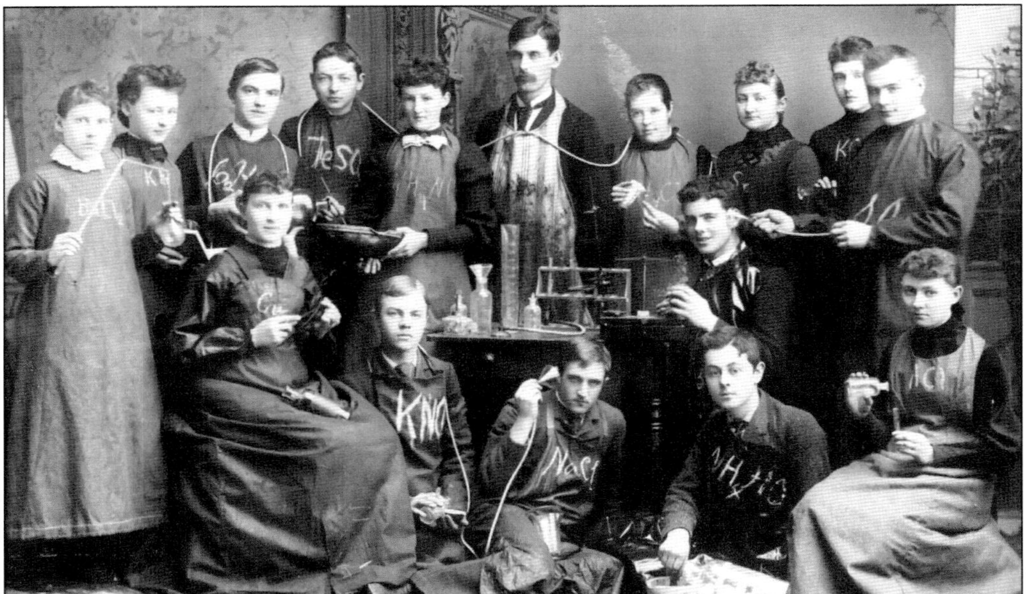

The Racine High School chemistry class is pictured in 1892. On the bottom row, from left to right, are Josie Van Ornum, Ole Olson, E.R. Burgess, Will Bolton, Martin Gillen and Lillian Jones Clifford. On the top row, from left to right, are Jessie Gibson, Agatha Pauli, Fred Rickeman, George Mead, Agnes Lynch, Ernest L. Talbert; teacher, Lillian Hansen, Alice Graves, M. Carey, and Fred Barker.

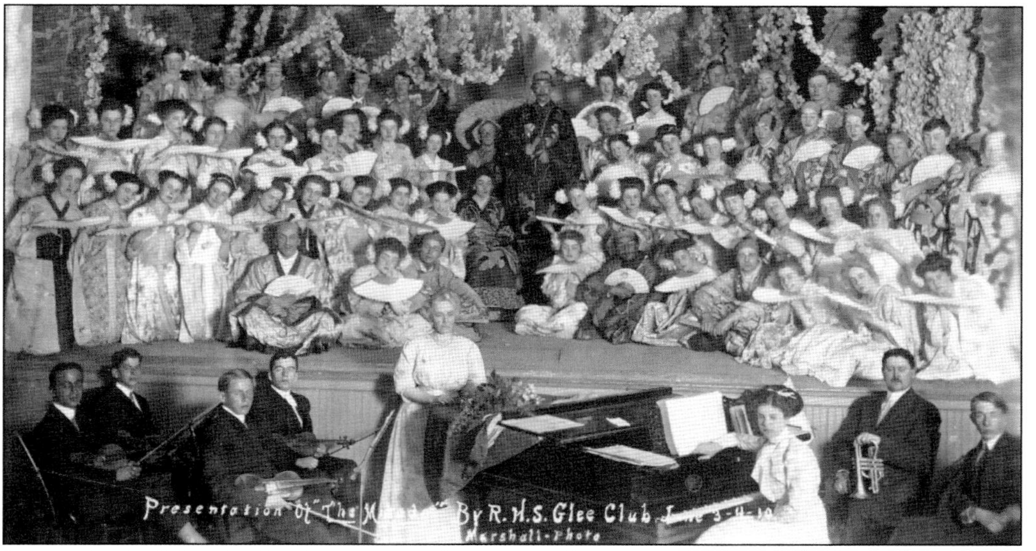

Racine High School offered a variety of activities that extended beyond the classroom. The performers of the comic opera *The Mikado*, organized by the Racine High School Glee Club in 1910, are pictured above. The costumes, stage decoration, and full orchestra are remarkable for a high school production of this era. *The Mikado*, first performed in London in 1885, remains popular with amateur and school productions.

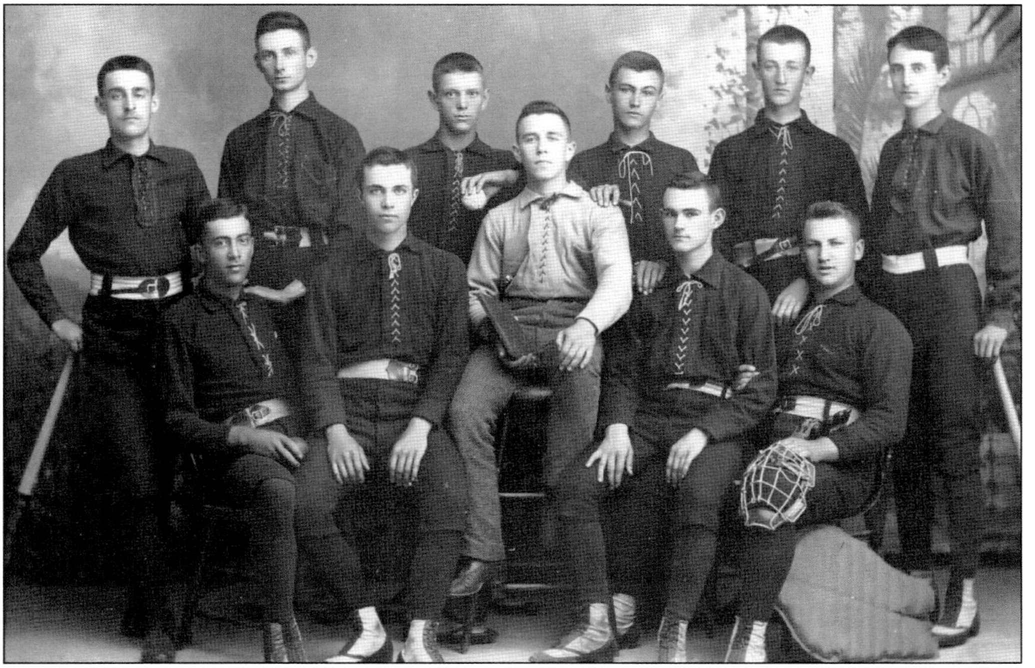

Interscholastic athletics were a part of Racine High School's culture from early on. Here is the Racine High School baseball team of 1886. Sitting, left to right, are Lewis Peck, Walter Tostesin, Guy Vaughn, Fred Foster, and William Lewis. Standing, left to right, are Arthur Guilbert, Albert Wheat, George Herzog, Charley Gorton, Herbert Patterson, and Walter Wheat. Guy Vaughn was the team's scorer, not a player.

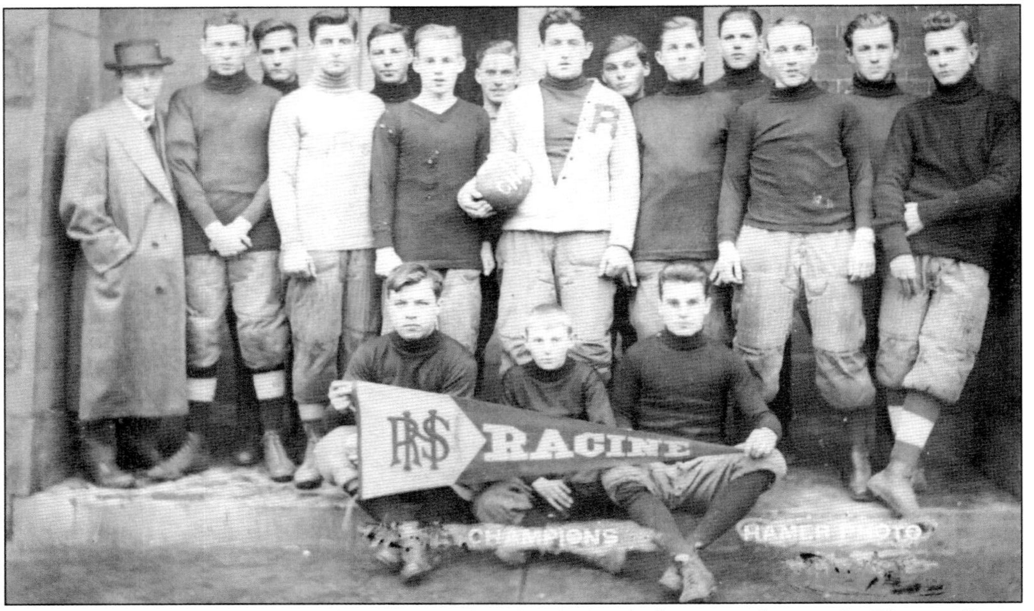

This is a c. 1911 photograph of Racine High School's football team. The coach, Thomas Rees, is standing at the far left, wearing a hat and overcoat. In 1911, the Racine High School football team went undefeated against the Milwaukee high schools, a very proud accomplishment. At this time, a great football rivalry had developed between Racine and Milwaukee's South Division High School.

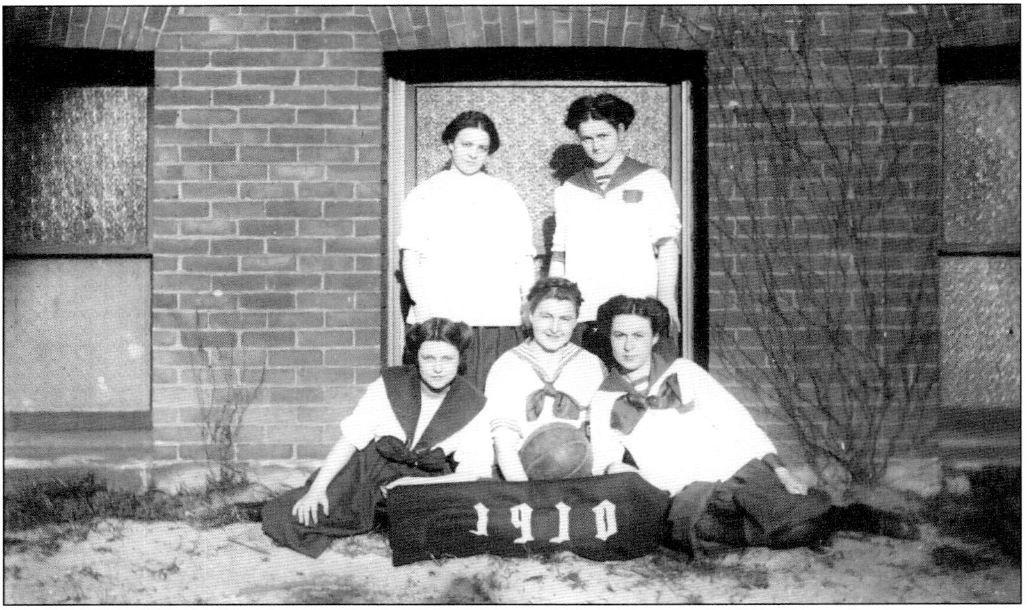

Racine High School also provided girls' sports. Seen here in uniform is the 1910 Racine High School girls' basketball team. Because Racine High School had no gymnasium, all home games for both the boys' and girls' basketball teams were held at the YMCA. At the time, the YMCA was located only one block north of the school, at Sixth and Center Streets. Girls' games preceded the boys' games.

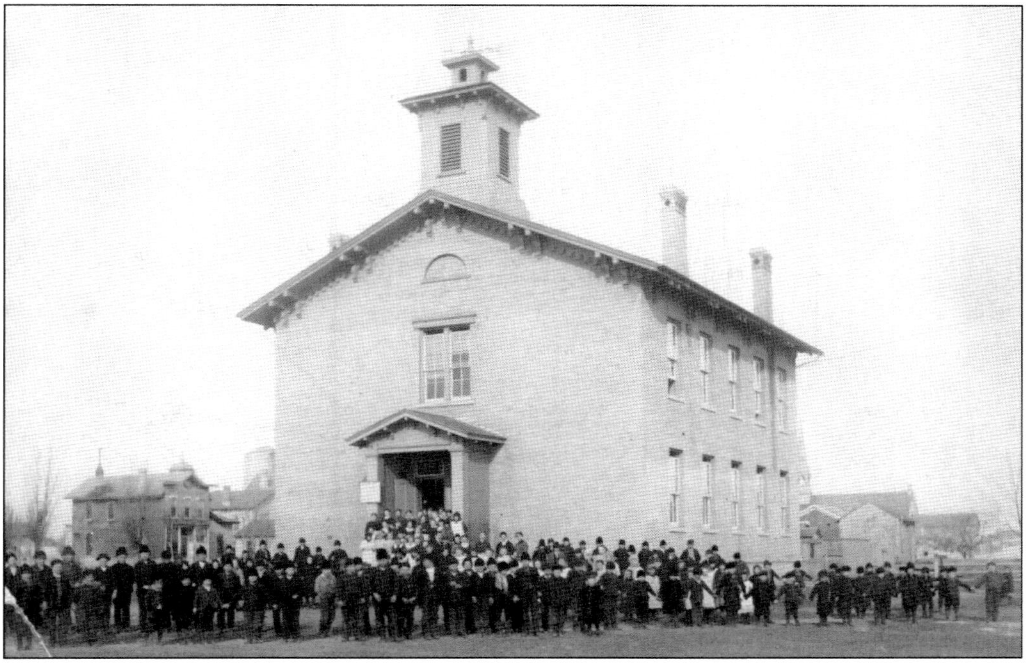

The Fourth Ward School on North Main Street was built in 1855 on land donated by Lorenzo Janes. Additions were made in 1883 and 1896 when the original building was moved to Barker and North Main Streets, and the name was changed to the Janes School. Janes was the first school in Racine with running water and bathrooms. The Fourth Ward School is pictured around 1880.

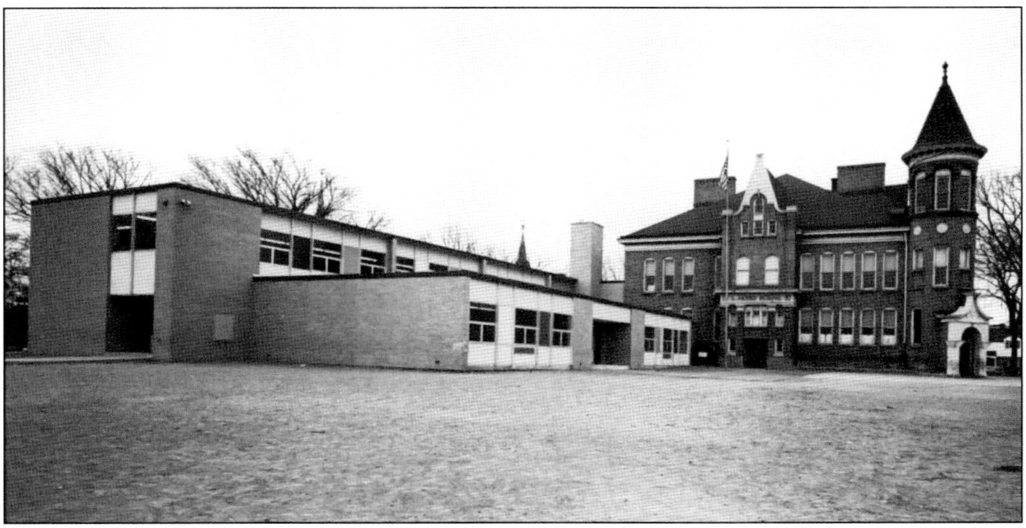

The Janes School is pictured at a later date. In 1959 and 1962, multipurpose additions replaced third-floor areas that had been closed by the State Industrial Commission, and the main entrance was moved from Main Street to Wisconsin Avenue. The Janes School is listed as a historic site and has the distinction of being the first year-round school in Wisconsin.

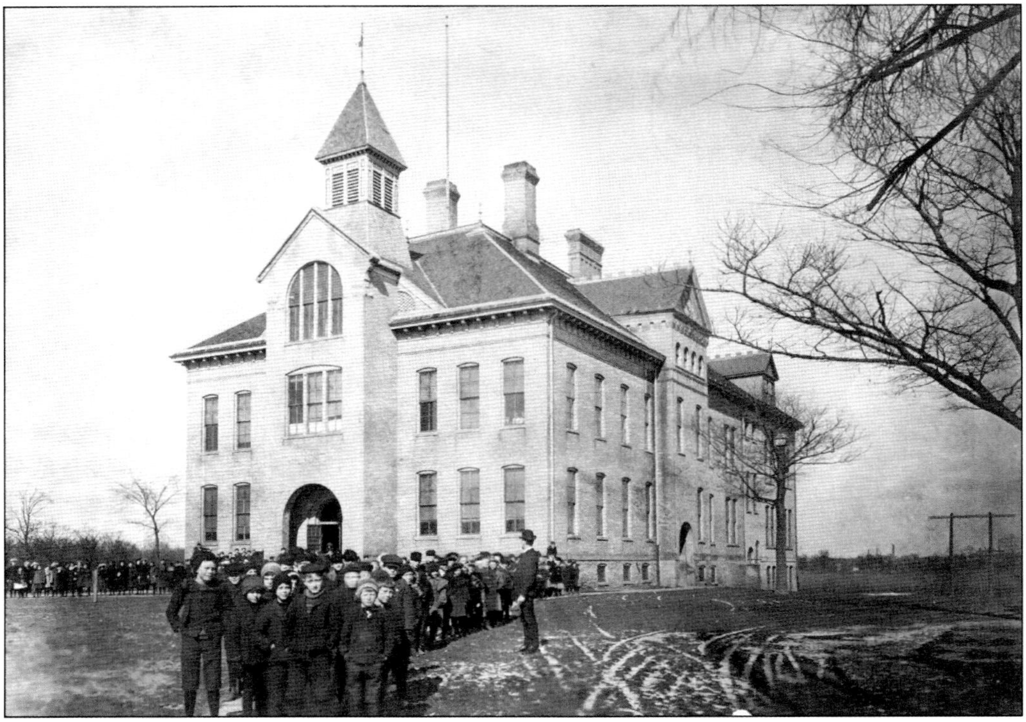

The Howell School, named for board of education member Richard Howell, was built on Washington Avenue in 1888. It was expanded in 1891 and 1902. The Gittings family donated the land behind the Howell School and south of the Washington Park High School to the City of Racine for use as a park. This c. 1910 photograph shows the school and principal John Sogard (standing to the right of the student body).

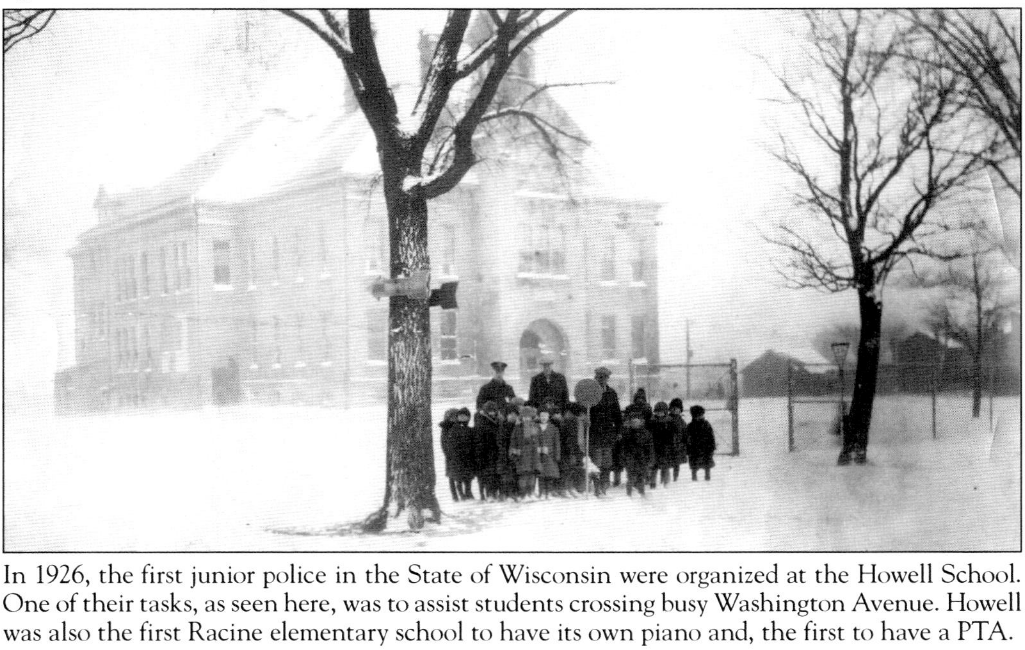

In 1926, the first junior police in the State of Wisconsin were organized at the Howell School. One of their tasks, as seen here, was to assist students crossing busy Washington Avenue. Howell was also the first Racine elementary school to have its own piano and, the first to have a PTA.

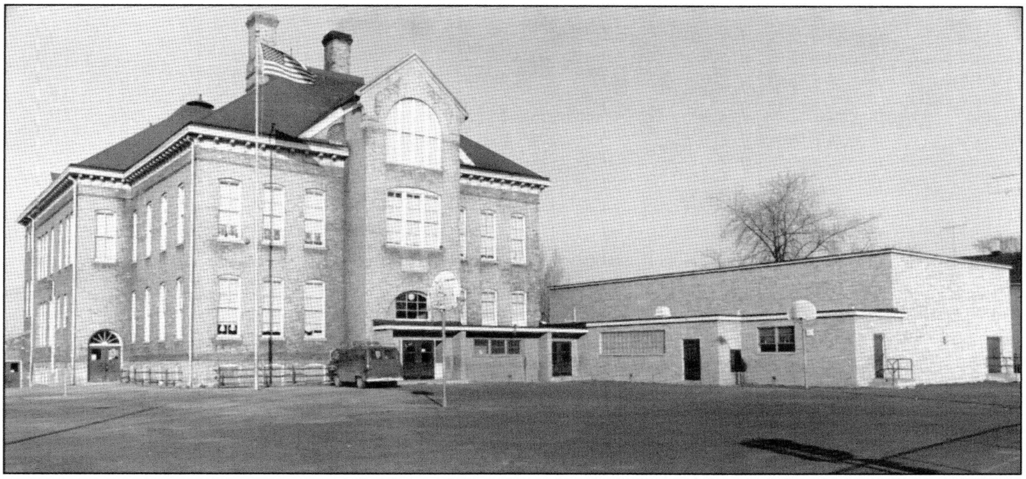

In 1954, a multipurpose building was added to the Howell School. By 1968, the Howell School was found to be inadequate for use as a school building. It was closed in 1968 and demolished in 1970. The 1954 addition remained in use as the Hilltop Preschool, until it was sold in 1982.

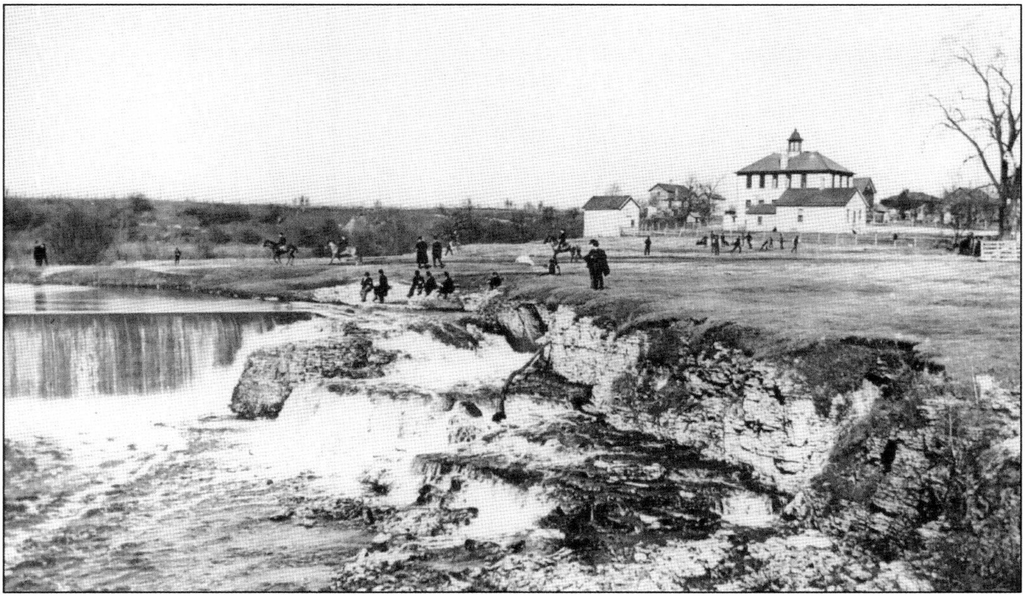

In 1903, the Rapids School, pictured here around 1910, was built just east of the Horlick Dam. An addition was made to the structure in 1954, and in 1961 the Rapids School became part of the Racine Unified School District. The school closed in 1976 and became the site of the Schoolhouse Shoppes. The building was razed in 1994.

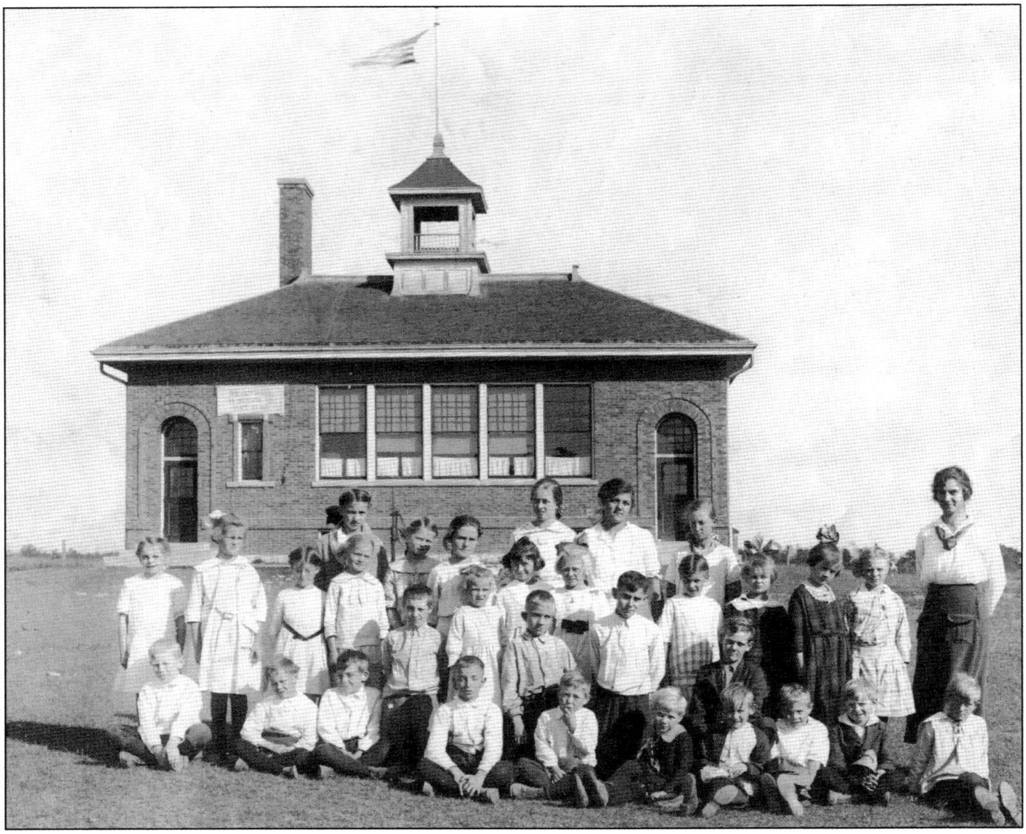

The Trautwein School was built in 1912, on the northwest corner of the intersection of Spring Street and Green Bay Road. In 1954, an addition was made which included a plan to remove the bell tower. Due to student petitions, the bell tower was saved. The Trautwein School, pictured below in 1978, was closed in 1980. The school building was then sold and remodeled. It is now home to a shopping center.

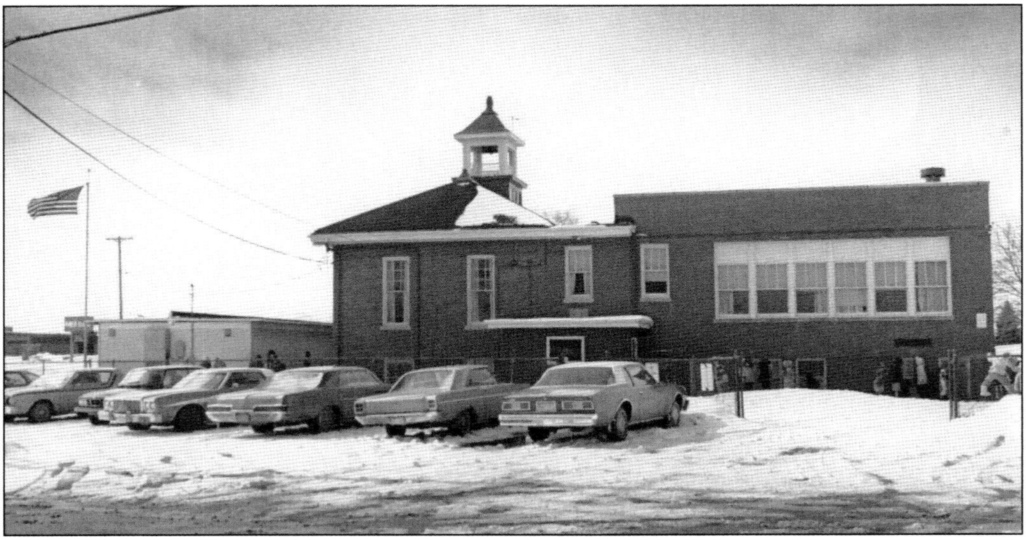

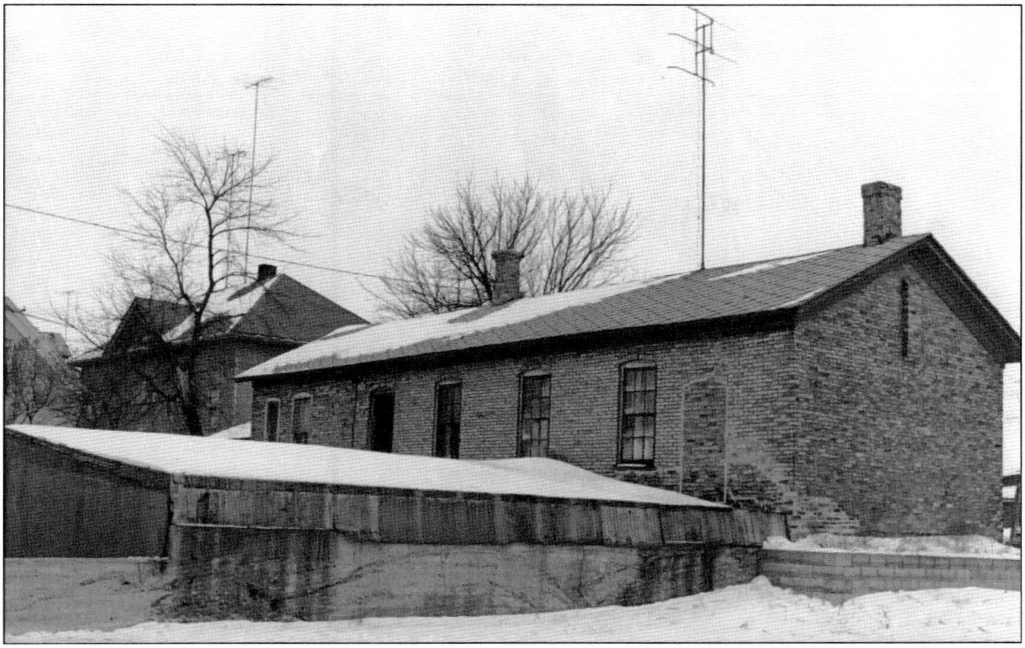

The original Lincoln School was built around 1862, on State Street. It was damaged by a tornado in 1883. When a new Lincoln School was built across the street in 1890, the original building was remodeled into a residence.

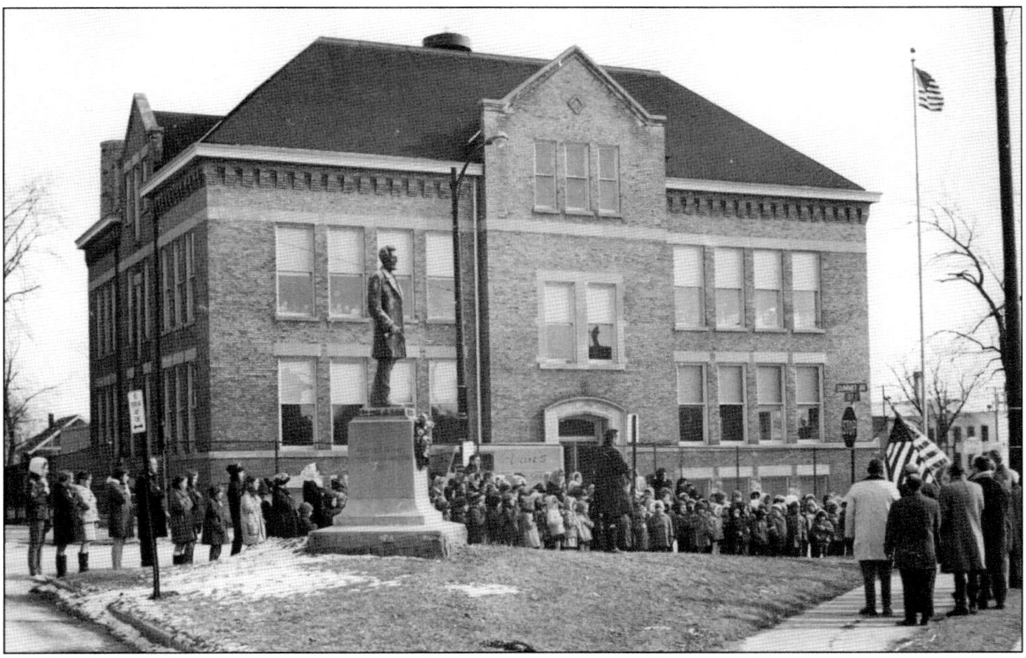

The annual ceremony marking Lincoln's birthday, pictured here around 1970, was a memorable custom at the Lincoln School. The statue of Pres. Abraham Lincoln, located across the street from the school, is one of only seven in Wisconsin. Opened in 1891, the Lincoln School was closed in 1981 and sold to a developer who converted it into a senior apartment complex in 1989.

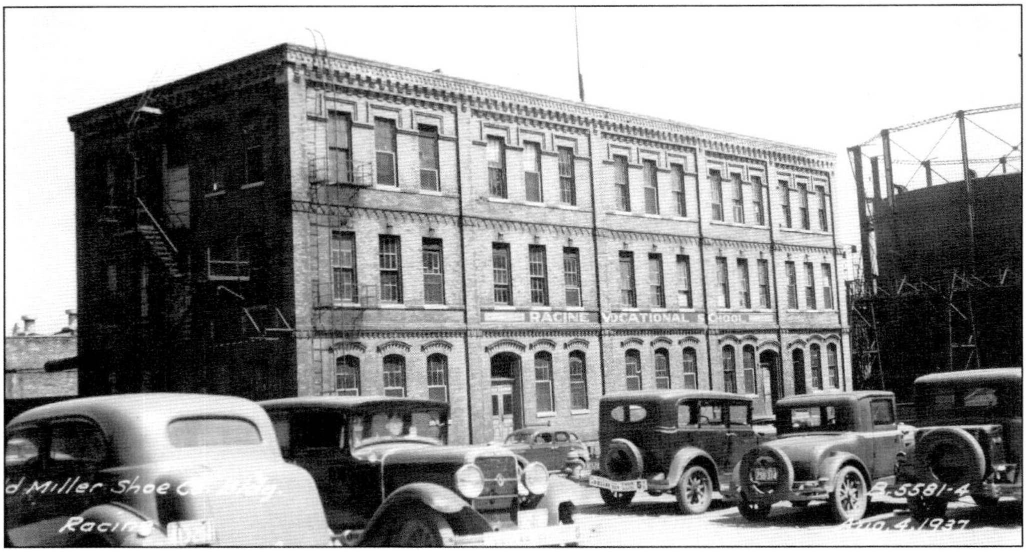

This building, located at 100 Third Street, had many tenants during its history. The Racine Vocational School and the Board of Industrial Education were tenants from 1923 through 1929. From 1939 through 1971, the Wisconsin Gas & Electric Company had offices located there. The building then became vacant in 1972 and was torn down around 1977.

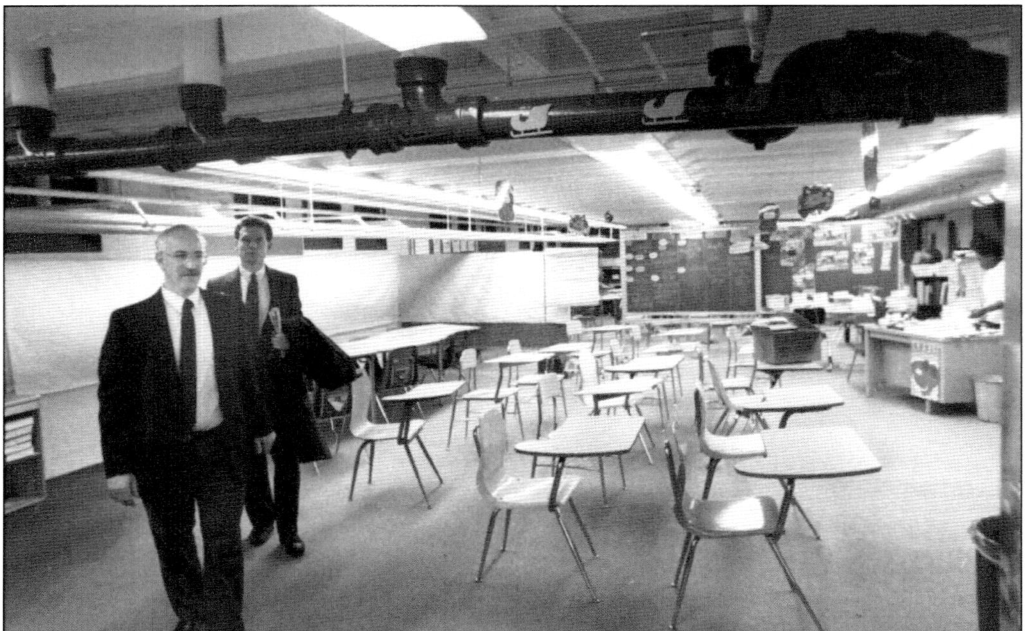

Mitchell School, located on Drexel Avenue, was built as a Public Works Administration Project. It opened in 1937 as a combination elementary and junior high school. Early students recall the huge mural that hung in a multipurpose room. Completed in 1941, the 40-foot mural done by Santos Zingale and funded by the Works Progress Administration, illustrated the arrival in Racine of Gilbert Knapp. The basement area, which included a rifle range, was changed from a "dungeon" to the library and learning center, pictured above, in the 1970s.

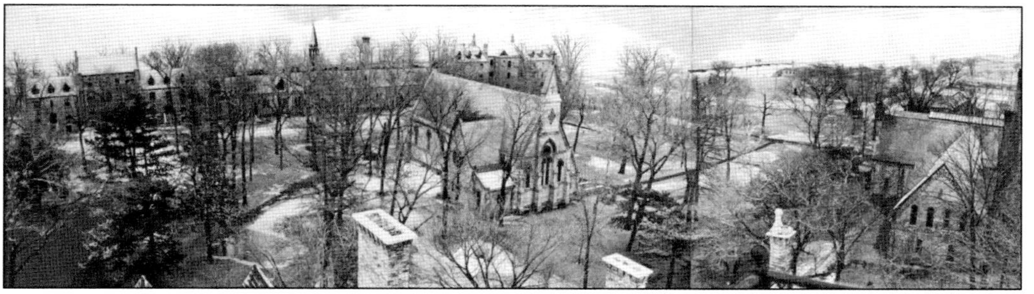

One of Racine's most venerable landmarks is the campus at 600 Twenty-first Street. Operating today as the DeKoven Center, the campus was originally the home of Racine College. This panoramic view was photographed looking southeast from the top of Taylor Hall's bell tower in 1952. All of the buildings were constructed between 1852 and 1875. They are recognized as the most outstanding examples of collegiate Gothic architecture in America.

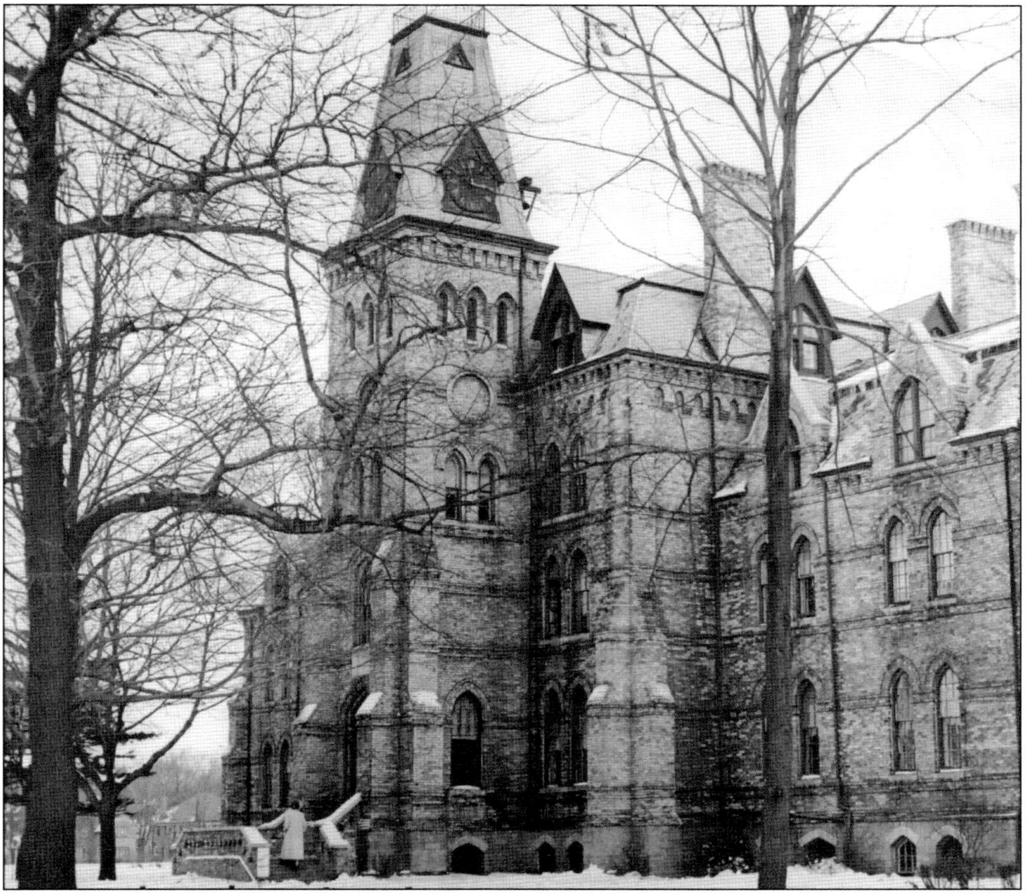

Taylor Hall, pictured above as it looked in 1952, was built in 1867. It contained Racine College's library, chemical laboratory, classrooms, and offices, as well as housing for about 50 students. On February 4, 1875, it burned to the ground. Because it was 20 degrees below zero at the time, little could be done to save the building. However, the building was quickly restored after the fire, and the new structure boasted the—then modern—innovation of steam heat. The last class graduated from Racine College in 1933.

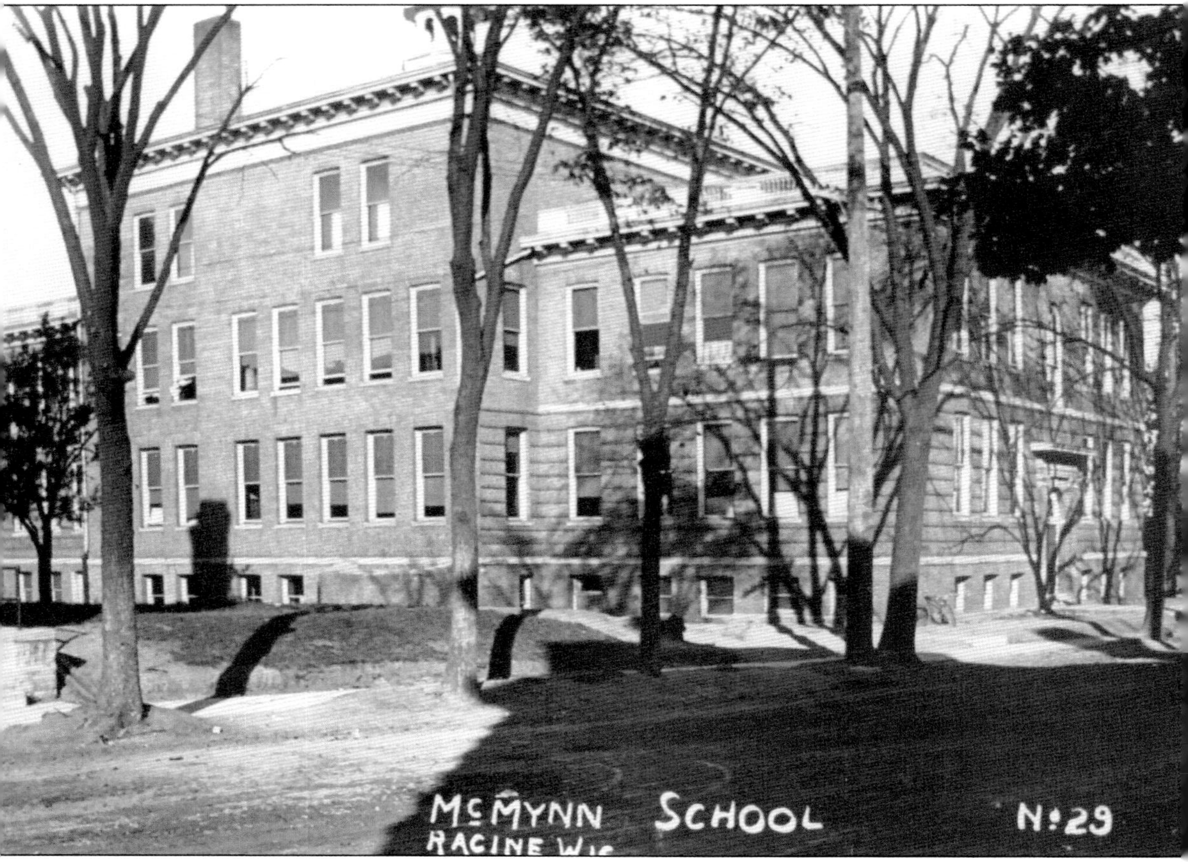

The McMynn School, above, was built in 1903, at Seventh Street and Lake Avenue. It replaced the original Second Ward School. Over the years, the building served a variety of purposes: annex to Racine High School in 1916; public library extension; annex to Racine Vocational, Technical, and Adult School in 1927, and again from 1964 through 1972; the Racine County Relief Building in the 1930s; World War II Ration Board Building; a campus for the University of Wisconsin-Racine, from 1946 through 1964; and, finally, as the Walden III Alternative High School from 1972 through 1975. The building was demolished in 1975 as part of a downtown redevelopment project. It was replaced with a parking structure and a high-rise apartment building.

Eight

Parks and Recreation

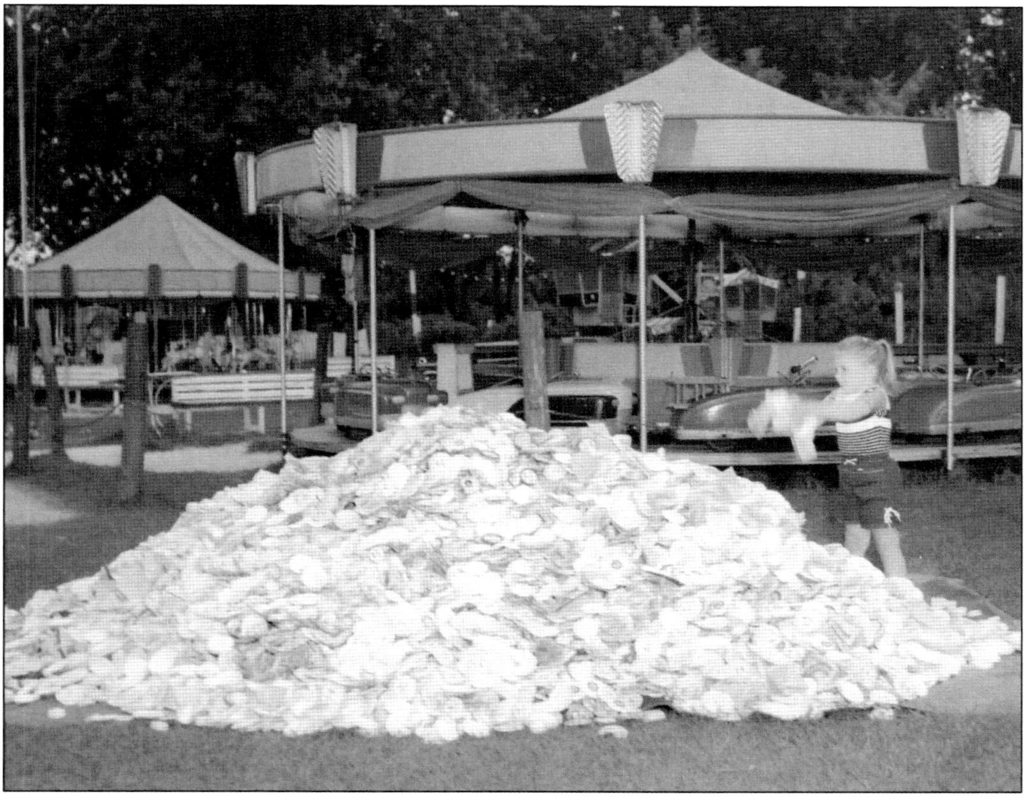

Horlick's Kiddieland was located at Horlick's Dam, just east of Root River. Operated during the summer in the 1950s and 1960s, it included a pony ride, the "400" train, electric cars, boat rides, a Ferris wheel, a chair-o-plane, and a merry-go-round. A large pile of coupons for free ride tickets is seen here. They were printed on the Progressive Dairy Co.'s cottage cheese lids, milk cartons, and bottle caps.

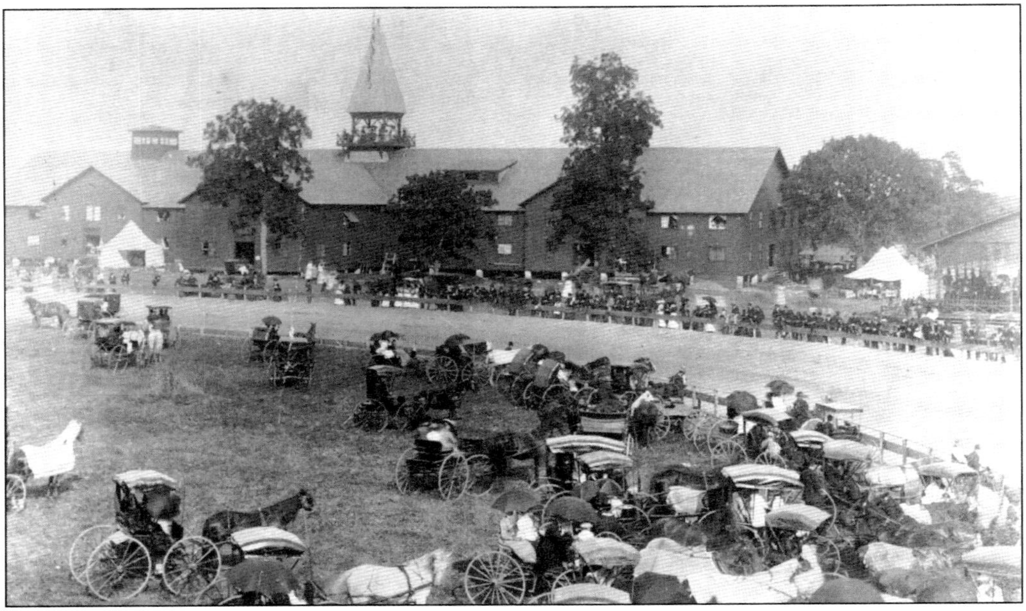

After first being held in nearby Burlington, the Racine County Fair was moved to a site on Taylor Avenue, southwest of Washington Avenue in Racine, in 1884. It was only held there for a few years. This photograph shows the old Racine County fairground on Taylor Avenue, with the bicycle track in the foreground and the pavilion in the back.

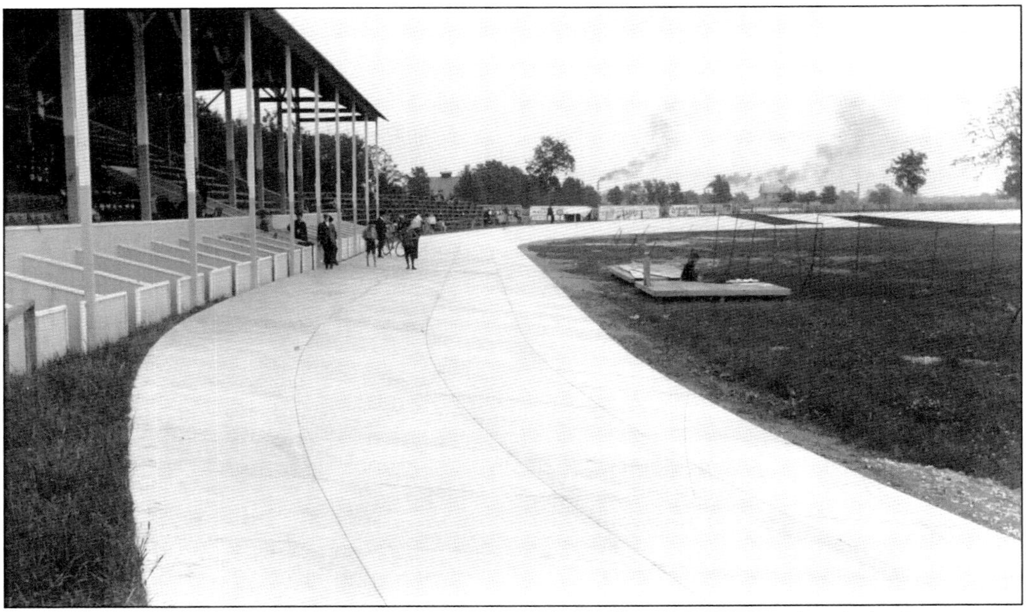

The Racine Athletic Association was incorporated in July 1896. It immediately built a quarter mile cement bicycle racetrack, bleachers, and a grandstand on the old Racine County fairground property on Washington Avenue, as seen above in 1897. At the time, it was the world's only cement bicycle track, and it encircled the Association's football field and baseball diamond.

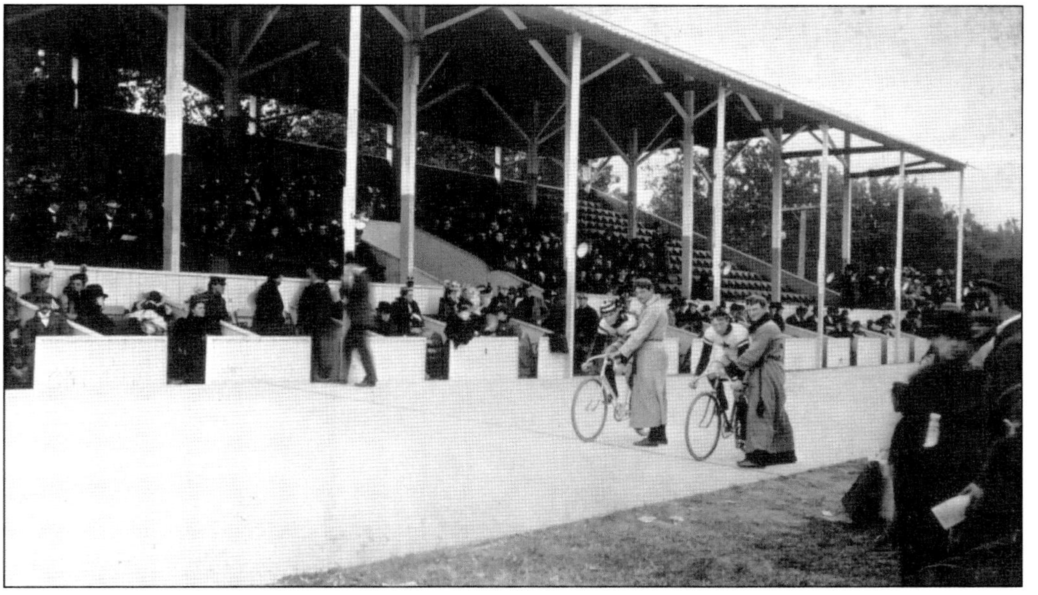

Taken in the late 1890s, this photograph shows a typical scene at the Racine Athletic Association's bicycle racetrack. On July 4, 1899, on this track, the Association held Wisconsin's first professional bicycle race for cash prizes. The winner received $20, with $10 going to second place and $5 to third. Previously, prizes had included diamonds, other gemstones, and jewelry.

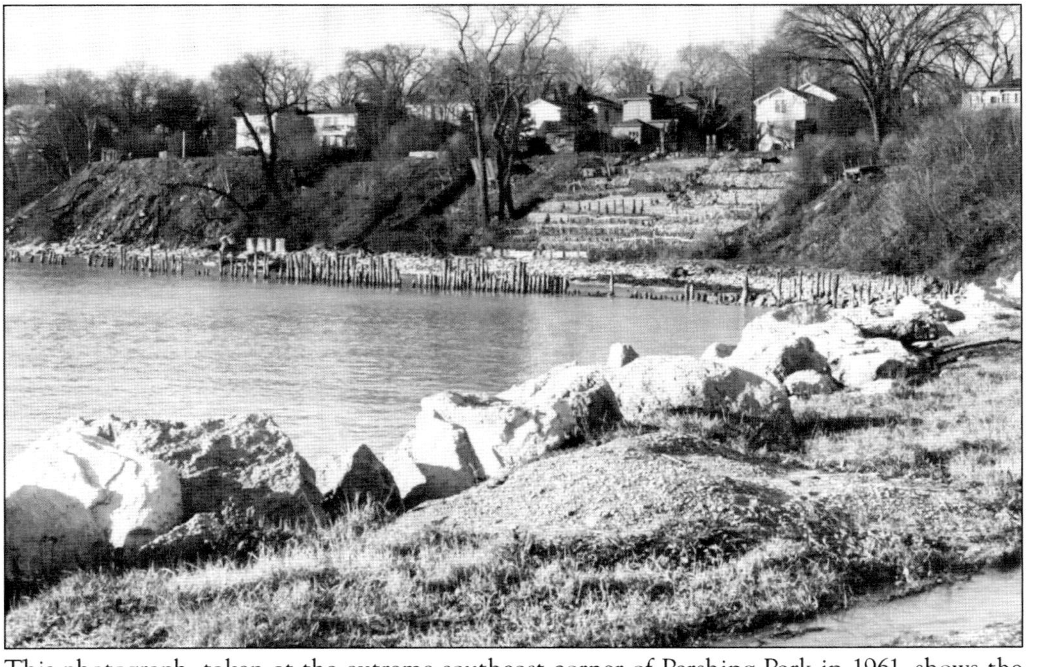

This photograph, taken at the extreme southeast corner of Pershing Park in 1961, shows the homes that were included in the land purchase for the UW-Racine campus. The campus site was extended by filling in the water area of Lake Michigan visible in the foreground. Today, this area is the Gateway Technical College campus. School buildings have replaced the homes, and the water area of Lake Michigan seen above is now the college's parking lot.

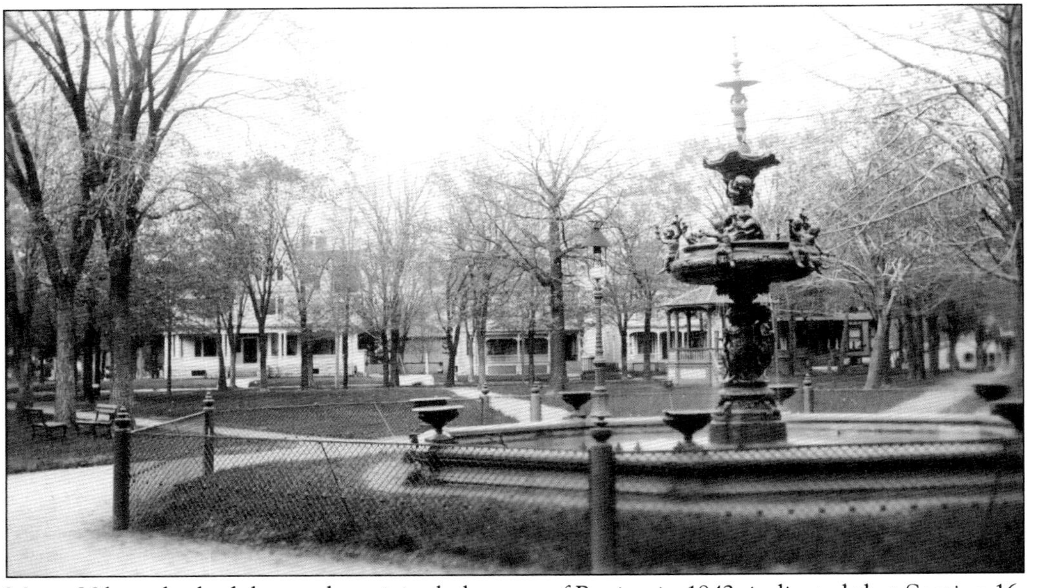

Moses Vilas, who had drawn the original plat map of Racine in 1842, indicated that Section 16, Block 25 was reserved and set aside as a public square. Located on the east side of Main Street, between Tenth and Eleventh Streets, it is known today as East Park. As seen here in 1898, East Park had a beautiful fountain in its center.

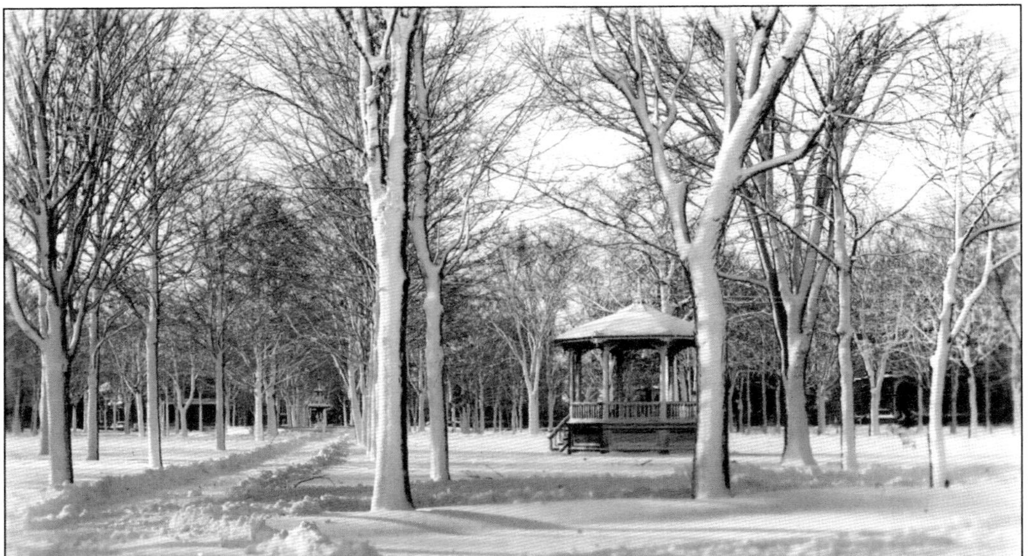

This snow-covered and serene scene looks southwest across East Park. Visible in the distance is the bandstand where popular summer concerts were given by the Schulte Band, the Racine Park Board Band, and other groups for decades.

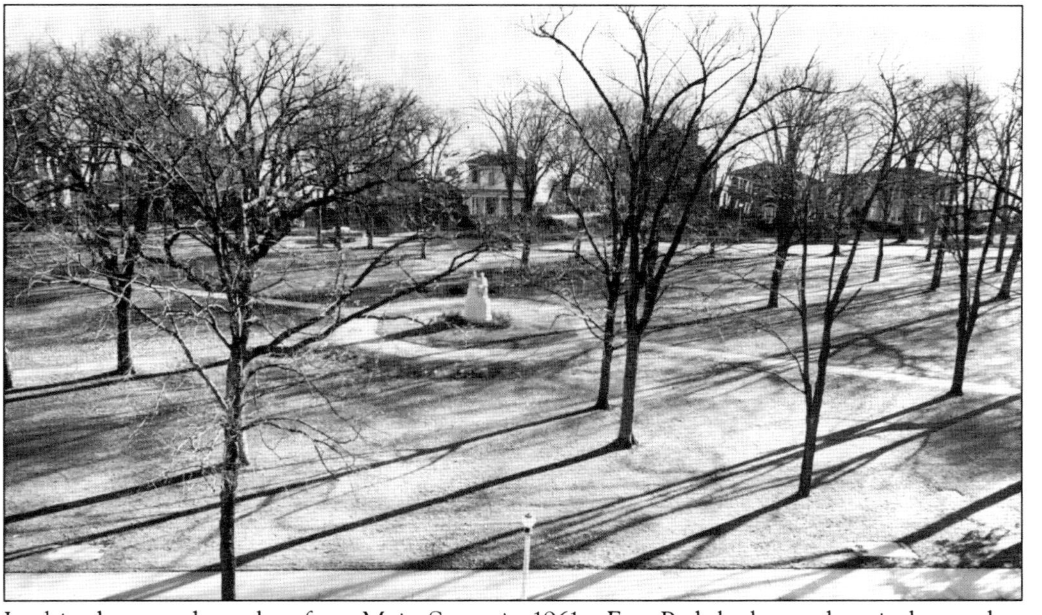

In this photograph—taken from Main Street in 1961—East Park looks much as it does today; with its many trees and the central statue of Abraham and Mary Todd Lincoln. The homes that once lined the east side of Lake Avenue have been replaced by the campus of Gateway Technical College. These homes, once desirable waterfront properties on Lake Michigan, had many owners who were very reluctant to give them up.

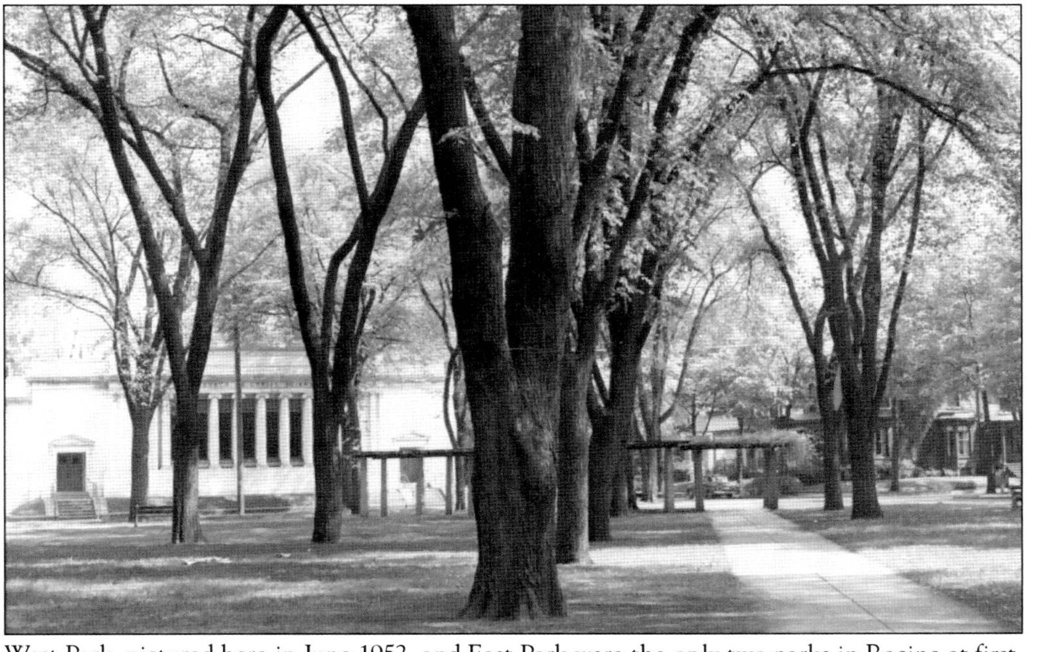

West Park, pictured here in June 1952, and East Park were the only two parks in Racine at first. Like its counterpart, West Park was a public meeting place, held band concerts, and was a favorite spot for picnics. Today, it is mostly used for strolling or as a momentary stopping place while out for a walk. As with East Park, there has never been any playground equipment on the site.

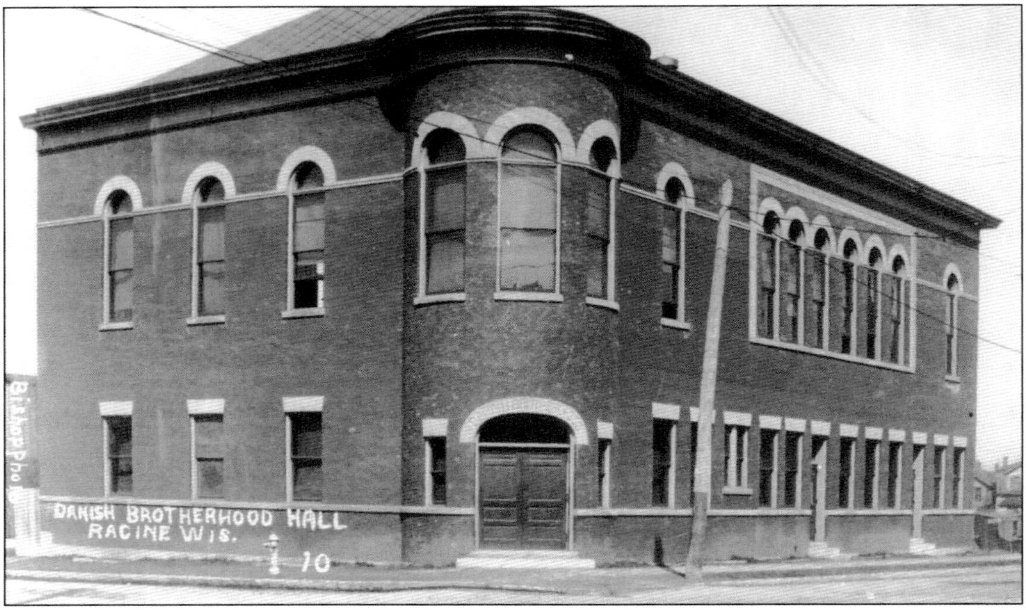

Racine Lodge No. 4 was one of the charter lodges of the Danish Brotherhood, a national society formed in Omaha, Nebraska, in 1882. Although primarily a benefit and fraternal society, the Racine lodge of the Danish Brotherhood also hosted an extensive library and put on plays, dances, and musical entertainment. The group's first lodge in Racine, pictured above, was erected in 1904 and was located at Sixth and Marquette Streets.

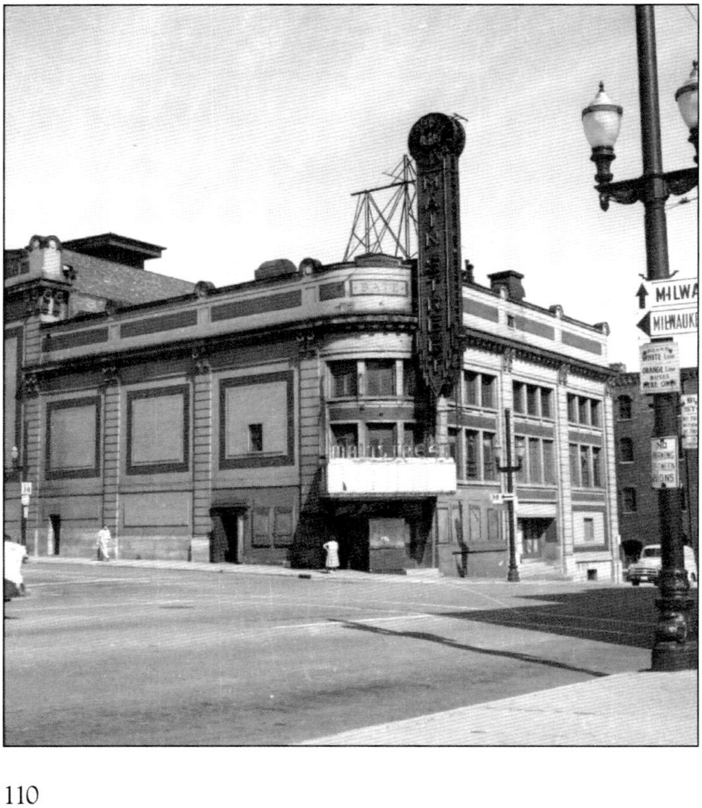

The Mainstreet Theater was located on the northeast corner of State and Main Street and cost $60,000 to construct in 1911. It was initially called the Bate Theater, followed by the New Orpheum, the Orpheum, the RKO Allen, and, finally, the Mainstreet. The theater was torn down in 1958.

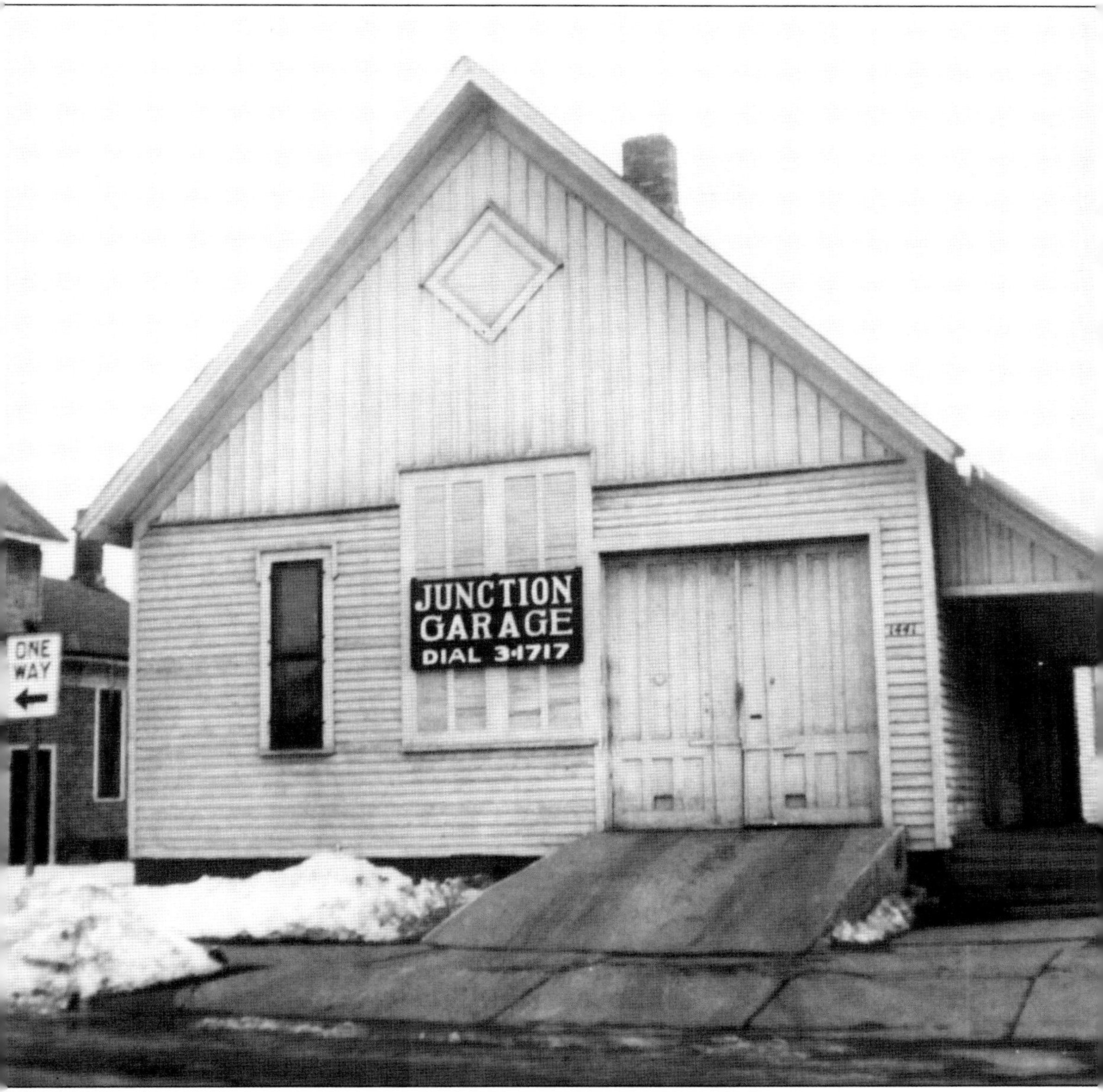

In the 1870s, people in the Junction area of Racine felt the necessity of having a Sunday school, as there were no churches in the area. Initially, this Sunday school met in the union depot building at Racine Junction and was called the Union Sunday School. It outgrew those accommodations within two years, and this building, called the Union Mission, was constructed at 1441 Ann Street. By 1879, a group called the Junction Library Association was holding fundraisers for the purpose of buying books to open a public library. In 1881, shelves were built in the Union Mission and, with about 200 books, the Junction Library was opened. Fundraising continued over the years, with the money earned divided equally between the Sunday school and the library.

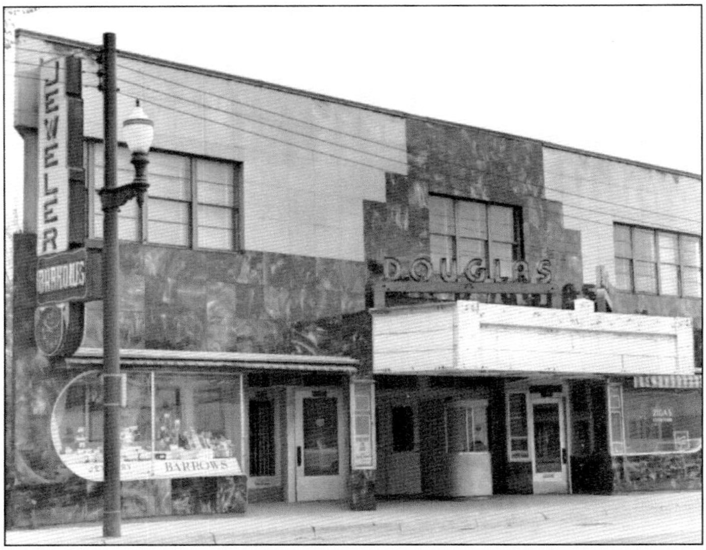

The Douglas Theater, located at 1639 Douglas Avenue, was built in 1923 by Walter Krusienski. Krusienski first operated the theater as a vaudeville and silent picture house and then, when talkies killed vaudeville, as a movie theater. Krusienski sold the theater in 1945 and retired. Sold again in 1955, the modest, one-level theater closed in 1961. Since then, the building has been extensively remodeled. Few traces of the theater remain.

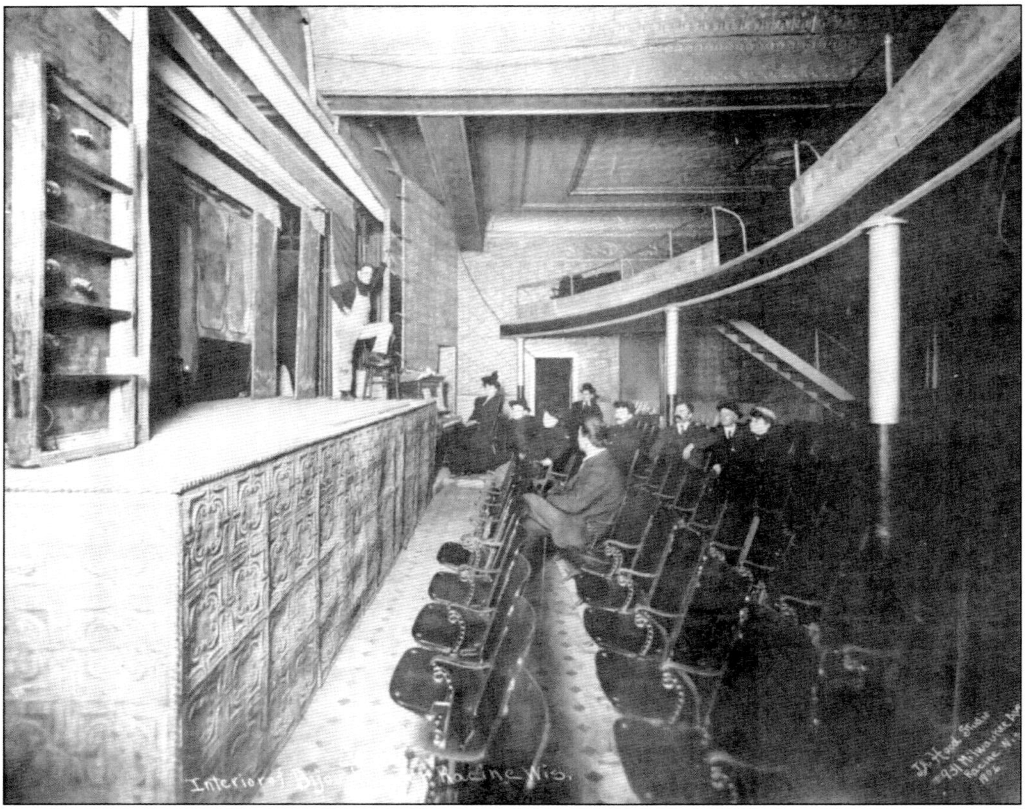

The 350-seat Bijou Theater opened with a matinee vaudeville performance on Saturday, December 24, 1904. Seen here in 1906, the theater was located on the first floor of the Secor Block at Third and Main Streets. The Bijou introduced the first motion pictures to Racine and combined movies with the very best and cleanest vaudeville attractions. A restaurant replaced the theater shortly before the outbreak of World War I.

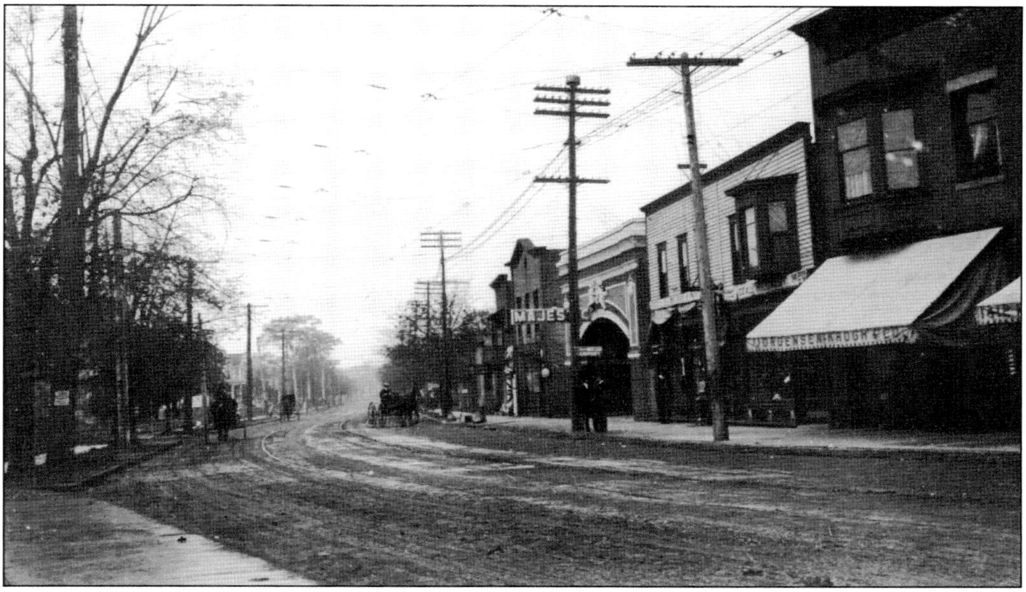

The old Majestic Theater at 1425 Washington Avenue is seen in the center of this photograph. It was in business at this location from 1911, through the mid-1920s. The old Majestic was eventually replaced by a new theater with the same name. The new Majestic opened a few doors down, at 1430 Washington Avenue, on May 2, 1928. This second location closed two years later, in 1930.

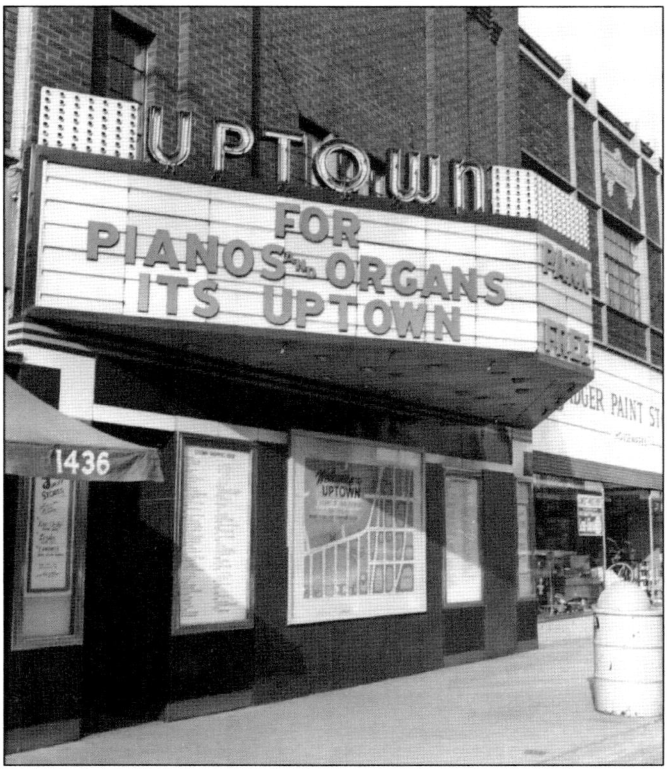

The second Majestic Theater, which had been close since 1930, reopened in 1940 as the Uptown Theater; named for the business district in which it was located. The Uptown closed permanently in late December 1959. Only the retail spaces at the front of the building have been used since. The theater remains abandoned, and there currently are no plans for its restoration.

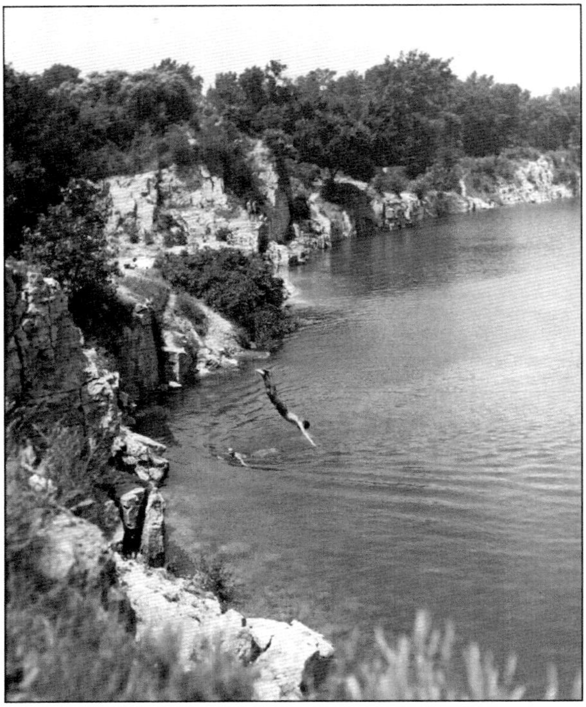

Once it filled with water, swimming was the principle attraction of the quarry on Northwestern Avenue, at Rapids Drive. On nice summer days, one could usually find people swimming and jumping from the rock walls, as seen here in August 1959. In 1966, after much urging from the community, Racine County purchased the quarry and turned it into a recreational area.

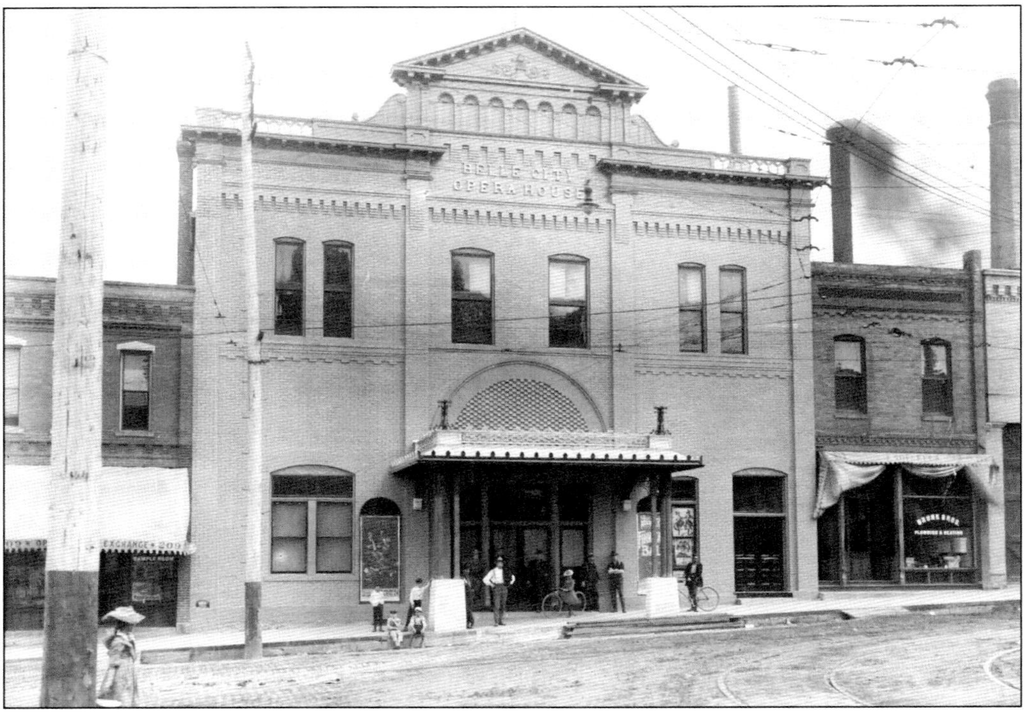

In the 1890s, the Belle City Opera House hosted many concerts, plays, and vaudeville performances. It was located on the east side of Main Street in the middle of the 200 block. The building closed in 1908 and later became a movie theater called the Rex.

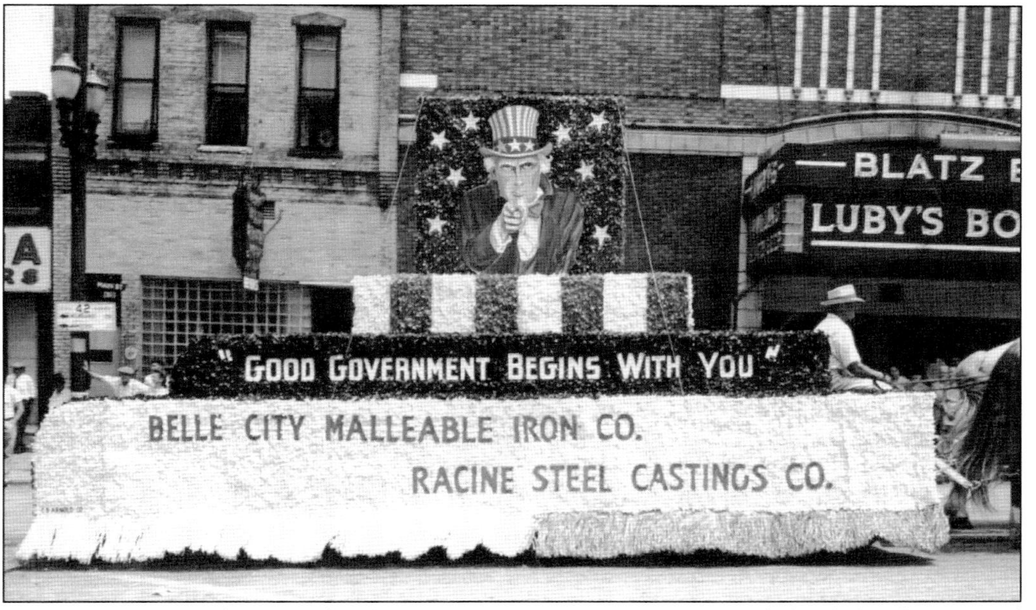

Luby's Bowling, on the east side of Main Street at State Street, is seen behind this float. David Luby got into the bowling alley business in 1942, when he took over the former Rex Theater and converted it into a bowling alley. He sold the building five years later, and it became J&W Lanes. Luby then built Luby's Recreation Center, a 20-lane establishment at 1400 Thirteenth Street.

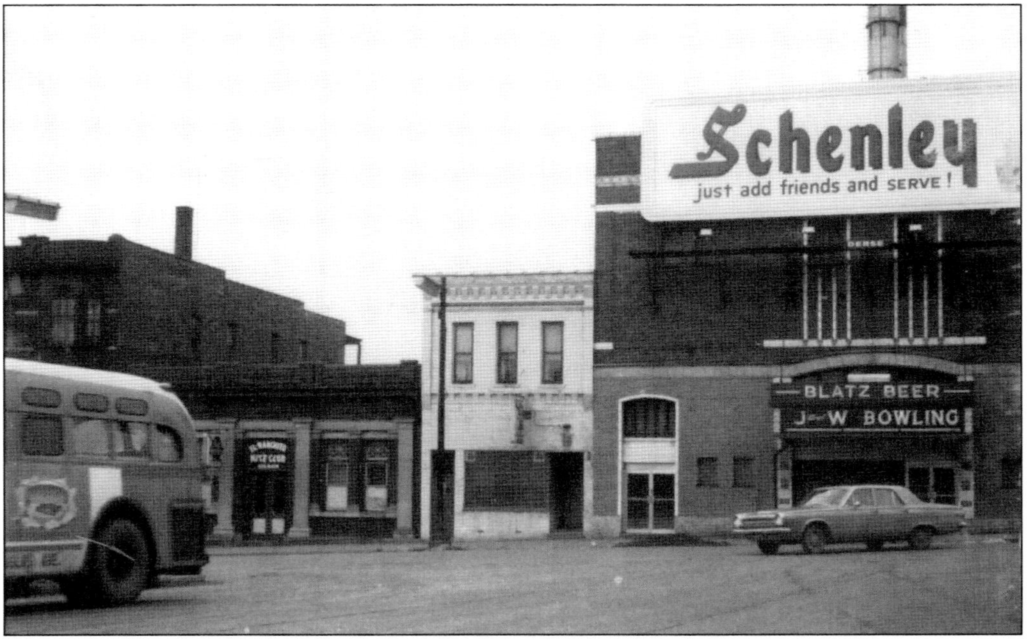

Looking east at what was then the intersection of State and Main Streets, sometime in the late 1960s, J&W Lanes is seen. In 1977, the building was acquired by the City of Racine so that State Street could be extended to Lake Avenue. At that time, the city also acquired 5.7 acres of land east of Green Bay Road, between Byrd Avenue and the Milwaukee Road tracks, to relocate the bowling alley. Castle Lanes was built on that site in 1978.

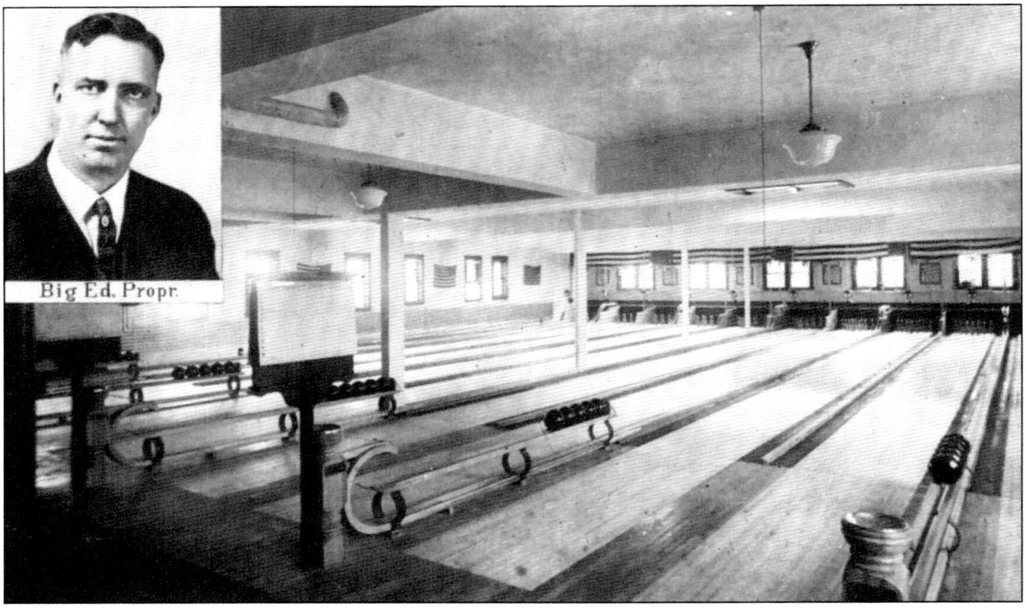

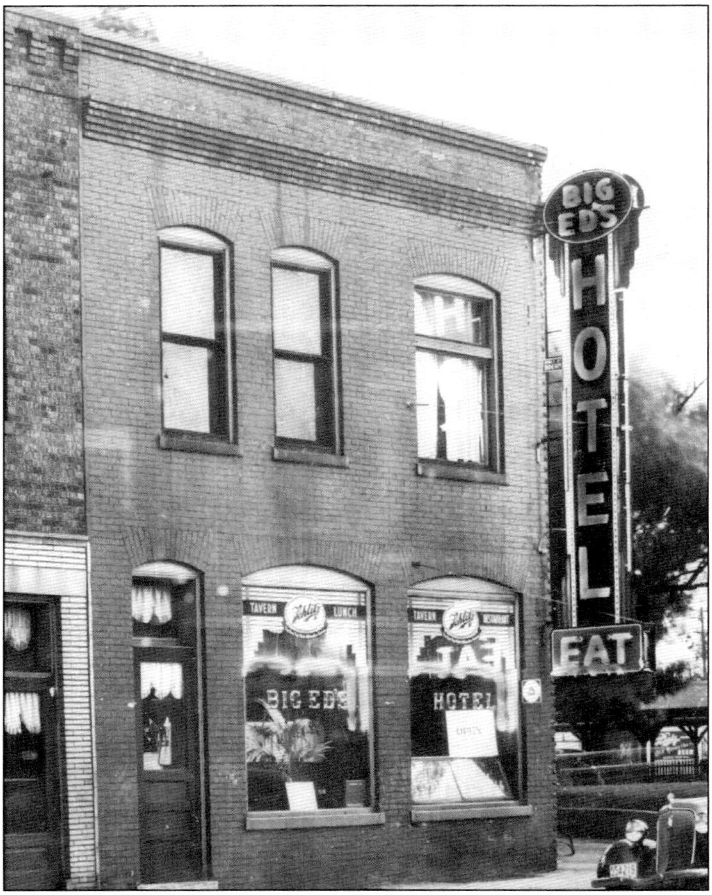

Big Ed's Hotel, 1347–1349–1351 State Street, had its grand opening on November 7, 1917. The hotel occupied the second floor, while a tavern, restaurant, and bowling alley were on the first. Ed Mandernach was the proprietor of all the businesses. Big Ed's Bowling Alleys led the way in getting women involved in organized bowling in Racine. The life of the Racine Women's Bowling Association began on September 7, 1924, with 150 members in two leagues, one of which was the Big Ed's Ladies League. Up to this time, few women frequented regular bowling alleys. The first women to bowl in Racine usually did so on the private alleys of the Racine Elks Club.

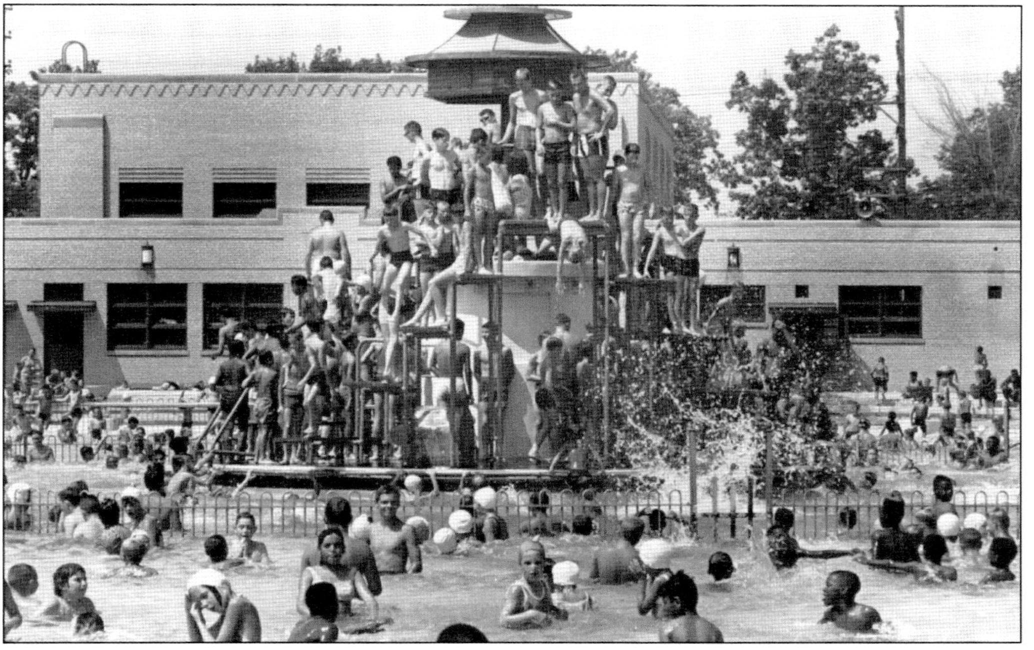

Racine took advantage of a WPA grant and built the Washington Park Pool and Recreation Center in 1939. The pool, seen here in July 1964, was opened on the third weekend in August 1939. The Red Cross held swimming classes at the pool each summer. Chartered buses would bring children to the swimming classes from as far away as Union Grove. The pool closed after the summer of 1969.

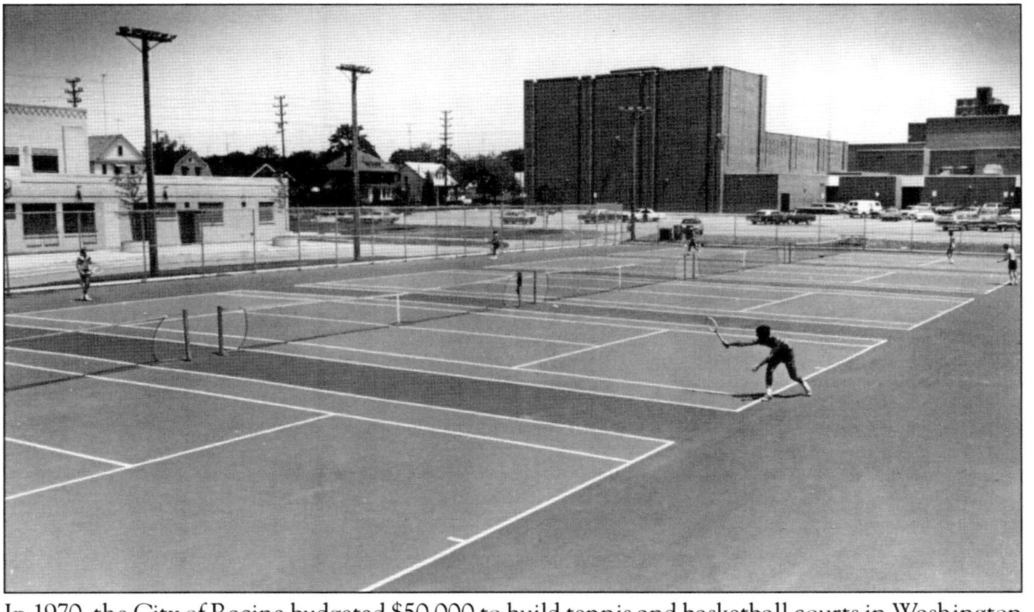

In 1970, the City of Racine budgeted $50,000 to build tennis and basketball courts in Washington Park, on the site of the former outdoor pool. In this photograph—looking east from behind the Washington Park Recreation Center in July 1971—five brand new tennis courts can be seen where the pool used to be. Further east, across the parking lot, is Washington Park High School.

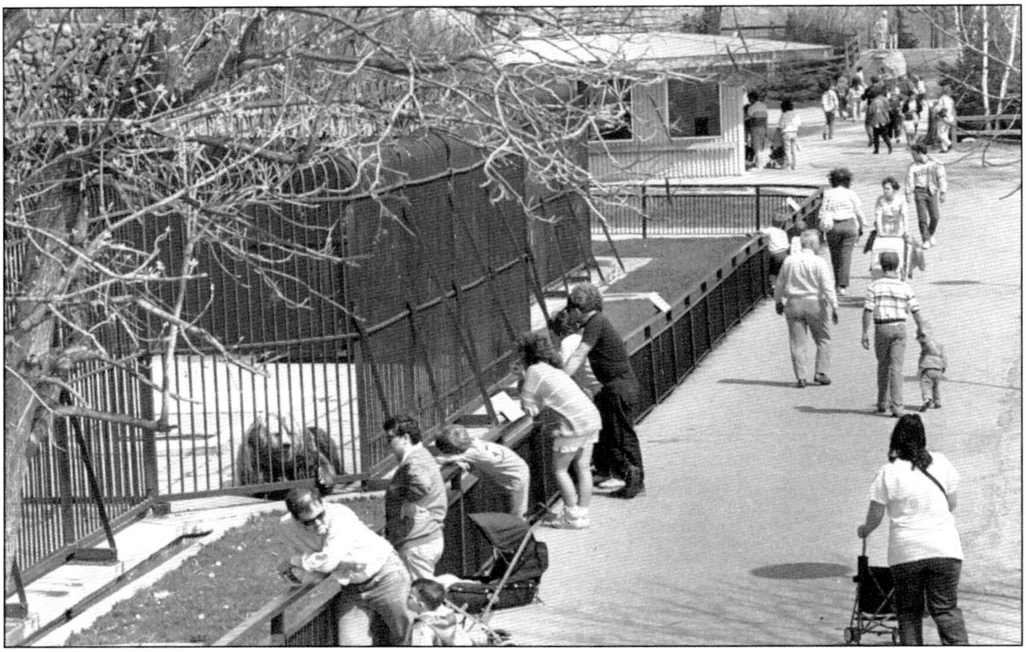

Nice weather always brings out the bears—and a large number of visitors—at the Racine Zoological Gardens, especially on weekends. The old concession building is seen to the right of the bear cages. The zoo was operated as a free attraction until January 2007, when fiscal needs prompted the introduction of an admission fee.

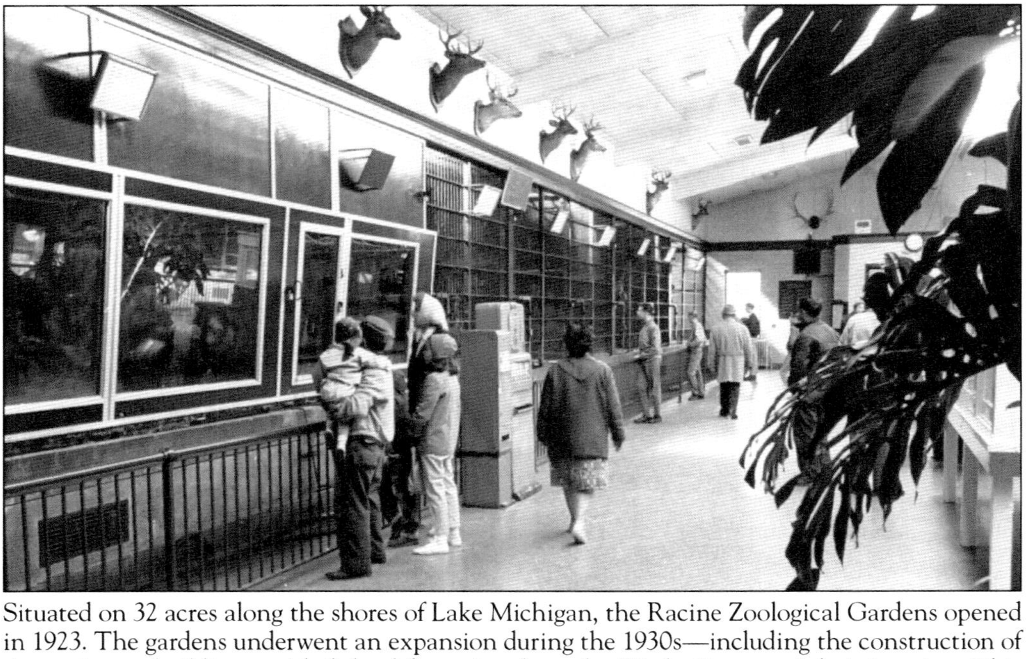

Situated on 32 acres along the shores of Lake Michigan, the Racine Zoological Gardens opened in 1923. The gardens underwent an expansion during the 1930s—including the construction of the main zoo building—with federal financing from the Works Progress Administration. This photograph shows the interior of the main zoo building many years ago, prior to its current remodeling. Here, larger animals such as lions, tigers, apes, and monkeys can be viewed.

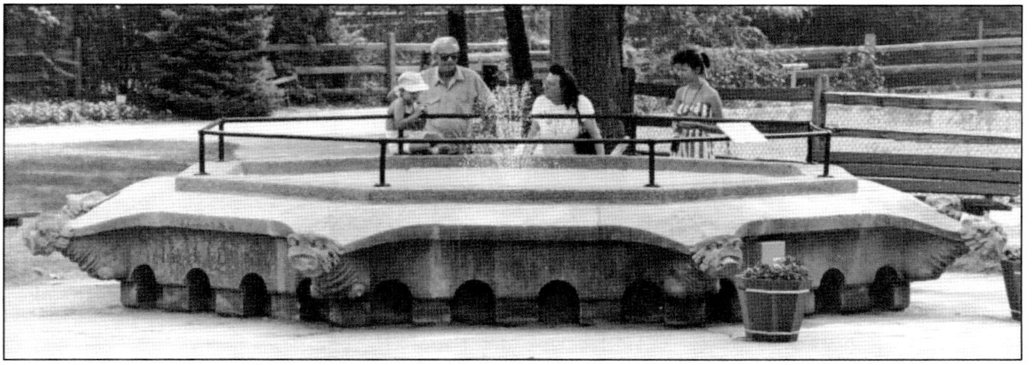

This fountain on the grounds at the Racine Zoological Gardens was once used to house and display alligators during the summer. In the middle was a deep pit, which allowed people to look down inside and view the animals. The fountains gargoyles once ringed the steeple of Racine's first Post Office, at the corner of Sixth and Main Street. This decorative cement ring was preserved and placed at the zoo when the post office was demolished.

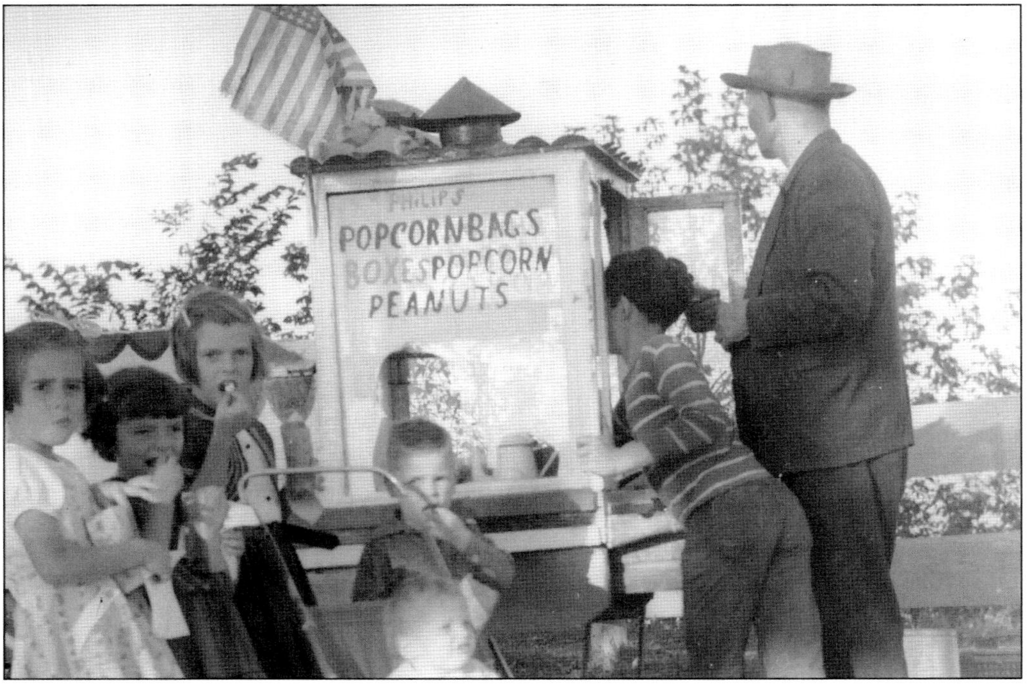

Philips's popcorn stand was always a popular spot with the children at the Racine Zoological Gardens. Theodore Philips is pictured at his stand, tending to his young customers.

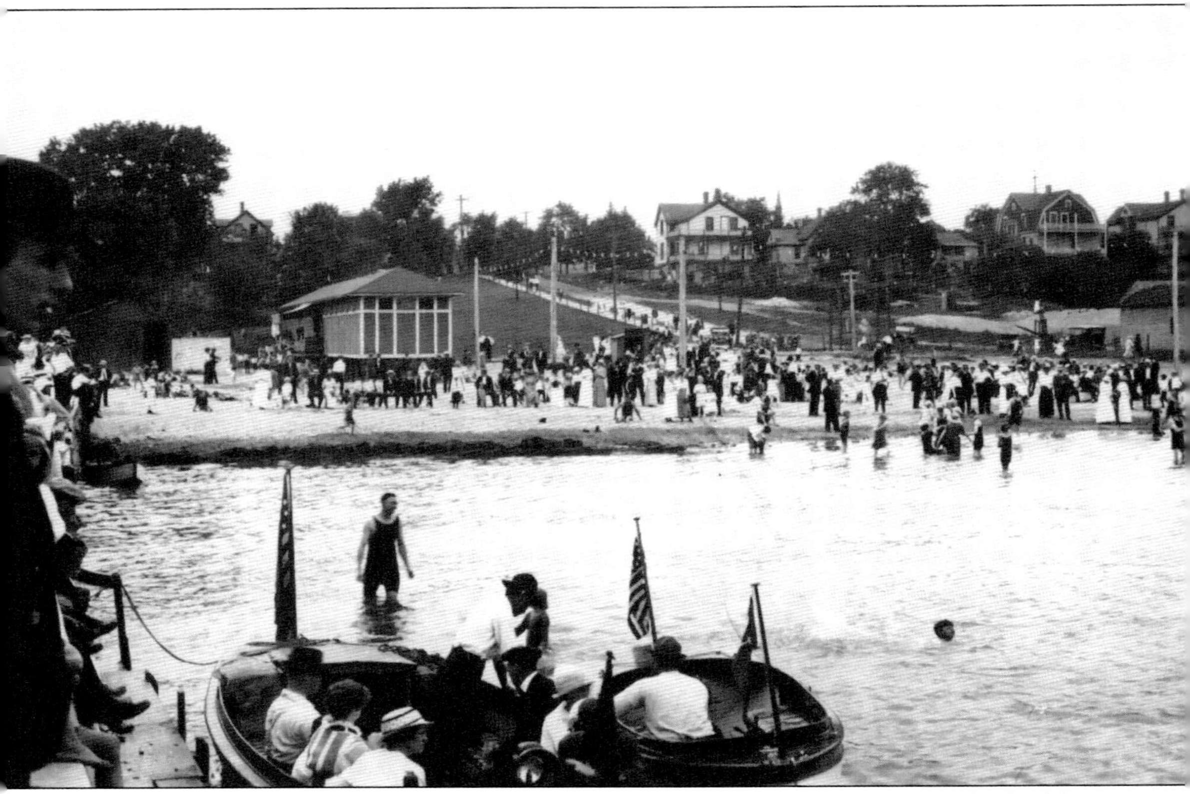

The North Beach Bath House is the long, narrow building seen on the left. The bathhouse was built by the parks board during the summer of 1908, on land that the City of Racine had purchased for this purpose from James Cape and Sons for $10,000. The bathhouse, which opened on August 20, 1908, was entirely paid for with private donations garnered during a local fund raising campaign. It featured rooms to accommodate about 50 bathers, with a male attendant always on duty to collect fees, maintain the beach, and serve as a lifeguard. The building was a temporary one, with the thought that a more complete and expensive bathing facility would be built sometime in the near future. After the bathhouse was built, the new North Beach Park also began hosting evening dances, band concerts, and even marshmallow-roasting parties.

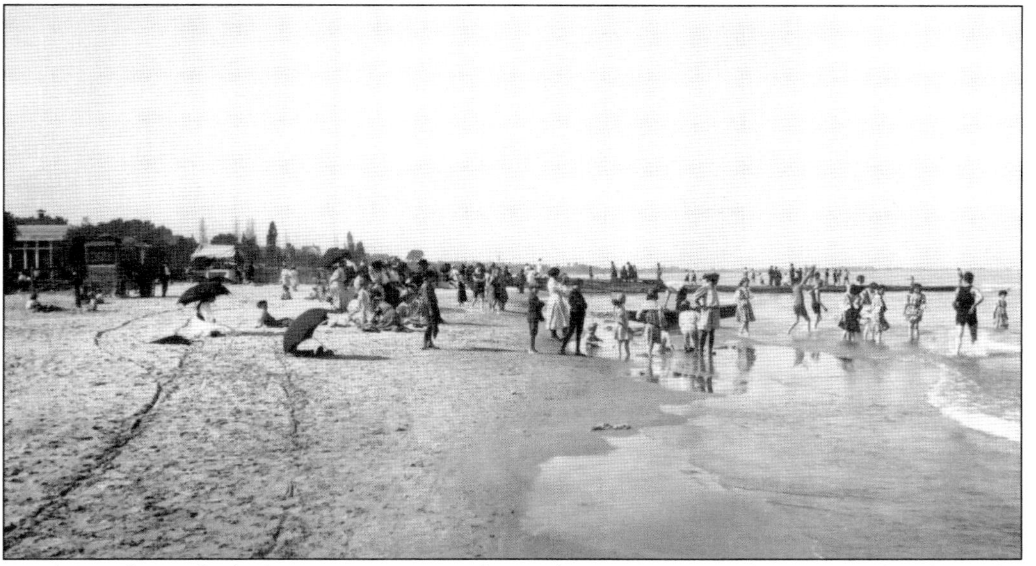

North Beach as it looked on a nice summer day in the 1910s. One of the most used parks in the City of Racine's system, the summer months bring thousands of swimmers and sunbathers to North Beach. It was originally established as a public beach in 1908.

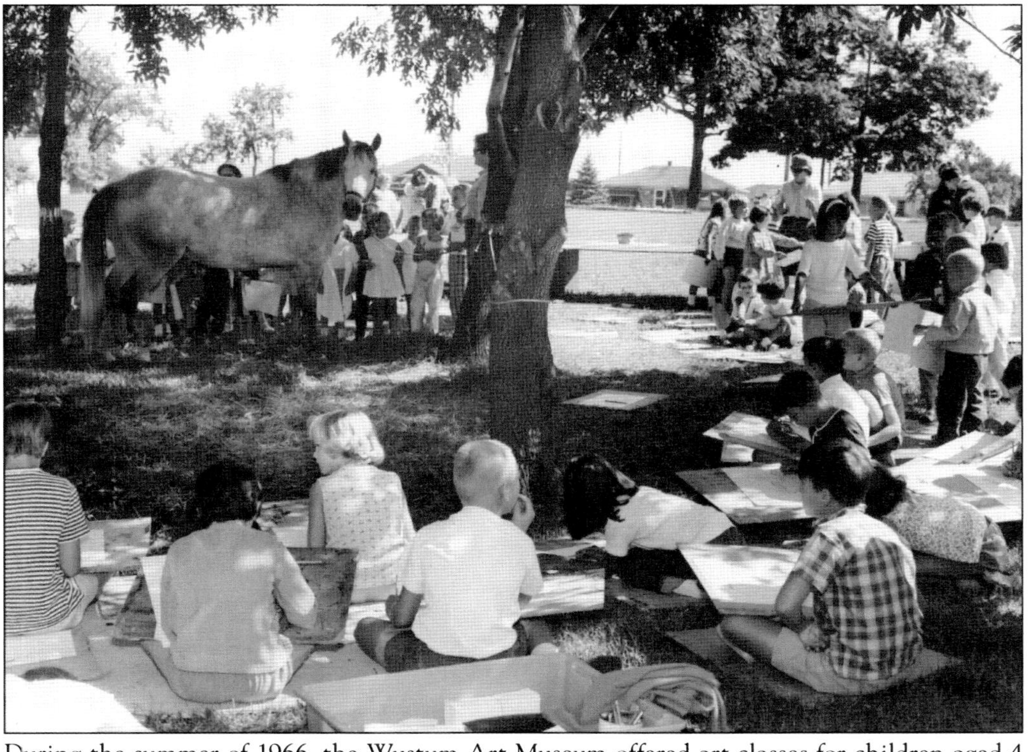

During the summer of 1966, the Wustum Art Museum offered art classes for children aged 4 to 14. Sponsored by the Racine Art Association, these classes were held from July 5 through August 8. During the pictured class, it looks like some of the aspiring artists couldn't resist petting their subject.

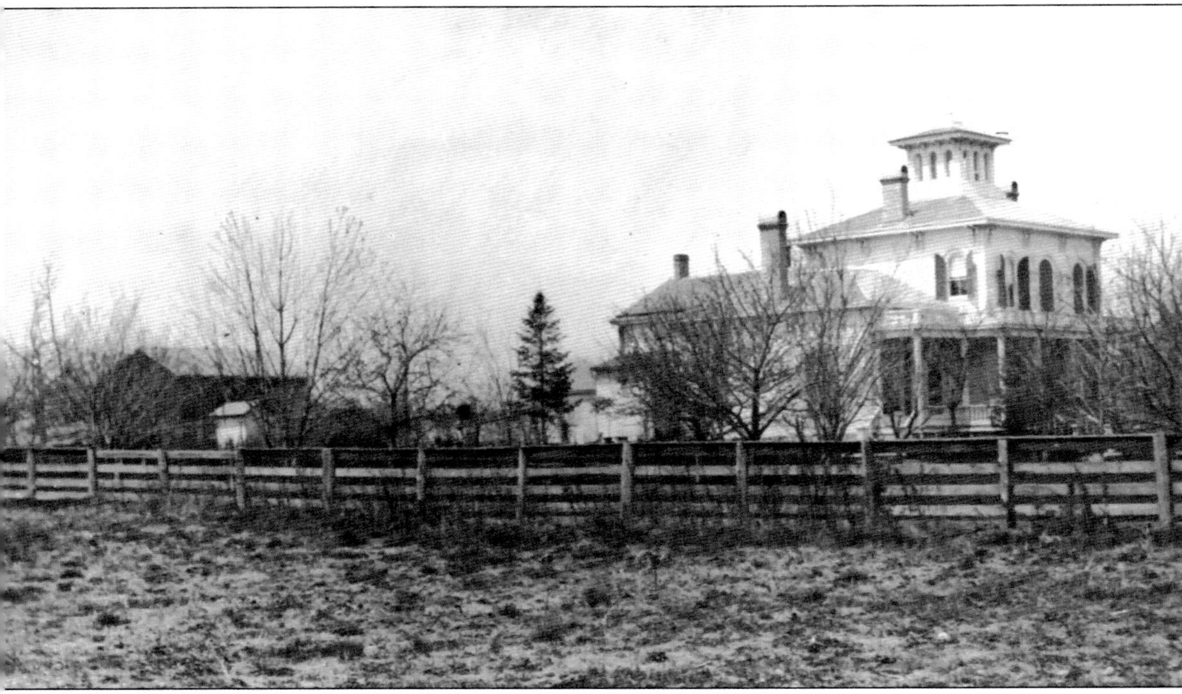

Now known as the Charles A. Wustum Museum of Fine Arts, this is how the property at 2519 Northwestern Avenue looked when James Walker and his wife owned it around 1880. In 1893, Charles A. Wustum and his wife, Jennie, decided to leave Billings, Montana, and come to live in Racine. They bought the Walker estate that year. In April 1940, Jennie left the estate to the City of Racine for use as a park and art museum memorializing her husband. The Wustum Art Museum formally opened on November 16, 1941.

Nine

MITCHELL

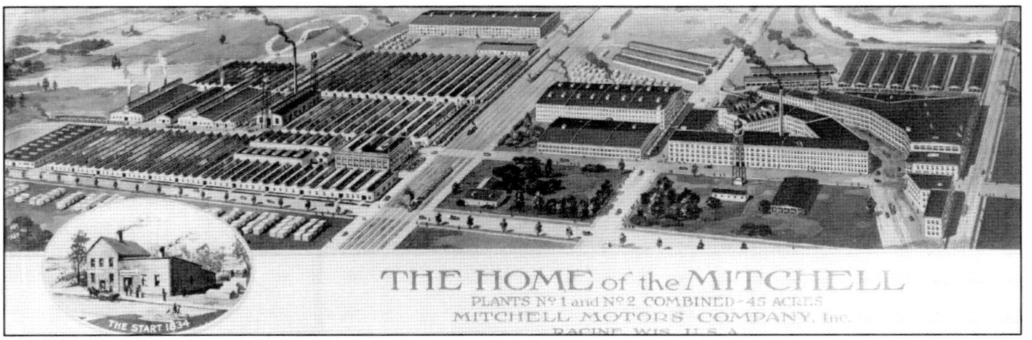

Mitchell, Racine's largest and best-known automobile manufacturer, operated out of two large factory complexes. One, the assembly plant pictured on the left side of the railroad tracks, was along Packard Avenue between Memorial Drive and Taylor Avenue. The other, the body plant seen on the right side of the railroad tracks, was located on Center Street between Sixth and Ninth Streets.

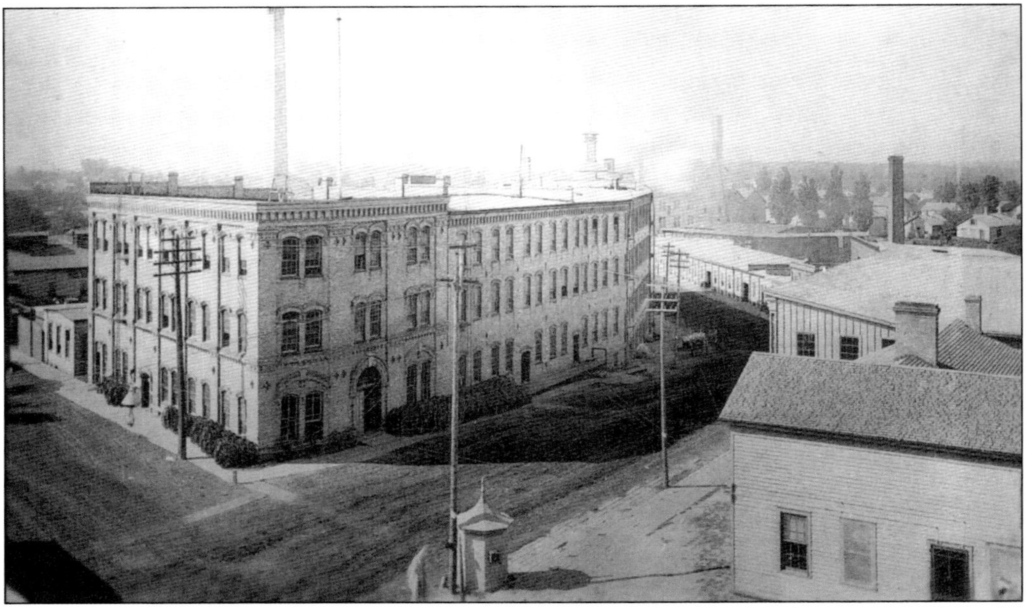

Henry Mitchell moved to Racine in 1854, where he established his wagon-making concern. In 1864, Henry Mitchell brought his son-in-law William Turnor Lewis into the company. Together, they reorganized the company. Before long, the name was changed to the Mitchell & Lewis Company Ltd. Its factory, pictured here in 1888, was located on Center Street at Washington Avenue.

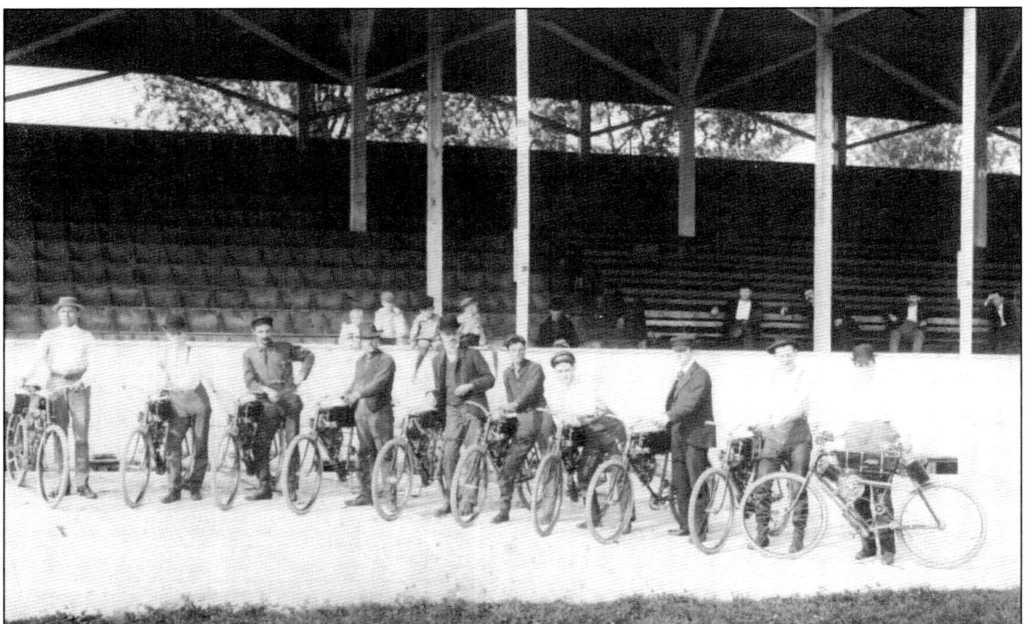

In 1896, William Turnor Lewis and his son William Mitchell Lewis purchased Beebe Wheel Works, changed its name to Wisconsin Wheel Works, and began to manufacture bicycles. In 1899, the company began to manufacture motorcycles. This photograph, showing a group of Mitchell motorcyclists, was taken at the Racine Athletic Association's bicycle racetrack around 1900.

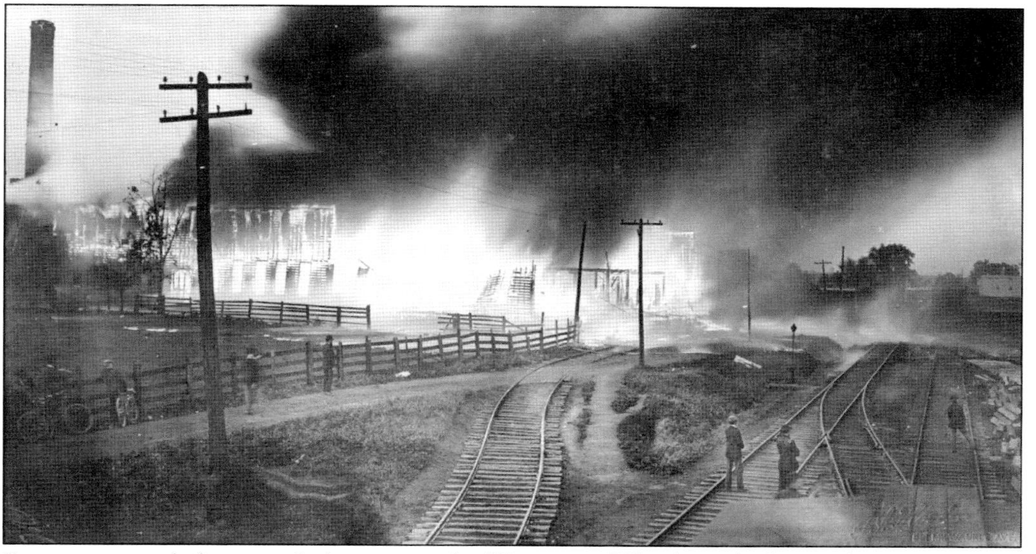

Spectators watch from a safe distance as the Wisconsin Wheel Works factory burns on June 7, 1900. Located at Seventeenth Street and Packard Avenue—next to the Chicago, Milwaukee and St. Paul railroad tracks—the factory was rebuilt on the same site and was back in operation making motorcycles on October 1, 1900.

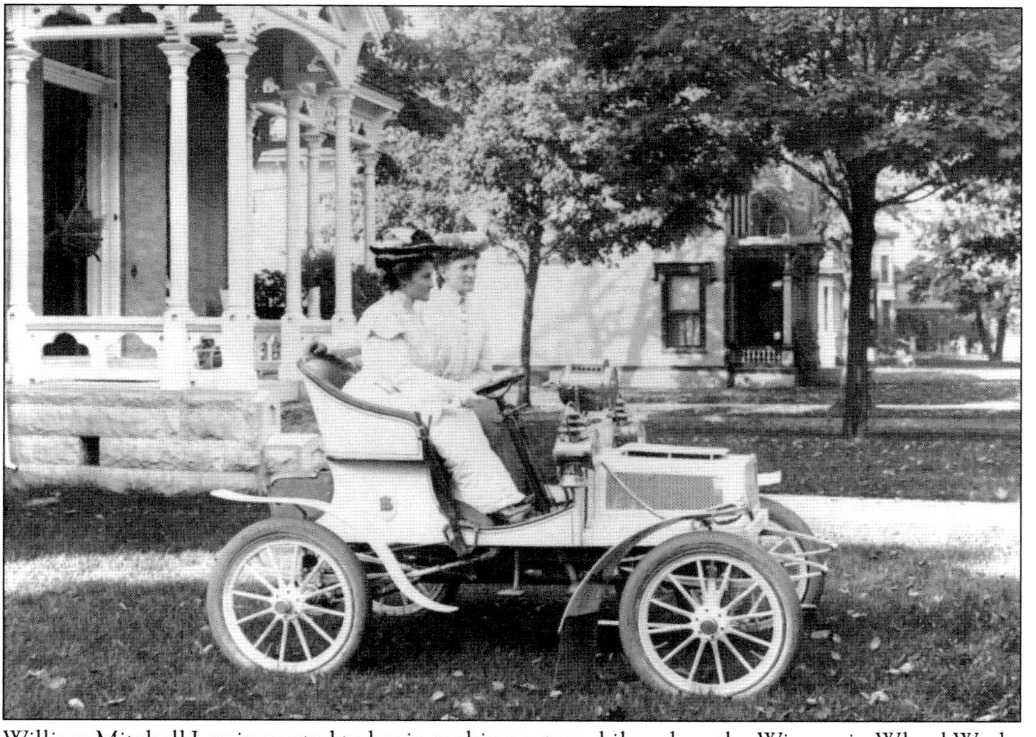

William Mitchell Lewis wanted to begin making automobiles when the Wisconsin Wheel Works factory reopened on October 1, 1900. However, it was not until February 1903 that the production of Mitchell automobiles finally began. Sitting in one of the first Mitchells, in front of 1012 Main Street, are Helen Lewis Wilson, left, and Mary Lewis Mosher, right.

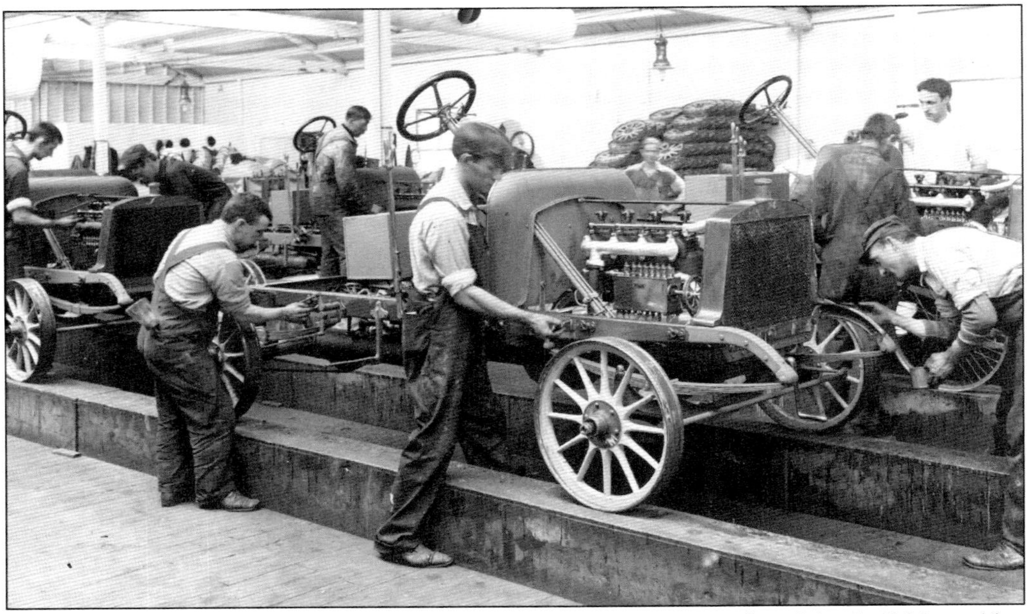

John W. Bate, chief engineer of the Mitchell-Lewis Motor Company from March 1904 until his retirement at the end of 1917, was instrumental in Mitchell becoming the first manufacturer of mass-produced, practical automobiles in the United States. In 1904, Bate began producing automobiles on an assembly line basis at Mitchell; making the company the first to do so in the United States.

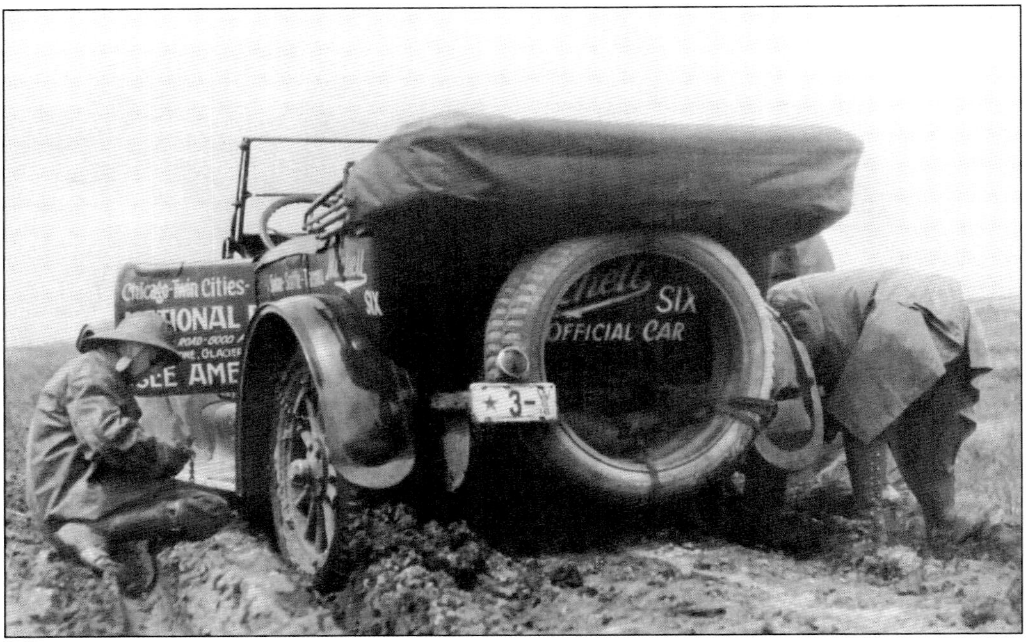

Paved highways were a thing of the future when these motorists chained their tires to help them get through the mud during Mitchell's 1916 Chicago-to-Tacoma publicity tour. The trip took 33 days in their 1916 Mitchell Six Touring Car. Standard equipment on this car included an engine-driven tire pump and reversible headlights for seeing into the engine compartment.

Mitchells were sold through a nationwide network of dealers. They were shipped to the dealers inside railroad boxcars, which were loaded at the factory. In February 1917, Mitchell became the first in the industry to use motion pictures to train their salesmen; doing so at a meeting of dealers in Chicago.

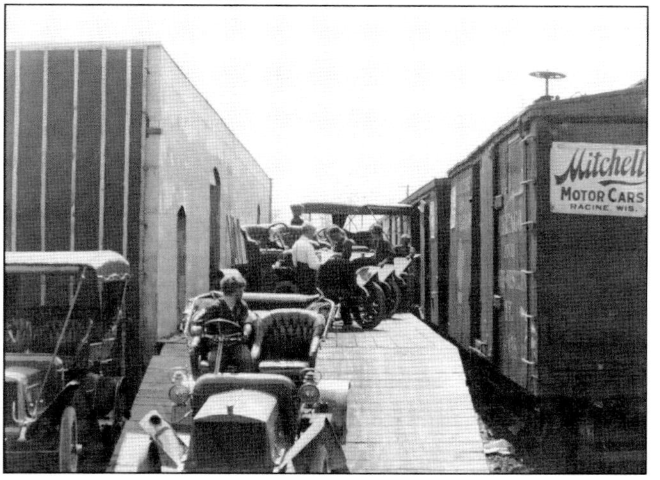

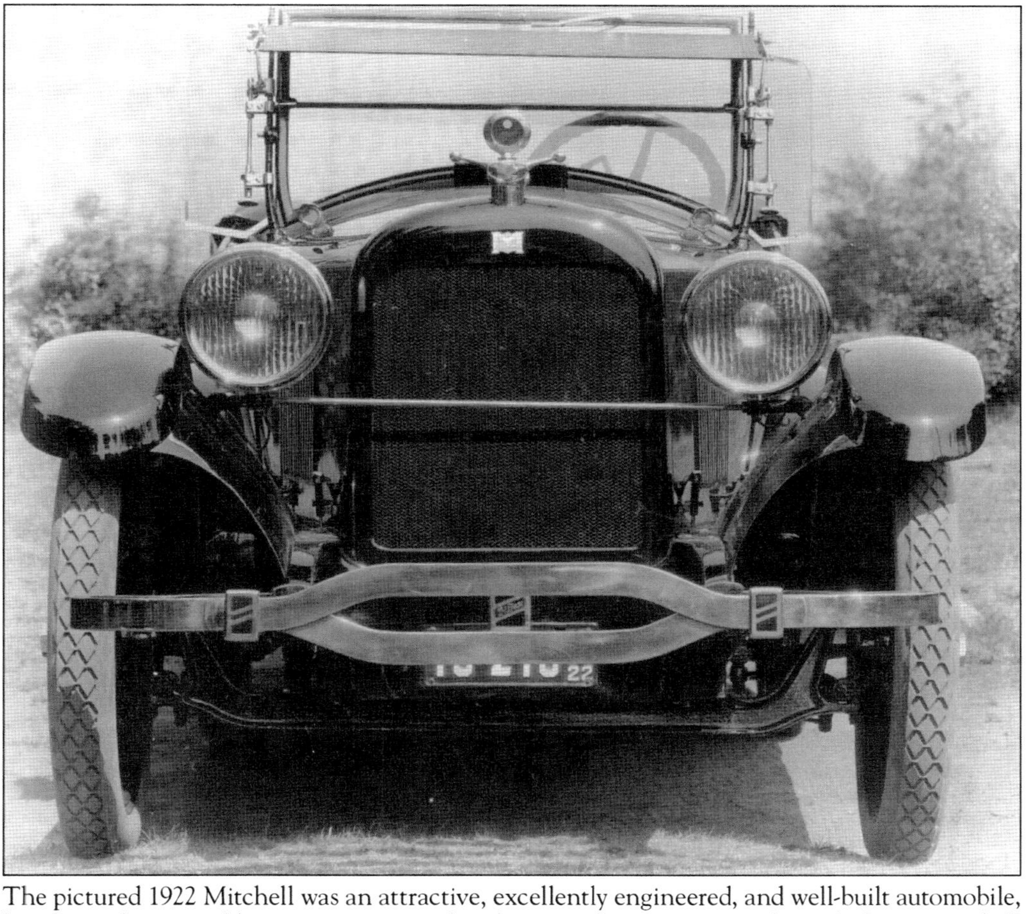

The pictured 1922 Mitchell was an attractive, excellently engineered, and well-built automobile, but the car-buying public was not interested in the company anymore. By the end of 1922, Mitchell was in receivership. Exactly 100 Mitchell's were built in 1923, before the factory shut down. In January 1924, Nash purchased the Mitchell factory complex and began producing the Ajax Six there in 1925.